HEADLINERS

Craig McGregor is the author of two novels, *Don't Talk to me about Love* (1971), which won the Xavier Society prize for literature, and *The See-Through Revolver* (UQP, 1977), and a collection of short stories, *Real Lies* (UQP, 1987). He has also written essays and books on political, social and cultural themes, twice winning the Walkley Award for Journalism with feature stories on Bob Hawke and Jill Wran. He now lives in Sydney and is head of Visual Communication at the University of Technology, Sydney and writes regularly for the *Sydney Morning Herald* and *Good Weekend* magazine.

By the same author

fiction

Don't Talk To Me About Love
The See-through Revolver
Real Lies

essays

People, Politics & Pop
Up Against The Wall, America
Soundtrack for the 'Eighties
Pop Goes the Culture

books

Profile of Australia
The High Country
In The Making
To Sydney With Love
This Surfing Life
The History of Surfing
The Great Barrier Reef
Bob Dylan: a retrospective
Australian Built
Life in Australia
Time of Testing
The Australian People

HEADLINERS

Craig McGregor's
Social Portraits

University of Queensland Press

First published 1990 by University of Queensland Press
Box 42, St Lucia, Queensland 4067 Australia

© Craig McGregor 1990

This book is copyright. Apart from any fair dealing
for the purposes of private study, research, criticism
or review, as permitted under the Copyright Act, no
part may be reproduced by any process without written
permission. Enquiries should be made to the publisher.

Typeset by University of Queensland Press
Printed in Australia by The Book Printer, Maryborough

Distributed in the USA and Canada by
International Specialized Book Services, Inc.,
5602 N.E. Hassalo Street, Portland, Oregon 97213-3640

Cataloguing in Publication Data
National Library of Australia

McGregor, Craig, 1933-
   Headliners: fourteen social portraits.
   1. Australia — Biography. I. Title

920.094

ISBN 0 7022 2344 1

CONTENTS

Acknowledgments *vii*
Preface *ix*

Clive James *1*
Simon Crean *18*
Jill Wran *38*
Bruce Dawe *55*
Peter Brock *63*
Paul Keating *77*
Leonie Kramer *85*
Allan Border *94*
John Cain *107*
Harry Seidler *123*
Bobbi Sykes *136*
John Howard *148*
Elizabeth Evatt *163*
Bob Hawke *179*

for my father
Allister Stephen Charles McGregor

ACKNOWLEDGMENTS

Bruce Dawe's poetry is reproduced with the premission of Longman Cheshire Pty Ltd and is taken from *Sometimes Gladness, Towards Sunrise*, and *Beyond the Subdivisions*. I would also like to thank Allen and Unwin for permission to reproduce from Harry Seidler's *Internment: The Diaries of Harry Seidler, May 1940-October 1941* (1986) and the University of Queensland Press for permission to use several of Bobbi Sykes's poems from her collection *Love Poems and Other Revolutionary Actions* (1988). The second part of the profile on Bob Hawke is taken from my book *Time of Testing: The Bob Hawke Victory* published by Penguin Books Australia Ltd, 1983.

PREFACE

"We are all of us, in our private lives, metaphors for some more general condition. If we don't understand the social significance of the merely personal we will never be liberated." I wrote that while trying to write about Jill Wran. Sometimes you don't understand something with real clarity until you write it down; writing is learning. Certainly that's the case with this collection of profiles which I've written over the last few years. The ones which have been published before I have rewritten and modified and, in some cases, restored to their original unedited form. In every profile, however, I have tried to write less about the people themselves than the social context which both constructs them and explains something to us, all of us, about ourselves. I've never been interested much in personality as such, so it's a bit strange to find myself writing about other people. But it's an honourable attempt, this effort to unravel the complex interaction between people and the society which shapes them and which they also shape. The underlying approach, obviously, is pluralist. And somewhere behind these portraits, I hope, some portrait of contemporary Australia and its social structure takes shape as well.

The forms are fairly self-evident. I try not to think too much about technique in case it becomes selfconscious or formularised. Nevertheless I've tried, quite deliberately, to use many of the techniques of fiction to enrich and expand the normal nonfiction forms. Behind it all, I suppose, is a quite ambitious though possibly misplaced attempt to force journalism into some of the arenas of subtlety and complexity which are usually reserved for fiction;

I can't see why, theoretically, a genuinely "new" journalism can't annex them to itself. Of course there are problems. Truth (objective) is a problem. So is the fragility of people's lives. So is the demand to communicate to a mass audience which needs, like ourselves, to be enlightened, not patronised nor treated to a pyrotechnic display. To be beautiful but plain is a lovely thing to strive for.

I wouldn't want to claim too much for these pieces: they are journalism-on-the-run. They've depended a lot on people who've been willing to give of their time and answer thousands of questions. I'd like to thank everyone who agreed to let me write about them; they were often incredibly generous. I could have included a lot more people, many of whom aren't "known" to the media, but it wasn't practical. Two of these profiles, of Bob Hawke and Jill Wran, won the national Walkley Award for Journalism. Most of the writing is of the profile genre but the John Howard feature tries to link, quite explicitly, the person with what was happening in the Australian community at the time. In a way it acts as a paradigm for what, less explicitly, is going on in the other portraits. The personal, as the women's movement recognised long ago, is always political; we enact in our lives the passions of our community, generations of the social.

Something like that.

As well as the people I've written about I'd like to thank all those who have helped in this project. Most of the profiles appeared originally in the *Sydney Morning Herald*, *Good Weekend* and the *National Times*; my thanks to their editors, Shelley Gare, Susan Wyndham, Shona Martyn, Eric Beecher and Max Suich, and in particular to John Alexander, editor-in-chief of the *Sydney Morning Herald*. The second section of the Bob Hawke profile originally appeared in *Time of Testing: the Bob Hawke victory* (Penguin, 1983). My thanks also to Craig Munro, publishing manager of University of Queensland Press; Nicola Evans, my editor; and my wife Jane, who read through each profile as I wrote it.

Craig McGregor
Bondi Junction 1990

CLIVE JAMES

"SATURDAY NIGHT CLIVE!" The logo is terrific, a postmodern bricolage promising intensity, vivacity, insight — whereupon on comes this short tubby bloke who reads some fake news items off the autocue, shows some corny American TV clips, carries out a couple of formula chat-show interviews with celebrities, exhibits a palpable sense of strain, and walks off stage to stunning applause and a fat six-figure BBC contract in his pocket. How does he get away with it?

The answer is a complex paradigm of how the media works in the late twentieth century, because Clive James is obviously better and smarter and funnier than the amiable buffoon he portrays on the box. Indeed there are many Clive James. To *Current Biography* he is "a polymath with an antic wit, one of the most scintillating figures in contemporary British intellectual journalism". To the general public he is a TV megastar. To Australians he is one of a group of expatriates — Barry Humphries, Germaine Greer, Bruce Beresford, all mates of James — who come home every now and then only to demonstrate how un-Australian they've become. To media watchers James is a phenomenon, a heavyweight literary figure who can make TV programs with twelve million viewers. To Auberon Waugh he is someone who "pretends to be an irreverent figure but in fact he is a cringing man on the make". And to Clive James himself?

He has described himself in the past as a clown, smart alec, Mummy's boy, teacher's pet, patsy . . . all of them true but right now what he is, basically, is a performer. An Electronic Media Entertainer. He's incrediably serious about it, it's taken over his life to the point where he works to a minute-by-minute schedule, has to program in having a haircut (it doesn't take long) and strives with the furious intensity of a man who has decided he has wasted half his life and wants to make every second count from now on.

"In many ways I've already lived my life, had a lot of fun. I really want to get on with my work, try to do something useful in the years that are remaining," he says with unexpected sombreness (he turned 50 in 1990). "I'm really good for the work I do and not a hell of a lot else. I'm not particularly original but I've got a way of saying things." Suddenly his mood changes as he laughs off suggestions that he is selling himself short, producing kitsch instead of culture. "Usually I'm portrayed as a terribly sad man who is trying to cover up a deep inner longing, but as far as I can see it's just not true! High quality entertainment is worth doing, I enjoy it. I'd like to do more of it. NONE MUST ESCAPE!" he shouts, storming around the studio, parodying the egomaniacal scale of his ambitions. "YOU MUST ALL HEAR WHAT I WANT TO SAY!"

It's the end of another horrendously long day in the BBC studios at Shepherds Bush, London, but Clive is still firing. He is jammed into a narrow room like a dogbox railway carriage with a metre-high black-and-white portrait of Frank Sinatra on the wall, a camp stretcher where he takes his daily after-lunch nap ("turns one day into two, look at Ronald Reagan!"), a grubby window, a tiny desk littered with scripts and scribbled notes and a wall of press pix of Clive with glamorous women: Joan Collins, Judy Green, Selina Scott . . . It is all part of his unspoilt Aussie ocker side, which has given him the immense advantage on British television of always being the Outsider: he shambles around in shabby Fletcher Jones menswear circa 1950, walks with the mincing topheavy steps of Merv Hughes's run-up, is affable and witty with all thirty members of the grandiloquently titled Clive James Unit ("he's a sweetie", says Joanna, his shared secretary) and generally comes across as a sort of balding overweight fuzzywuzzy koala . . . in unmatching socks.

"Strikes me as kind of weird, a 50-year-old man wearing odd

socks . . . look, one black, one blue . . . no time to check . . . it's crazy, I'm neurotic . . . I'm capable of almost insane feats of concentration and workload," he says. "Why I'm neurotic is a question I can't answer. But I certainly am. I've got a feeling it's because . . . if you lose one parent early it's such a demonstration of the law of chance that it really makes you feel every day is precious."

So he's an over-achiever? "I hope so!" he says, grinning. "I'm an over-achiever who feels like an under-achiever. I suppose one day I'll make the fatal mistake of trying to create a major work of art. Probably a novel. I'm basically a writer. I'm in the verbal construction business even on TV, I'm writing it in my head just before I say it. Little Vivian runs off at the mouth. I was a talkative little bastard when I was young. It's as simple as that."

What this doesn't do justice to, of course, is the famous James wit, the quicksilver intelligence which plays over the torrent of banter, puns, jokes, allusions, aphorisms and lighthearted verbal gambits which make up a Clive James conversation. When years ago I lived in Chelsea there was a blue plaque just five houses away which read: "Oscar Wilde, Wit and Dramatist, Lived Here." The Wit came first: so it should be when James gets his plaque. He is the most eloquent of people, a quality he shares with fellow ex-Push members Lillian Roxon and Murray Sayle. That doesn't make him right in what he says: behind that blinding facility he is often old-fashioned, conservative, sexist and just plain wrong, a sort of Beerbohm/Chesterton/Belloc figure wrapped up in tellytinsel. But to the TV networks he's gold. The BBC bought him from London Weekend Television for a reputed three-quarters of a million dollars a year; James says that's "absolute bullshit", he went for half his ITV salary to get the extra air time for his new shows, but anyhow it's made him a very wealthy man. "I'm in demand, you've got to make the most of it; TV likes to use you up and throw you away," he says. When I talked to him, James was working on three shows at once: Saturday Night Clive, a Jane Fonda interview special and a documentary on Miami, part of his cities-of-the-world Postcard series. Coming up is a new late-night interview series, more city docos and a secret

Big Project which he is piloting. It's a challenge even for a polymath with as many personas as Clive.

> *Just watch me use a whip, I can give the dawdlers gyp*
> *I can make the bloody echoes roar and ring;*
> *With a branding-iron, well, I'm a perfect flaming swell*
> *In fact, I'm duke of every blasted thing:*
>
> The Flash Stockman

Clive the Gymnast

The day starts early, a bit after 6.00 a.m.; he has stayed up until 1.00 a.m. working on his Miami script in the city apartment where he lives all week; he only goes home to see his wife and two teenage daughters in Cambridge at weekends. He's no family man, has little social life; ambition dominates him. By 7.30 a.m. he is down at the gym near Cannon Street tube station. He is badly overweight at 15 stone plus and last year Ron Clark, the former Australian long distance runner, took him over. His edict: eat less, exercise more.

James trudges off to get changed and reappears in a torn blue T-shirt, faded boxer swim trunks several sizes too small, and incongruous mulberry joggers; surrounded by weight machines and a roomful of aerobic disco dancers, he looks like a Moree pigfarmer (or maybe Henry Bolte) who has wandered into the wrong saleyard. "Underneath this flabby exterior is a wonderfully hard physique," he says, starting on the treadmill. Next up is a series of exercises on the Nautilus machine which James performs to an explosive series of wheezes, groans, sobs, grimaces and outright cries of pain. "I'm an addictive personality," he pants. "Light head for booze. Affects my mouth, which is how I earn my living (puff). Had to give it up. Just about. Boring. Just like Hawke (grunt). Quit smoking fifteen, sixteen years ago. Kissing me was like licking an ashtray (howl). I'm slowly becoming more and more self-disciplined, ascetic . . . yes, I'm slowly becoming perfect."

Sweat drips from his nose as he cools off in front of a fan. He has all the ailments of a successful man: a shoulder hurt skiing in Switzerland, rolls of fat at the waistline, freckles on his bald pate from sunbaking in Florida. He strips to his trunks to weigh himself, revealing a hairy back and thickening torso ("horror story!"). Next a few jabs at the red punching ball, a quick perv on the dancing girls, a 10-minute sauna and a couple of lengths of the pool. He swims like a suburbanite, too much roll and armlift; it's what you'd expect from the self-styled 'Kid from Kogarah'. (Growls Don Henderson, a songwriting mate of mine: "Anyone should be able to leave Kogarah behind. If you can't, stay there!") Throughout it all, James keeps up a threnody of comments, bon mots, self-revelations and self-concerns; he's friendly, monologic, waving to get your attention, the perfect communicator. "It's the size of my ego that drives me on," he confesses. "Self-confirmation? Possibly. In fact probably. The self is my big subject. I intend to explore it further! Also I've been lucky; that's another of my big subjects. I've had more than my share of luck."

Over a quick cereal-and-fruit breakfast in the gym, James explains he is two-thirds through his next novel, about a Japanese man visiting London and reflecting on the British lifestyle, and has completed the third volume of his "Unreliable Memoirs", but won't be writing any more. "My memoirs are really about when I had time to spare; they'll stop after this volume because my life changes," he says. "Marriage. Responsibility. A couple of friends got killed, young, died in accidents; it reinforced my belief that there's only so much time available. The change snuck up on me. Finding out how much I enjoyed writing for the *Observer*, becoming part of the landscape, that was part of it." He laughs. "Like Monet, finding out I was on to a good thing."

We catch the crowded tube to Shepherds Bush, something he does daily and which astonishes the BBC . . . I mean, he's made it, he's a 'personality'. But James says it keeps him in touch with his audience and besides, he doesn't like 'images' or smoothness or sophistication. "It's very necessary to retain that raw, strong reaction to things. I'm sceptical but not cynical, it's very important to retain one's naivete. We writers are in the business of having thin skins. Maggie Thatcher's got a thick skin!" James's fellow straphangers are listening in that bored, eyes-averted English way, but James rattles on, impervious. "I'm a bit of a larrikin; you don't get over that early vision of yourself," he says. "These days it's called . . . western suburbs, I guess. In those days I hadn't heard the term. I knew there was an eastern suburbs railway. And I knew there was a north shore. And I wasn't it." Pause. "And I didn't mind."

Euston, Notting Hill Gate, Holland Park . . . James is explaining how he moved deliberately from being TV critic on the *Observer* to being a TV performer because he wanted the exposure. "I love it, I love being at the centre of things, getting all the glory," he says. "I even like being recognised in the street. You tell this to people in England and they get embarrassed, they don't believe you. But I also want to get a lot said. I'm not there for my baby blue eyes." Shepherds Bush. As we get off, a lady in her late middle age touches Clive gracefully on the shoulder and says: "I enjoy your show, Mr James." Clive James, gymnast and westie-of-the-mind, dimples.

Clive the Performer

When he strides into the BBC studios everybody looks up. "Hi," says James in his best Groucho Marx/Sam Goldwyn voice. He's a star and there's no doubt he deserves his enormous popularity: he is a very funny man, a consummate performer, friendly, self-deprecating, never bitchy, and capable of communicating an easygoing warmth across the cool edge of the TV screen to millions of viewers.

It's heartening to find he is much the same in real life as on the box; it was said Oscar Wilde's plays never did justice to his conversation and even the best of James's scripts barely live up to his minute-by-minute wit. He is probably the most articulate man in the world. Yet his shows are always a bit disappointing; you turn them on with great expectations and turn them off feeling cheated. There's a lot of cleverness, and precious little insight; they're as formularised as any Australian chat show and bear hardly a trace of James's intellectuality. The Saturday Night Clive show displays him at his worst; the end-of-the-year specials at his best; the late-night interviews at his most serious. Somewhere in between come the documentaries and the one-off specials. He attacks them all with great gusto, puts his scripts through up to seven drafts and insisted on three full pilots for Saturday Night

Clive before it went to air. "I never talk down. I try not to underestimate the intelligence of the audience," he says. "I think people depend to a much larger extent than is commonly recognised upon the voices they hear, and I want to be one of the sane voices. I stand for the reasonable view. We know what it's like when insane voices are in control. I manage to get a fair bit said. I send up everybody and leave the common people with their dignity. Let's take the worst possible view of what I'm doing on TV and say that it's got nothing of what I'm really capable of. I still think it's worth doing."

Q: Has he really tried to push the limits of what he admits is "sheer entertainment", or has he succumbed to the formulas?

JAMES: "TV is critically short of time. You've got to give up trying to provide answers to problems. There are some things you can do on television, some you can't do; all this has to be lived with. A talk show is fundamentally hard. With the Saturday Night shows, there's a limit beyond which you can't go."

Q: Doesn't that castrate him, turn him into a eunuch?

JAMES (smiling): "The harem can't run without eunuchs."

Clive the Producer

Miami Postcard. James and his team are in the editing room, watching a rough cut of the documentary on the monitor screen and laying down a draft voice-over from James. The trick is to match the picture and voice seamlessly; James is reading from his typed script which is festooned with last night's scribbles. "You might say leave well alone, but well can be better," he says as he sets about injecting extra "gagettes" into a narration which is already chocablock with gags, puns, allusions, sexual innuendos, extravagances . . . just like his books. "OK, here's my latest fun line: 'That's like Miami: you brace yourself for a blackjack in the neck and get a frozen yoghurt in the face.' How's that? We'll save the girls in swimsuits till later. OK, mod coming up. Here's what I'm going to say: 'We Australians, with our magnificent bodies, are natural water experts . . .'." The images of Miami flash by with James in his familiar role of the gormless patsy, bumbling from water-skiing to girl-lusting to vice-searching; the real Clive, meanwhile, is peering over his gold-rimmed half-spectacles at himself and giving instructions in the arcane gibberish of the electronic media: "Dip it after big city ... ditch that ... OK, another mod ... picture's good ... well-spotted, Richard ... we're gonna boost those popguns, make 'em sound like cannons ... another layer? I'm game."

A train roars by outside the studio. "FUCK OFF!" shouts James. He's still not satisfied, so after a sandwich lunch, a half-hour kip on the camp stretcher and another hour of scriptwriting he returns to the studio. He's feeling good after his sleep and sings "Give me a kiss to build a dream on ..." into the mike while cueing up; he croons it beautifully, deep and mellow, just like his hero Frank. He's got massive earphones on which transform him into an avuncular Willie the Wombat figure or maybe even Bumper Farrell, the infamous police sergeant and Rugby League heavy, but when the green light comes on the familiar trans-Pacific Clive James accent rolls out of the studio speakers:

> *If you drive down Florida till it comes to a point you finally get to Miami, an old Seminole Indian word that means 'Look out, here come the tourists'. Nowadays, thanks to the TV series Miami Vice, tourists come here expecting a pastel-trimmed gun battle between drug runners and undercover cops with designer bulletholes in the T-shirts and chins carefully unshaved. They come here looking for stubble. I wasn't exactly planning to get killed, but I'd made my will and filled in the forms so that my body could be flown home packed in ice: Miami ice!*
>
> Right. The titles: da da dada da dada da. Here comes the second speech. Ready? Go.
>
> *A hundred years ago Miami was a sandspit that a slow alligator could cross in half an hour ...*

And so it goes on. You don't learn anything much about the subject in James's documentaries, of course; they're just carefully scripted scenarios for James's grandstanding, a film set backdrop for James as punster, voyeur and lovable buffoon. It's fun. And it's funny. But, as Dylan says, "nothing is revealed."

The voice-over ends. *Clive*: "Jake?" *Producer*: "It's a wrap."

Clive the Mummy's Boy

On his shows Clive James constantly seeks the company of celebrity women, calls them "beautiful creatures", babbles on about "the fair sex". There are a lot of strippers and "glamorous gals" as well, usually being ogled by a fat man (James). There's an uncomfortable feeling of prurience about it all, something a bit abnormal, which hasn't escaped viewers or critics; *Punch* magazine had a go at James's "double standards" and described him "bobbing around in Hugh Hefner's pool like a mangy walrus that can't believe its luck"; *Private Eye*, more seriously, has written about his "womanising".

Off the box, he's just as bad — but uses humour to defend himself. "It's good news, I encourage these rumours," he says. "Like Diamond Jim McClelland, I'm a great one for the fair sex. I love 'em all, I have something of a conqueror's fantasy, played out in part in relationships with women. Flirting is the answer. Thank God for AIDS and feminism; they made flirtation not only respectable but compulsory. I'm very interested in Don Juan as a figure and in Don Giovannis in real life. Like John F. Kennedy. To be compulsively trying to run up a score is a condition. I'm very grateful to feminism, I wouldn't have been able to figure all that out myself."

Nevertheless the worries remain. He admits he's a Mummy's boy, an only son who never knew his father (he died on the way back from the Changi POW camp) and was brought up alone by his mother. He's very close to her still, rings her all the time. In *Unreliable Memoirs* he gives a hilarious account of his masturbatory early years, when he was "as queer as a coot", and his terrible lack of success at sex. In London, eventually, "women were very kind to me, probably because I was so pitiful". "I think sex is a bit of a joke. I'm glad I'm not at the right end of the joke. It's a very, very comic thing to do."

James says that being a Mummy's boy taught him that if he cried loudly enough he got what he wanted. It's also made him the sort of man who measures himself by his achievements, in this case a one-man media factory perpetually turning experience into videotape: "I've at last lived up to some of my mother's expectations."

Has he kept up with his gay experiences? "No, no," he replies, laughing. "I didn't have the courage." Could it be said he's adjusted too heavily to the masculine role? "Many, many gay men have told me this; they say they're not convinced, they say 'Clive, you're covering it up, you're gay!' I have to tell them that as far as I'm concerned I'm not! It might be true, but I don't think it would be the end of the world if it were."

> *I'm a stockman to my trade, and they call me ugly Dave*
> *I'm old and grey and only got one eye*
> *In a yard I'm good of course, but just put me on a horse*
> *And I'll go where lots of young 'uns daren't try.*
>
> The Flash Stockman

Clive the Englishman

Then there's Clive James the Antipodean-Ocker-turned-British-Gent, who talks about the British as "we" and is anti-Republican. He has even come to see the value of the old Empire link, but after all, he's been there thirty years and you'd expect him, as he says, to become "Anglicised to a certain extent; I get in the back of the cab instead of the front. I like privacy."

A more serious criticism is the one made of the way in which he peppers his shows with excerpts from corny Japanese, American and European TV shows, in theory holding them up for ridicule but revelling in them at the same time. It's the old *Daily Mirror* double-standard double-take, and it's pretty nasty.

"He apes an Englishman taking the piss out of wogs," says one Australian expatriate. "He's taken on board a lot of English insularity, holding up all other cultures as funny/peculiar." Another thinks he has "made a compact with the British public to parody everything they dislike — including Australia".

In the media he's been criticised for being anti-Japanese, something which might be understandable, given the circumstances of his father's death. James claims he's not, though his defence that it's better the Japanese be cruel to each other on quiz shows than go slaughtering the peoples of Southeast Asia doesn't go down too well either.

At the BBC, during my time with James, the most dispiriting session of all was the one in which James and his producer, Richard Drewett, assembled their "troops" to preview material for

Saturday Night Clive. The eight-person team had assembled cruel/funny/horrific hidden camera material from all over the world, and once again the Japanese was the worst. For hour after hour, slumped back in his chair, patting his tummy with his left hand, James selected the juiciest for his own show.

"Love it," he says to the man getting an electric shock when he pinches the woman's tits. The sneezing dog is in (someone must have shoved pepper up its nose, says his team leader). The home videos — too cruel? Drowning is never funny; falling over is. A red-robed American evangelist: "He's fabulous." George Hamilton, Zsa Zsa Gabor for satellite interview? Clive's keen on Zsa Zsa, his producer isn't. "You'd be doing a Wogan interview," he says (Wogan being the housewives' choice on British TV, a sort of local Ray Martin). Everyone throws up their hands. "Pass!" shouts the producer. Zsa Zsa's out, but another Jap game show clip is in. "Try to get clearance," orders James. "The commentary will save it; I'm going to get clubbed for the usual thing, but that's OK."

And so it goes on, an endless succession of cranks, nutters, freaks, the weird world of masscult telly. It very quickly becomes clear that any idea of sending the shows up is a pretence; the team is simply choosing what it thinks will make good TV. At the end of it all James levers himself to his feet, says: "It's great. Well done, troops." Walking back to his room he says proudly: "That's what goes into a light entertainment show; it's all in the preparation." Earlier, rejecting some material and selecting other footage, he had said: "You take a cross-section of garbage, you still get garbage.

Exactly.

Clive the Literateur

Clive James has a formidable reputation as a literary figure. He is extraordinarily erudite and well read, contributes to international journals like *The New York Review of Books*, learnt Russian because he could "no longer bear not to know something about how Pushkin actually sounded" and has published several books of criticism, poetry, essays and television columns: indeed, there are those who pine nostalgically for his *Observer* TV columns and maintain they are the best thing he's ever done. He still rips off the occasional heavyweight critique to remind everyone he can do it and thinks he'll move on from TV in a few years, maybe into a synthesis of film/TV production, or writing and acting for the theatre, or "longer books". His first two novels were hammered by the critics. "No-one takes him seriously enough to be nasty about him," says one of his anti-fans.

He's the target of some pretty stupid spite and envy, not least because of his success as a mass communicator. Yet the critics who are so quick to praise his literary work and eager to drag him back to that arena may be doing him a disservice; James is such a brilliant performer, as he has been from his youth, that television may turn out to be his natural medium, his major achievement. James agrees. "I love it. It's a terrific art form," he says. Yet the idea of "a book that interprets the temper of the times" lingers in the back of his mind. "I wouldn't like to say too much about it, I'd hate to have that one hanging over me," he adds, grinning. *"Like, 'when are you going to write that big book? We're still waiting for that big one!' "*

He is also, somewhat surprisingly, much more of a literateur than an intellectual. He hasn't read much contemporary cultural or political theory, plays the philistine (but means it) in his documentaries, reckons he "knows enough about architecture to know what I don't like", and defends himself ironically: "Postmodernism? Doesn't mean a thing to me. I don't know what they are talking about. I can give you a whole list of things I'm not interested in: structuralism, semiotics, deconstruction, the list is endless, because they're empty of content. Anything that tries to remove the author from the centre is anti-humanist, and I'm a humanist."

His political stance is similarly elementary: he's a social democrat, he says, anti-Thatcher, but abstained from voting Labour because he opposes public ownership, finally found a party he could vote for when the dead-centre SDP emerged, and now it has self-destructed doesn't know what to do. "People get more conservative as they get older," he admits. "One becomes a member of the propertied party; if I thought Labour policy would cost me above a certain percentage in income tax, I wouldn't vote for them."

So what does he do with all his money? "I stick it in the bank, pay the mortgage, and save. I'm a saver. If I have enough money in the bank I can tell anybody to fuck off . . . even Rupert Murdoch. It's crucial not to need the next job. I haven't needed the next job for years." For the first time all day James shows a glint of anger behind the humour. Yeah, Murdoch's an interesting figure; he might work for him one day. "In the meantime I make a point of getting stuck into him. Somebody has to. He's got to remember somebody is out there who can't be bought."

> To watch me skin a sheep, it's so lovely you could weep;
> I can act the silvertail as if my blood was blue
> You can strike me pink or dead, if I stood upon my head
> I'd be just as good as any other two.
>
> The Flash Stockman

Clive the Middlebrow

He loves Frank Sinatra, Andy Newman, The Lovin' Spoonful, good American movies, country-and-western, songs with lyrics you can follow (with a bouncing ball?), motor racing, adorable actresses and the telly. "I'm a bit old hat," he admits. He believes in an integrated culture, he's vehemently opposed to niche marketing and he approves of the BBC because it delivers him a unified audience. He likes the middle ground. "Oh yes, I really do love coherence. I really do. I'm a traditionalist," he says.

A distrust of conflict seems to be at the heart of his fears; though he was influenced by philosopher John Anderson at Sydney University he's rejected Anderson's pluralism and retreats from the fragmentation and dynamism of the contemporary world. "I like unity, I like the idea of one world. I'm fearful that if cultures lose their coherence you get real conflict, war, as in Europe and the Pacific in the Second World War," he says. But the concept of a unitary culture is, of course, banal and runs directly counter to James's belief in democratic theory and the safe, old-fashioned liberalism he espouses in his essays; it makes you wonder about the depth of his other beliefs. He is anti-reformist, believes politics is simply about "governing the country", took part in the anti-nuclear marches years ago, but now regards that as "a colossal mistake, a real lulu".

He wears his fame and wealth lightly, though his helpers are careful to support him when he turns to them for endorsement: "Yes, Clive, it's marvellous. You've done it." He worries too much about "husbanding my energy", won't disclose his movements in case thieves break into his house or apartment, loads up every minute of the day so he becomes inaccessible to the press or Aussie callers; these days he doesn't even see that much of old friends like Germaine Greer and Barry Humphries: "Germaine is tough company, she wears me out," he grizzles, "and Barry, he's never off!"

In fact there's a bit of a mean streak in James, a legacy perhaps of a genuinely impoverished background. The tube saves money. Doesn't own a car, gets chauffeured from Cambridge so he can work in the back seat; "driving in traffic is dead time." Still, he wouldn't buy a boat, owns a Clifford Possum Aboriginal painting and some work by younger English artists but isn't really a collector ("no expensive tastes"). Instead he reads, watches movies while jetting around the world (he's just back from a trip to Rome, Shanghai, Perth, Miami and Los Angeles), holidays in Biarritz because there's a great cafe there where he can sit outdoors and write his books in longhand, and works works works works works works works . . .

Clive and Jane Fonda

Back in the editing suite, Clive James is about to replay his interview with Jane Fonda. "This is a different story, this is about her, not me," he explains, contrasting it with Miami Postcard: *"Short Overweight Australian Meets The World's Most Beautiful Woman."*

The interview starts with Clive and Jane on the beach, Clive first. He wants the order reversed: "You don't want to see my three chins before you see her," he growls. "And drop that story of the two mules fucking, that was stupid, I asked her too early just to get the story." Clive's accent gets more American as the interview rolls on. "Sensational. Sensational stuff," he says. "We should use Beach Boys, *California Girl*, for the soundtrack. Perfect. Problem? OK, get someone else's version."

Then he catches sight of a big fat blob in the foreground of the screen picture. "Is that my knee? Is that cameraman blind?" he shouts. "It's a program starring my knee. Clive's Knee!" The hapless cameraman has now switched to a back view of Clive's bald cranium with Jane Fonda somewhere in the far distance. "My God!" moans Clive, kneading his forehead with his fist. "What a fool. It's a terrific interview, she looks great . . . the critics will praise its deliberately raw technique." Later he adds: "It shows the value of research. I knew beforehand every answer she was going to give."

This raises a bit of a problem about Clive James the Interviewer. When he returned to Australia for his ABC shows he revealed himself as fairly laughably out of touch, reduced his interviews to quick grabs, programmed his questions and their answers beforehand, and came up with some profoundly unsatisfying results . . . including reducing author Frank Moorhouse to inarticulacy — no mean feat! James always seems ill at ease and self-conscious as an interviewer, and there is very little "seeing into" in this or his other work; the typical James approach is to use the subject material as mere grist for his own performance. He's uninvolved, the gagster, the funnyman, but behind the pyrotechnic facade a void. You get lotsa humour from James but you don't get perception.

On the other hand, those critics who praise his late-night "highbrow" interviews, and feel he should restrict himself to them, misjudge the breadth of the man's talent and his genuine Aussie populism. James has broken out of the intelligentsia stockade and gone for the mass audience, and he's right to do so. Right now he's planning a BBC Channel 1 show which will give him an even bigger audience; then the USA; then the universe . . . "NONE MUST ESCAPE!"

Clive the Australian

"I feel Australian. Absolutely. Never more so than when I'm with the English! I'll go to my grave that way. There are all kinds of inhibitions the English have that I don't. I'm quite outgoing and most English people aren't. I show my emotions more than the English — and less than Australians do, but I've been here a long time. So Australians think I'm a Pom and the Poms think I'm an

Aussie, so I'm caught in the middle, but I quite enjoy it. I still have an Australian passport. Professional Australian? I've never understood that one. You can't win: if you kill your accent and be English you're a turncoat, if you don't then you're a professional Australian. The chief advantage of being an Aussie here is that it makes you hard to place; nobody can tell where you're from, you can talk to anyone, penetrate the class system. It makes you very flexible. Until recent times an Australian in Britain was on to a winner. Only a small, bitter group of British journalists regard me as a parvenu. I'm accepted. There may be some club which prides itself on keeping me out but I've never applied to it! When I went back home I got less flak than I'd have expected. I suffered colossal culture shock because I'd waited too long but within a day my accent had reverted. Being an Australian expatriate is a very interesting thing to be. Auberon Waugh wrote an article some time ago actually saying the Australians here should be sent home . . . rounded up, shipped off to the east. He's berserk, he doesn't recognise what he's saying. I think it was because I got an award and Bron didn't. No, I think I'm as Aussie as ever."

The Real Clive James

It was the end of the day. In the cutting room Clive James had interviewed Jane Fonda, waterskiied in Miami and walked along the beach to the sound of Bryan Ferry. In the conference room he had previewed half a hundred scenes from game shows, candid cameras, home videos, comedies and Japanese teleclips. In his anti-star study he had rewritten a dozen script pages, thought up half a dozen gagettes. In the recording studio he had laid down a complete voice-over. In the gym he had run over a thousand metres, swum four laps and exercised more than three hundred muscles. In the canteen he had indulged in badinage which had wasted some of his carefully husbanded energy. He had also answered, with great charm and humour, what seemed like several hundred questions.

He slumped back in his studio chair, the Shepherds Bush sun beating down on his freckled scalp, and screwed his knuckles into his eyes. He had a right to feel tired.

Did he love anyone? Yes, but it was a private matter. He didn't love mankind but he loved individuals. He thought Swift was right. Swift said you love them one at a time but not altogether. At least he thought it was Swift. Was there a deficit in his, Clive James's, ability to love? Yes, quite possibly true. "Yes, I'm slightly vulnerable on that one. Not generally vulnerable. Slightly vulnerable. I'm too busy to give people the attention they should have, yes." Clive paused. He looked as though he was about to screw his knuckles into his eyes again. "I forgive myself."

I figured it was time to go. Mankind cannot bear too much scrutiny, says Eliot (or was it Schwarzenegger?). James, for his part, thinks Schwarzenegger is a condom filled with walnuts. I remembered the corny shows he had done in Australia and tried to forgive him, but couldn't. James had done it for himself, anyhow. I remembered his hilarious New Year's Eve special and rejoiced. I remembered his Saturday Night shows and didn't. On the tube the ambience that remained clearest was of a self-aware, very funny, dazzlingly articulate man who had triumphed over the very worst he had managed to throw at himself in *Unreliable Memoirs* and was still accelerating — the best may be yet to come.

I have one reservation: a long time ago Clive Vivian Leopold James, a nice young bloke from the southern suburbs of Sydney, set out to confront the world, and life, and whatever lay within, but he ended up skating across it, thrilled by and thrilling the cheering crowd as he dwindled flashingly into the distance . . . flared up again . . . disappeared from sight. Mediaised. Only the sound of glittering skates remained.

> *I've a notion in my pate, that it's luck, it isn't fate*
> *That I'm so far above the common run*
> *So in everything I do, you could cut me fair in two*
> *For I'm much too bloody good to be in one!*
>
> The Flash Stockman

SIMON CREAN

He's another Hawke! they say enthusiastically. *He's the Next-Prime-Minister-But-One!* And the parallels between Simon Crean and Bob Hawke are certainly amazing: right-wing Labor man, union career, president of the ACTU, move to politics, a fast track to the top . . .

Crean's friends and supporters believe that, despite his union career, he has had his gaze fixed on politics for most of his life, that he has been deliberately grooming himself for the Prime Ministership, and it is probably only a matter of time before he gets there.

Consider: he has already successfully made the transfer from the ACTU to Minister for Science in Canberra. When Hawke steps down and, in all probability, Paul Keating ascends by Divine Right to the Lodge, Crean could well become Treasurer in a Keating government. He's got the economics degree, he's in the correct (Labor Unity) faction and he's got the backing of Hawke, who has been a hefty part of the push to get Crean into Parliament and then the Ministry and doesn't mind keeping a couple of balls in the air even if it does discomfit the titular heir apparent, Paul (The Knife) K. The fact that Crean could be seriously considered to lead the party despite having so little experience in Parliament ("yes, he obviously has the capacity to be a Prime Minister" — Hawke) shows just how highly regarded he is. Simon Crean, in fact, has been very much the Golden Boy of the Labor movement. Question: does he deserve it?

When you meet Simon Crean it's quite a surprise: here's this young-looking, very ordinary, low-key suburban bloke with two lively daughters, Sarah, 5, and Emma, 4, hanging off him as he tries to make the tea, keep the TV down and generally look after the house on a Sunday morning while the Port Melbourne rain drizzles down and trams slosh by in the street outside and it's quite unexpected to find him much more mundane and light-hearted and easygoing than the rather wooden Talking Head persona he projects on television. He has a hooked Bob Dylan nose, thin bum, slight pot belly, endless patience, a pretty friendly and direct manner, and, greatest shock of all according to Carole, his wife, who is a boilermaker's daughter and as sharp and fast on her feet as they come — he's funny.

Funny? Simon Crean, the uptight, articulate, business-suited spokesperson whose public language is positively eye-glazing and whose public image is almost as much so? Crean's aware of all that, but he has an explanation: "People come up to me at the footie and say 'it's great to see you smile, I've never seen you smile' and I say, 'look, most of the time on TV I'm not asked to come in as part of a comedy routine, I'm there to deal with the hard issues!' " Which is fair enough, and though Crean has nothing of Hawke's 'charisma', whatever they may mean, he's got something which may be even more valuable as he makes the transition from trade union heavy to fasttrack political leader: a commonplaceness, a down-home friendly Australianess which people warm to because they recognise themselves in him, there is a typicality they respond to.

It takes a while to pick that up because Crean has a certain defensiveness, even shyness, which shows in the way the side of his mouth curls up when he is talking, an ever-present self-control ("the more I worry the better I perform") which can come across as an inherited Presbyterian dourness; after all, Frank Crean, his father, first Treasurer in the Whitlam government, was a Presbyterian elder!; but when Crean does finally smile his face is entirely transformed, his countenance lights up, and you get this sudden and marvellous illumination as though he has accidentally revealed a true and uncomplicated spirit beneath the Economic Guru mask.

Now everybody knows politicians are not like that, especially those who are so successful so fast as Crean has been, and Crean has a reputation for being manipulative and a tough and tenacious negotiator, as well as being very conscious of his image: "if he's been image-conscious *before* going into politics, what the hell's he going to be like later? I mean, fibbability is nascent," says one Melbourne commentator. He's very opinionated, doesn't like being interrupted, slices the air with the palm of his hand when he gets worked up, give the impression that once he has explained something so brilliantly, how could anyone of any intelligence possibly disagree?

It sounds just slightly familiar, and indeed the parallels between Crean and Hawke are so close that sometimes Crean has to point out the differences, though he insists: "I don't compare myself with anyone." Explains Crean:

"Sure, there are some parallels. We're both consensus operators, but that's like Keating, Willis, Kelty, Carmichael. I got to the ACTU because I had a power base that elected me, I got there as an elected official, not an appointed one — that's a fundamental difference between me and Hawke. We've got different styles. Bob is very much the populist, he has enormous public approval rating. I haven't got the same natural appeal, or developed appeal, but we both come over naturally in the media. I don't see myself, quite frankly, as a self-promoter, I've promoted issues and causes instead. Why? Well, I think basically I'm a fairly reserved sort of person! (laughing). It's causes, not personalities, that count. I got the support to go into Parliament not because I'm good on TV, not because I can string a few words together, not because I was ACTU president, but because I've been seen to be contributing positively to a very successful process in the trade union movement. I think I can take it further in politics."

There are reservations about Crean. He hasn't got any old-style fire in the belly; he's a technocrat, a manager, a middle class careerist who's been zooming fast up the class and success scales. Says a trade union friend: "He's *safe*! He's *moderate*! What people want at this time is certainty, they want solutions without great upheaval: with Simon they've got it." Carole, his wife, confirms that he is balanced, not cynical, very practical, spends most of his time with men . . . yeah, he gets on well with women, but she keeps them at arm's length! He's a good listener. Doesn't swear (in fact he swears all the time). Doesn't get passionate about anything but the footie, where he gets so carried away barracking for North Melbourne she gets embarrassed to stand beside him; no, he's not emotional, hardly ever gets annoyed or angry at home though he does sometimes. Oh, and he's nice.

A woman who knows him well uses the same word: "*nice* is such a devalued word these days, but that's exactly what he is. He's extremely affable, very social, there's a gentleness about him, he's good with people on a one-to-one basis; Frank Crean's like that." Says a writer: "I was a real doubter for some time, I thought he was a fixer, too calculating, no ideas, but I've come around; there's a kindness or something about him, he goes out of his way to help people."

Whatever the reason, Crean is completely bereft of the "side" which disfigures so many politicians. When he goes down to the corner shop to buy some chewing gum for his kids and the fat, jovial Italian grocer calls him "Meester Prime Minister!" he seems genuinely embarrassed, smiles, walks off down the wet footpath with the kids trailing half a block behind, absorbed in the serious business of unwrapping their chewy. He reckons he's got a strong ego, doesn't want to appear cocky, and deftly sidesteps any questions about his final destiny in politics. But maybe that's because he believes he *is* going to be Prime Minister anyhow.

Where does Crean stand politically? He sees himself as "of the Centre, leaning towards the Left". In the labyrinthe world of Labor politics he belongs to the Labor Unity faction in Victoria, which is well to the Right (it's Hawke's faction), though on the ACTU he and Kelty took a Centrist position. As he says himself, he's basically a pragmatist, a moderate, a gradualist. Sometimes, surprisingly, he claims to be more than that. "I respond to the idealism of the Left; I think we are putting in place a much more planned, forward-thinking society and if you can condition people to accept that then later you're capable of taking them further, getting them to accept more profound change."
Q: Why aren't you of the Left then?
CREAN: "Maybe I am!"

Q: "What's the evidence?"

CREAN: "Well . . . OK . . ." He hesitates, seems about to declare something important, but then he says: "Look, it comes back to a question of what's achievable, what's realistic. If the concept of the Left is some idealism based about redistribution, about more influence, more power, more affecting of political direction from a working-class perspective, that's what I am trying to achieve — but using different methods, using the existing structures. You don't get the chance to change things if you telegraph too many punches that frighten hell out of people."

That, of course, is very close to Victorian Premier John Cain's dictum "DON'T FRIGHTEN THE HORSES" and ironically Crean criticises Cain for not having done more with his term in power; also, Cain sacked Crean's mate and patron Bill Landeryou from the Victorian Cabinet because of "irregularities". On the other hand, Crean does have some very clear strategies (his discourse is larded with the terms of the political fixer: *deals, options, strategies, trade-offs*) to achieve the changes he's after.

At the heart of Crean's approach is economic management. Like Keating, Button and others, he believes the Australian economy must be dramatically restructured to make it competitive and to generate the wealth which can then be redistributed through Labor policies. In this restructuring the unions have a crucial role to play, and they should have a voice in the redistribution process as well. "Industrial relations has to be seen not just as a mechanism for settling disputes but as contributing to the change the economy has to undergo, through the raft of labour market policies: wages policies, training, skill formation," he says. "Our ability to affect redistribution isn't just through the wage: it's through taxes, it's through welfare payments, it's through employment growth, it's through industry policy. The one thing we can deliver on is wages policy, and we have used that to bargain for influencing a wider agenda."

The Accord is the basic instrument for this: it has given the unions a major impact on government policy. "I don't agree that this government has moved away from traditional Labor aims, not at all, the Accord's been a remarkable success. Yes, I'd like to

accelerate the redistribution side, but the capacity to do that is severely limited unless you're into wealth creation."
QUESTION: Wealth for who?

When he talks like that Crean can sound quite abstract, as though he were reciting something by rote; in fact Crean has two voices. One is the formal, jargon-ridden mode which journalists in Melbourne have dubbed *Creanspeak*; the other is the direct, curse-laden mode he uses with trade unionists and political mates. This is the first, with Crean explaining his pro-privatisation stance:

"If the Labor movement wants these enterprises to grow, we have to free them from their constraints, we are obliged to look at alternative means for raising those monies if they are required to subject themselves to certain sorts of procedures, like going to government, saying we want this approval; it's those sorts of things that have got to be assessed, they should be freed of the constraints in raising capital and decision-making, we have to look at the question as to how its fund-raising and loan basis impacts upon the public sector borrowing requirement, because that has broader implications in terms of the overall economic situation, but I think that if the sole source of government revenue, of additional revenue, for the capital base is government and government is not going to pay it then as a movement we have to be seriously considering what other options there are that enable it to raise it . . ."

And this is Crean in Mode 2, explaining his relationship with Eddie Kornhausser, the Gold Coast property developer and friend of Bob Hawke's who was mentioned in the Fitzgerald Inquiry:

"Eddie Kornhauser's just a long time family friend! I knew Larry Kornhauser, they've known Dad, the Chevron Hotel was in Melbourne Ports, it was one of those sorts of connections, together with the Jewish community. Eddie was part of that group, people who were strong supporters of the Labor Party, fundraisers; y'know, it was one of those political-cum-family connections. He went up to the Gold Coast, did the big development up there. Yeah, I still see him, when we had the ACTU executive on the Gold Coast I had dinner with him and his brother Jack,

he's the quieter one; Eddie rang me the other day when he was down in Melbourne. The annoying thing, that article that links me with Kornhauser . . . Queensland wanted us to see Expo, so we agreed to take the May executive meeting up there, but by the time the Queensland bloody Labor Council gets around to fucking organising it there's no accomodation around, so they ring Eddie up, Eddie who used to own the Ramada Hotel but sold it; he's able to get us in, but we paid the commercial rate . . . so Eddie organises us to get up to Expo by bus, get him on the bus, so I said to the executive, 'We don't want the Press coming with us on the bus, it's a private bus', but silly Harry, a couple of these reporters then go to Harry, and say 'can we go?' and Harry says yes at the last minute, and he gets on the bus, and fuck me dead, I just knew all this was going to happen, they call in a photographer, desperately trying to get these shots of me with Eddie, it was such an outrageously distorted story, the caption on the top was CREAN CUTS CAKE WITH KORNHAUSER! Right? The concept of the cake was this: when we got on the bus, for lunch the hotel had organised these picnic boxes, which was a sandwich, a banana, a fruit juice, and there was a bit of cake in the bottom, everyone on the bus including this prick that wrote the story ate it. Just outrageous blow-up it was, just outrageous. Favour, what favour? We paid for the bus, we paid for the cake, we paid for the journalists who ate the cake, and the bus, and the entry to Expo, we paid for every fucking thing! Did not take a favour! And we were there at the invitation of our host state. Not one favour!"

Crean is sometimes accused of being too close to business, too self-consciously upwardly mobile, too bourgeois. The media made great fun of the fact that he helped the *Age* with its good food guide, that not-so-simple-Simon was something of a Toothsome Man. But Crean can be absolutely scathing about the inefficiency of business, describing some enterprises as "absolutely fucking hopeless" and others as "obscene" because of their tax and profit behaviour. He believes in a mixed economy but argues "you can't rely on creating the right economic environment and hoping the necessary thing's going to happen because business, left to itself, won't fucking well do it! We've got to develop a system that corrects the deficiencies of the market. I've never been a believer that deregulation works better than regulation. In some cases we may have gone too far. You've got to find the mix that produces the best outcome."

That means not waiting till a crisis hits an industry but picking those which need help and using the AIDC (Australian Industry Development Corporation) or special assistance packages, as happened with the steel plan and the vehicle industry package. "Planning frightens people," he says. "We've got to use incentives; the successful economies are those that are given some direction and our government ought to be doing more."

As for the deregulationists in the Coalition parties: "They're wankers. Christ Almighty . . . what's Greiner done? Business knows that the best way to get what they want, to get stability in labour market arrangements, is by involving the trade union movement. The deregulationists, the enterprise bargainers, all lack that balanced approach. They all translate it to a *laissez faire*, libertarian-type economic morality. It's nonsense, it's never worked and it never will."

In the city the placards read HAWKE ADMITS ADULTERY. Crean grimaces. He is wearing a silver wedding ring on his left hand and a gold watch which has slipped below his wrist. Later, when he flies up to Canberra to officially open the ACTU headquarters there, the media descend on him with their barrel lenses and boom mikes and ask him about his political career. One of the reporters asks Crean, jokingly, if there's anything *reely personal* he'd like to get off his chest? Crean gives his quick, funny grin and turns it all aside: "I have a very happy family life!" he says. And walks out into the bathroom to wash his face clean.

In fact you see Crean at his best, and most normal, when he's at home with Carole and the kids. He spends most weekends with them, plays with the children and fixes up their toys, talks to them straight without babytalk, likes mucking around in the back garden and doing odd jobs while the girls keep interrupting. Dinner parties and the footie have languished because of lack of babysitters and because raising the kids has become a dominating part of his life. He calls Carole *Caz*, and Sarah *Sare*, and Emma *Em*, and family dinners tend to be the usual mix of TV, kids' crises and banter:

SCENE: *the Crean family kitchen. Carole is putting some samosas and three sauces on the table. Crean is opening a Yarra Valley white and talking about the need for "structural readjustment". The girls are watching TV. Emma is grizzling that her plastic piano won't work.*

Did Carole make the samosas?

CAROLE: *"Yeah."*

Crean bursts out laughing. "Her best friend's in a cakeshop!"

CAROLE: *"I'm a much better liar than cook. I hate cooking."*

CREAN: *"I like cooking. Specially Saturdays in winter, kids are in the house, you can paddle around the kitchen . . . yeah, sometimes it gets to me."*

EMMA: *"Dad . . . DAD . . . DAAAADDD! Can you fix this for me?"*

CREAN: *"Bring us a knife, darl. Looks like something's missing!"*

CAROLE: *"He's not a chauvinist, but he's not helpful. He's just not around when something needs to be done. Y'know, I'll ask him to do things, and he'll say yes, but it doesn't get done!"*

CREAN: *"I try to contribute. I think it's a shared responsibility, bringing up the family . . ."*

CAROLE: *"He does with the kids."*

CREAN: *"I really try to work on that."*

CAROLE: *"Turn that volume down!"*

CREAN: *"I like pancakes. I cook the kids pancakes for breakfast. I try to get them to school, lessons, that sort of thing. I'm not a great gardener but I like getting the place neat, being out in the garden with the kids . . ."* He is having trouble with Emma's toy piano. *"I'm hopeless at this."*

EMMA: *"When's it gonna be ready, Dad?"*

CREAN: *"I'll make beds and vacuum floors if Carole asks me to."*

Bit of a puritan?

CREAN: *"No, what makes you think that?"*

CAROLE: *"He's been led astray by the Stormos (Storemen and Packers' Union) a couple of times."*

CREAN: *"It takes alot to get me led astray these days."*

CAROLE: *"Hates the disco scene."*

Crean finally fixes the keyboard and is rewarded with Emma playing *Ba Ba Black Sheep* and *Jingle Bells* a few hundred times. Sarah goes to bed. Crean is explaining: "I believe Australian society can be changed radically, I *do* believe it, I'm a fundamental democrat, I have great confidence in the electorate's ability to understand, appreciate sound argument, make a rational judgment . . ." When he and Carole eventually turn in for the night, Emma is still up, waiting. "She likes to sleep with us. Same bed." He grins.

Next morning Crean gets up, reads the papers, showers, switches on the radio for the news, listens to it through breakfast, gets into his car, listens to the ABC while he drives into Swanston Street. I am struck, once again, by the parallel with Hawke: the immaculate suit, the slightly bouffant hair, the friendly and communicative body language. He's a close mate of Hawke's, has been for a long time.

HAWKE ADMITS ADULTERY. Outside in the street, the newspaper placards are turning soggy.

Port Melbourne. Grey hard-edge horizon like a Michael Johnson painting, ships balanced on it like models in a waterfront Monopoly game, the sirens of the container cranes screaming like wounded seabirds. Crean grew up around here and would have liked the Melbourne Ports seat but got bustled into accepting Hotham. He may have to go and live there, but he doesn't want to. He's still cranky about that because he feels local: his Dad and Mum live just a couple of blocks away, and his daughter Sarah goes to Middle Park Primary, exactly the same school he went to.

But this portside, former working-class electorate has become marginal, it has been gentrified by affluent young professional people who have moved there to be close to the bay and the city, it needs only a 3.1 per cent swing for Labor to lose it, so maybe Hotham in the industrial-and-ethnic northwest is safer. Crean himself is part of the same gentrification process: he's moved, as a friend puts it, "from the wrong to the right side of Victoria Street", built a major living room/bathroom/kitchen/patio on the back of their modest Federation house, saddled himself with such a big mortgage that Carole got quite worried, and got helped over the hump by a timely Qantas directorship worth $17,000 a year. Is he worried that moving into Parliament may mean a drop in income, below his $53,000-plus-expenses salary from the ACTU? Crean smiles. "Depends how far I go," he says.

Crean is down here at No. 3 Dock to have his photo taken; he used to be head of the blue-collar Storemen and Packers' Union. But Crean has changed more than his address over the years; he is wearing a tailored suit with ever-so-slightly-flared trousers and highly polished black shoes and politically groomed hair and he looks bloody out of place as he poses on the loading dock next to *The Bass Trader*, a roll-on roll-off container ship.

"HARDHAT AREA" says the rusty sign. Huge 24-tonne forklifts are moving blindly around like post-Mad Max behemoths, trundling containers into the gaping black maw of the ship; the safety precautions are extreme, the gantry sirens are wailing — two men got crushed to death here last year; the ambience is one of immense industrial power, a neverending TWILIGHT SHIFT lifeline which feeds directly into the Melbourne city skyline in the distance and Paul Keating's worrying billion-dollar current account deficit. The men who keep it going are wearing red safety jackets with big diagonal yellow crosses on them. Unskilled workers? They look uncannily like targets in a telescopic rifle sight.

Crean chats to the dockmaster, checks out the ship manning levels, and asks why there are fifty or more container lorries queued up outside the port. He's meeting the shipowners tomorrow. As Crean leaves, the gatekeeper, who recognised him and let him in, calls out: "Is that news true about Bob Hawke?"

"What news?" says Crean.

"They're gonna make him an honorary member of the Liberal Party!"

Crean smiles, shrugs it off, climbs into his silver Ford Falcon Executive. Maybe they'll be saying that about him soon? "Some people say that about me already!" he says.

But it's a problem. Crean now has two constituencies: the union movement, which is demanding that the Labor government deliver on the wage-tax tradeoff after accepting years of real wage cuts from Labor/ACTU connivance; and the burgeoning middle-class Australian electorate, which wants no strikes, the unions kept in their place, and a good safe middle-of-the-road leader who will reassure them that everything will be all right, honey. In the past Crean has balanced the two out; the higher up the greasy pole he goes, the harder the balancing act.

* * *

Family Day, North Melbourne Football Ground. Crean is going to be made the club's No.1 ticket holder, a real honour in this city's exuberant footie culture; the club offered it to Keating first of all but he was non-committal so they gave it to Crean, who has been an ardent supporter of the team ever since . . . well, he was born and grew up in South Melbourne, and there are a few sceptical remarks about his transfer of loyalty to Norths, but there are a lot of woolstores around there and when Crean was working with the Storemen and Packers he naturally gravitated to the local team; anyhow, there's no doubting his dedication these days, even though the team has transferred to the MCG because it's bigger and so Simon, Carole, Sarah and Emma jump into the car and head off to the old ground.

It is an amazing scene: North Melbourne is one of the original cradles of Aussie Rules football, a decrepit working-class sportsground with wooden sheds, bleachers, faded signs, bitumen under foot, a tacky grandstand and a big gal iron shelter shed which used to double as greyhound pens and where the club's fans are now huddling out of the rain. They, too, are basically working class: muscly blokes in check shirts and shorts, women in beanies and sneakers, kids in tracksuits and blue-and-white North Melbourne jumpers, a fair number of Southern Europeans, a lot of them wearing party hats and swigging cans of soft drink while they wait for the ceremony.

When it starts it takes place on the back of a truck, the coach introducing the team one by one as "a fighting side, a side that will not give in". Bob Ansett, one of the club sponsors, introduces Crean and hands him an envelope with a club tie and his No.1 ticket inside. Crean, who is dressed in a green striped shirt, light casual pants, black shoes and the brightest gold sweater in Christendom, thanks the club, jumps down from the truck, hoists Sarah on to his shoulders, her legs around his neck, and goes off in search of ice creams, train rides and a go on the Jumbo Jumping Castle. It's Simon Crean at his most unguarded and admirable: there is something so straightforward and endearing about his love for the kids, and the time he spends with them, and his unselfconscious involvement in the family, that he could well be Mr

Aussie Average, a symbol of ordinary, suburban, twentieth century life.

Carole watches him. Does he get worked up about anything except the footie? Not really. Politics sometimes. "He's not doing it just for his own sake, but for the good of other people." Why did they wait ten years before having children? "We wanted to have some time before the kids arrived. I was teaching. We did the restaurant scene, the travel scene." But why wait quite so long, especially as so much of their life is now so obviously centred around the children? Carole looks directly at me. "Because I wanted to make sure he'd be a good father."

Not everybody loves Simon Crean. He's a lightweight, say some, a front man. Never worked with his hands in his life, which is strange for a trade unionist who came up through the blue collar Storemen and Packers (or maybe not so strange, as the workforce turns inexorably from deep blue to white collar). He's sometimes compared unfavourably to Bill Kelty, ACTU secretary, who has more of a traditional, cloth cap, I'm-on-the-side-of-the-worker style about him. Kelty was often described as the ideas man, the real power at the ACTU, while Crean handled the media. The conventional wisdom is that, back in 1985, the two rivals/colleagues did a deal: Kelty was to be the powerbroking secretary, the administrator, while Crean handled the upfront presidential role. When Crean moved into the union movement there was a lot of criticism of "academics" taking over Labor and some of that resentment lingers on. It tends to focus on symbols like first-class air fares and overseas junkets. Crean, for his part, laughs when it's suggested he's "well-off". He has, he says, no shares, no investments, no weekender, just a house with a mortgage. However, they were DINKS (Double Income No Kids) for a long while before the children arrived, teaching science and maths. Simon has a new Falcon, Carole has a newish Laser.

Are they Yuppies? Carole says: "nobody thinks of themselves as yuppies, it's always somebody else". Crean tends to think they're just fulfilling the aspirations most Australians have. In class terms he's moved from lower/middle to upper/middle. He was never a battler; he went to Melbourne High, the "old school tie" state school, and being the son of an MP, says a friend, "gives you a reasonably elevated view of yourself and your position in the world". As he's moved from success to success Crean has developed a taste for a few things: good white wines (he has a few dozen at home, dislikes reds), and excellent restaurants, expensive suits, and travel — especially travel, which he wants to do more of. He was going overseas four or five times a year for the ACTU and ILO (International Labor Organisation), likes Paris, regards Geneva as a work base only, and is sometimes jetted around the country in Lear jets provided by business groups. None of John Cain's puritanism there.

But he's not a high flier in the Paul Keating manner; indeed, his general style is reassuringly suburban: despite his natty suits he has appalling clothes sense, wears insurance salesman green shirts with RSL ties, and must be one of the few men in Australia to still wear a tieclasp to keep his collar in place; at weekends he slops around the place, answers telephone calls from the media. There are a few nondescript prints on the wall, the front of the house needs a good paint, there are plastic kids' bikes and dolls and kindergarten cut-outs everywhere, and the headiest leap into luxury he is contemplating right now is a CD player. In fact if you wanted a photograph, for a time capsule, of the quintessential living environment of Middle Australia, this is it.

Nor is he a cultured man, despite his university background. He doesn't know much about art, has started going to the opera to see things like musicals and *The Gondoliers*, the last films he saw were *Roger Rabbit* and *One Hundred and One Dalmations* (for daughter reasons) and his reading, apart from documents and economic reports, is limited to spy thriller stuff like Le Carre. On his bookshelf: Len Deighton, encyclopaedias, bushwalking guides, a globe of the world, a framed photo of Carole, *The Two Bad Mice Pop-up Book* and Jeffrey Archer's *First Among Equals* (hmmm). His father used to get *The Listener* but Simon admits he hasn't read any political theory since leaving university almost twenty years ago.

There is an upright piano in the almost Edwardian sitting room, though he doesn't play it; he was forced to take piano lessons as a kid and it turned him right off. He's locked into the pop music of the 1960s. In the dining room there is a large and formal dining table where, when he turned 40, Simon and Carole hosted a dinner party which included Bob and Hazel Hawke, Paul and Anita Keating, Ralph Willis and his wife, Bill Kelty, Gareth Evans' wife, and other assorted political glitterati. With mates like those, who needs style?

Crean is an asthmatic. He takes medication, carries a squirter with him wherever he goes. He says it's allergy related, not stress related, though sometimes the pressure gets him down. "I work hard," he says. "You can burn out. I give myself another fifteen years." Because of his asthma he doesn't smoke; in fact he remembers trying it when he was a kid, "I was up a tree, did the drawback, felt giddy, gave it away." He does sit-ups every morning, swims in the pool at his father's home unit to help his breathing, doesn't do much beach swimming despite being just a block away, reckons he ought to lose weight but doesn't do much about it.

Ambitious? Yes. Had it easy? Now that riles him. "Why have I had it easy? It's one of the hardest electorates to succeed in, the trade union movement. It's been a torrid time; I mean, I've had some very difficult periods!" He includes in that three defeats for positions he's gone for, including his failure to win preselection for his father's Melbourne Ports seat in 1977. That could have stopped Simon Crean in his tracks.

"I lost by one vote," he says, with palpable bitterness. "I had worked my butt off in the area. It taught me who to rely on, what you can believe in terms of personal commitments, what the individual power plays were. No, it didn't make me cynical. The important learning curve for me was to cop a defeat and not let it set you back; I just set my sights on a new goal, which was to stay with the union." Did being Frank Crean's son help? That annoys him as well. "If anything my background made it harder, critics thought I was riding on my father's coat-tails. But you've got to remember he didn't come from the trade union movement, he was the most surprised of anyone when I came home and announced I was going to work for the Storemen and Packers' Union." So did he learn anything from his father? Crean thinks about it. The family went to church regularly, and Crean says he himself is still a believer: "I wouldn't be anything so silly as an athiest." So: "It teaches you values, compassion, concern for the underprivileged. That's important for a caring sort of role. Frank is a philosophical, rational thinker, very moral." Pause. "I consider myself to be a moral person."

One of three brothers, Simon Crean grew up amid dinner table political discussions at home, but at high school, says Crean, "in a strange sort of way I withdrew from political life, you tended to be ribbed about your father being a politician. I gave up Social Studies, which should have been a shoe-in, for French, which was the only subject I've ever failed in!" He went to Monash University to study Economics and Law, got involved in the anti-Vietnam moratoriums, joined the ALP, and credits his time at Monash with getting him back into politics. After finishing economics, "I wanted to get out and work, didn't know what to do, and the vocational guidance adviser there told me that there was this new president of the ACTU, Bob Hawke, who had been talking about bringing in a research capacity. I wrote to see what opportunities there were, didn't get a response, so I decided I'd persist with Law." But Crean never saw himself as an advocate and one day when he met Bill Landeryou, then secretary of the Storemen and Packers' Union, in the John Curtin Hotel, Crean arranged to do some work over the Christmas vacation and ended up working with the union fulltime. He was involved in a couple of big wool-handling disputes, became union secretary himself, and eventually moved to the ACTU.

That long experience has marked Crean. He understands, but is wary of, the media, uses Creanspeak to avoid answering questions, and saves his trade union language for his mates: he sneers at "the mad Left", talks about "attracting the flies" had he stood for Melbourne Ports, dismisses one journalist as "a prick" and recalls how Hawke thought he would "shit it in" when he first challenged Bill Hayden for the Labor leadership. The perceived closeness between Labor Unity and the New South Wales Right, he explains carefully, is the result of the exercise to "get Bob up". Well, they got Bob up. Next task: get Simon up.

* * *

The environment is one of those issues which may determine whether Simon Crean is a genuinely 'new' politician or just another old-style Labor machine man. On the fridge in the Crean family kitchen, amid the magnetic alphabet letters and stickers and kids' scribbles, is a snapshot of three generations of Creans out in the bush. Crean says he is "sympathetic" to environmental issues and declares "I'm a great lover of the environment. We took the kids camping at Christmas time up at Halls Gap, the Grampians, I'd like to take them to the Flinders Ranges, I'd like to take them up to Kakadu, I like outdoor living. It's not a question of saying I'm not interested in the environment, that's crazy."

Yet when the Wesley Vale pulp mill controversy blew up, Crean, as then head of the ACTU, took a conservative and pro-development view and attacked the "illogicality" of the Labor government's decision, by which the government imposed stricter environmental guidelines on the proposed pulp mill in Tasmania and the developers walked out. It is hard to know whether it was the decision itself or the unfavourable public reaction to Crean's comments about it which made him so sensitive. Whereas the general public response had been to praise federal Cabinet for standing up to the developers' threats, Crean attacked the government for not setting up overall environmental guidelines. Retribution was swift: Senator Graham Richardson, Minister for the Environment and New South Wales Right-wing heavy, said he "had thought I'll be supporting him (Crean) for the Labor leadership" but now "I think . . . that support will be a few years further off than I thought originally." Tandberg had a cartoon showing Richardson with a chainsaw having lopped Crean off at the knees. By the end of the day, according to the *Sydney Morning Herald*, Keating had called Richardson to heel and a chastened Minister admitted his comments were excessively harsh. Still, Crean's timing had been less than brilliant; he'd picked the wrong issue with which to try for a high profile, and a few days later he was still smarting.

The restaurant is Fanny's, which has to be one of the most exclusive places in Melbourne, with slightly more waiters than diners and patronised by trendy financiers, moustachioed advertising gurus, bouffant-haired Porsche types, and the occasional trade union leader. There are no STORMOS, as the Storemen and Packers militants are known. Crean is entertaining Clive Jenkins, the former president of Britain's TUC (Trade Union Congress), who is visiting Australia, and his partner Sherie, who runs a restaurant and cottages on the east coast of Tasmania. Crean orders, carefully, a Lilydale Chardonnay from Victoria, casually joins in the conversation about brilliant wines, the exquisite properties of Tasmanian walnuts and Port Phillip crayfish and the anti-union successes of Margaret Thatcher and Rupert Murdoch, talks with his usual clarity and good sense about the need for the Australian union movement to enlist the new tertiary and service workers created by post-industrial society, and agrees with virtually everything Jenkins says until it comes to the environment. Over Wesley Vale he is fierce, provocative and unrepentant. The greenies say they want balanced development but don't mean it. They can't deliver their constituencies, they can't keep to an agreement. Their peak councils are undisciplined. Labor needs jobs, the economy needs value-added industries, the government and the developers should have fixed up an agreement. As for Senator Richardson: "It doesn't bother me, it's crazy, he regretted it afterwards anyway."

Listening to him, it's like hearing an old-style Tammany politician who is unable to grasp that a new politics has developed which is focused on issues like the environment and nuclear power and minorities and the quality of city living, issues which aren't susceptible to a quick fix or bargain, and in which principles are more important than Crean's anger at pressure groups which can't "deliver". It's also a reminder of how conservative Crean has been on other issues: he gave the casting vote which reversed Labor's anti-uranium policy; he's still running on the privatisation issue, he's an economic rationalist who agrees with the Keating line in most debates. In his four years as ACTU president he "delivered", in one union leader's words, "a well-disciplined trade union movement".

Crean goes to the toilet. Clive Jenkins, to my surprise, leans over to me and says: "You're right." (I have been outlining the green case over Wesley Vale and arguing the need for a "new politics".) Of course, it's easy for him, he's retired while Crean is in the frontline. When Crean returns to the table he is as affable and charming as ever. A friend of the family says he gets his phlegmatism from Frank Crean: "He doesn't run on his nerves, he can handle monumental amounts of pressure." Crean himself thinks he gets his strength from his mother, Mary, a formidable woman who always sounds faintly surprised that, of her three sons, Simon's the one who's done so well. He loved study but he never knew what he wanted to do; she'd always assumed he'd just drift into Law. He never seemed to be that interested in politics, he never read any of Frank's books or talked about it much; maybe it just rubbed off, unbeknown to them all.

Crean farewells his guests, thanks the waiters and strides off to the ACTU in Swanston Street. A few people in the street recognise him, call out to him, wish him well. He's not famous but he's popular. One day he may be both. Hawke made the ACTU presidency a supremely political job; Crean, through the Accord, made it even more so. When he made the move into Federal Parliament, a close friend said: "He's been in politics all his life, so what else is new?"

Amongst the media who know him well the consensus is that Crean is "good but bland". He's a skilful operator, he communicates well, but where is the general program, the agenda? Says one commentator: "It's a bit late at 40 to start developing a vision." There's the pervasive feeling that he's had it too easy, never experienced any underprivilege itself — it's all been secondhand. No crises. A few years ago he lost his elder brother, Stephen, when he died on a skiing trip at Kosciusko. Otherwise it's been all straight ahead, one goal after another, swimming safely in the mainstream.

Crean rejects that. He says he doesn't see any need to change course from what he's done; if you ask him what he stands for, he replies "efficiency with equity". He believes in change and significant redistribution, but it will take time. How long? "I'll be around for a while," he says. "I'm still a young man, I'm only 40 — though I feel older at times!"

He has many of the qualities you'd demand of a national leader; the labour movement, by producing people of the calibre of Hawke, Crean and Kelty, has outstripped management over the last few years and has organised itself a major role in government policy as well. Crean's particularly proud of that. "We had this historic nexus between the union movement and the party, goes back almost a hundred years, but it's only in the last five years we'd tapped into that," he says. "It's been the main achievement to date. Very few people believed it would work."

In Canberra there is a lot of feeling, even among his supporters, that he needs another couple of years to prepare himself for whatever lies ahead. Bit more experience. Maybe a few defeats. There's a bit of the Golden Boy syndrome about Crean which he will have to live down. That probably doesn't matter. The perceived narrowness, the limitations, the easy pragmatism is more of a worry. *Personable, successful, liked by nearly everyone, but no real program for the future . . .* oh Jesus, they say despondently, not another Hawke!

JILL WRAN

When Jill Wran suffered some sort of nervous collapse a while ago she began worrying that she is two separate people. Or several. And she doesn't know which to choose. It only happens when she feels bad about herself, which is more often than you'd suspect. Because she seems so privileged you'd expect her to be less wounded, less easily hurt. Most of the time Jill (Wran) Hickson comes across as formal, glamorous, confident and very stylish. She is a successful businesswoman and agent in her own right and probably one of the busiest women in Australian public life — just the sort of woman you'd expect as the wife of Neville Wran, the former premier of NSW. That's the familiar Jill, the woman she has programmed herself to be.

The other Jill Wran is just below the makeup: obsessive, highly strung, vulnerable, very emotional — the sort of person whose friends are always trying to protect her, and who always feels under immense pressure to justify herself. Sometimes she becomes fearful she is self-destructive as well. No wonder she feels, as she says, "so much turmoil on the inside". She keeps busy "to keep from being churned up all the time; I'm partly well-controlled on the outside because I know I've got to mask quite a lot of uncontrol inside". Says a close friend: "she feels constantly on trial".

It sounds like a cliché, and there is something conventional about Jill Wran, from her designer watch to her high-caste brushed-back blonde hair to that impossibly cultured, almost theatrical voice. Early in her privileged/underprivileged life young

Jilly, as her husband Neville calls her, discovered an image of refinement and she has been trying to conform to it ever since. "I would rather be respectable than popular," she says.

But clichés, as we all know, are truths worn simple by the telling. In this case the complicated truth is that Jill Hickson, now aged 40, married to Neville Wran for 14 years, has had a damaging and hurtful past and, at the time I interviewed her, she felt she couldn't take it any more. "I've been really sick," she said. "I have just bust a gut, over and over, of every kind. I've found myself getting ill, and falling about . . . I ask myself every day, what *else* have you done? . . . I've had enough trauma not to ever want to cause any."

She is sitting in a restaurant. She is trying to explain her life to an outsider. "So long as it's not hurtful, and it doesn't harm anyone else, I cop it, I just cop it . . ."

Jill Wran is crying. She cries like the man in Les Murray's poem *An Absolutely Ordinary Rainbow*, "not like a child, not like the wind", with dignity, sitting at the table, the tears dribbling down on to the tablecloth . . . She gets herself together, apologises. "Why am I so upset? Because I feel so inadequate. And showing I'm so emotional. That's so stupid." Later: "I've been so totally disciplined all my life. By myself, partly, but also by my grandparents. I'm so goody-goody. Why don't I let more of myself come through? Because it churns me up so much. I suppose I'm frightened that, at bottom, I'm disturbed." She thinks about it, smiles, shakes it off. "No; I think I'm unbearably, excruciatingly sane and managerial."

A few months earlier she had reached a point of no return. Wran had decided to resign. Jill decided to try to have a child. July 4, 1986, the day Wran stepped down as Premier, was Independence Day in more ways than one. As she talks she entwines the fingers of her left hand around each other. She gets PMT badly, worries, gets exhausted — "I'm a nervous person, socially," she says.

But most of the time the more public Jill Wran takes over, that mellifluous voice sounds over the airwaves, she talks measuredly and self-assuredly about what Neville's resignation means to her, and says, quite unselfconsciously, things like: "I'll love him more than ever. I don't just say that. I think we'll always love each other. It's an extraordinary relationship, so highly charged, very tough at times. The most disturbing thing about Neville's blowtorch is that afterwards he says 'I didn't mean it, Jilly — I just like to win an argument.' But we've never thought of separating, never thought of breaking up. In every marriage there's a kind of power struggle that goes on. In a political marriage that power struggle is much more urgent than usual. If I was independent to begin with, being part of a political marriage has made me even more so. Because it would be easy for one's personality to be . . . if not crushed, then eclipsed, or absorbed. That's happened to me, but as I've been absorbed I've struck out in other directions: Qantas, the MBA (Master's Degree in Business Administration), my music . . . I've found new selves."

Says a close friend: "She's an old-fashioned lady, really. Not of this century. She's straight. And loyal. And very, very sensitive."

Jill Wran: The Public Image

Height:	171.5 centimetres (5ft 7½ inches)
Weight:	54 kilograms (8½ stone)
Size:	Clothes 10–12
Eyes:	Grey/blue
Hair:	Blonde
Scars:	Sole of right foot, from broken glass; left kneecap, fall on rocks; sundry hockey scars.

Appearance:
Most of the time Jilly Lesley Norton Hickson projects an image of beautifully groomed, self-assured, upper class elegance. She dismisses such descriptions as "nonsense", and says: "I really don't think I'm on about how I look. I mean, I don't spend hours shopping, I dress very quickly . . . I love slumming it all day and then getting into an evening dress at night . . . I see my approach as understated, toned down; I don't wear a lot of jewellery or makeup." Continuing, frowning: "I've always had this problem of people deciding that I'm a certain type of person because I look the way I do. I don't think my appearance says much about my personality, they don't necessarily relate. Sometimes I think that

it's just because I'm angular, that I've got Dad's paws and feet and bony structure."

Nevertheless her style is unmistakeable. She always seems to be impeccably and untouchably polished, like a Richard Avedon model. She wears her hair fairly long and straight and brushed back from her face in a way which emphasises her aristocratic forehead and cheekbones; the mode is, of course, high classic. Because she is short-sighted she wears enormous, fashionable plastic-framed glasses but, mercifully, never pushes them up on to her head. On her left wrist, a gold watch, on the third finger of her left hand, a plain gold wedding ring with three inset diamonds. She often wears long, draped clothes which emphasise her height. Her gestures tend to be faintly theatrical and she uses words like "wonderful" and "beautiful" and "absolutely marvellous" and "dishy" and occasionally when she laughs her voice moves into that familiar soprano trill — she loves singing, was a mezzo at school, warbles under the hot shower and stays there so long her legs come out in spots — but she never calls people "darling" and she detests snobbery of any kind and as she says, "I won't go to fashion shows or to all those society do's where the only objective seems to be to show off 2000 dresses."

Jill as Class Stereotype?

OK, so why does she seem such a class stereotype?

"Oh shit!" she says. "Why am I like that? I don't know. It wouldn't be Annesley, the boarding school I went to, because the one good thing about Annesley was that it was far from exclusive. Yes I *am* North Shore. I don't have the regulation proletarian background, but I'm *lower* North Shore, I remember waiting at the train station to go to see Mummy at Cremorne and being surrounded by those horrible Frensham girls . . .

"Look, I grew up with my grandparents who held it as a sign of healthy self-respect to always look well-turned-out. I am living out and reinforcing their standards; even if I do place a good deal of emphasis on respectability and refinement, surely scruffy people don't have a monopoly on sensitivity and soul? Glamorous? I hate that. Don't you see I could easily be a big brassy blonde with a thick wavy flowing mane, big thick red lips, diamonds and so on. Isn't it possible that the thing I most abhor is bad taste, that what I seek out is the *best* in everything?

"Why should I deny that North Shore element? It's there. That's where I grew up, in Neutral Bay with a grandmother who carried herself magnificently and a mother who went to Abbotsleigh and who was always beautifully dressed. But you must understand I see the North Shore thing as a jumped-up thing, whereas my family was different. I felt superior, because I wasn't bunging it on. I was always a loner, I never felt ordinary. Y'know, at school I was usually writing thank-you letters to other people who had me to stay, I always wanted other people to thank me. Achievement was the way through."

Her mind jumps off at a tangent which turns out to be a metaphor. "The first time I remember looking in a mirror, the Matron materialised magically behind us and said if she caught us at it again she would paper over the mirror. Can you imagine that? We were aged about 4. God, it's awful to be so ego-bound."

Jill Hickson, aged 4 to 40, perpetually looking in the mirror, knowing she shouldn't.

"I am, or have been, ambitious, competitive and proud. But always I'm looking for the best: the best performance, the best solution, the best in relationships." She stops. "It's all about where you are coming from, isn't it?"

Where She Comes From

Shortly before Jill was born, her mother began suffering from a lifelong mental illness which left her incapacitated. She is still alive and Jill obviously loves her deeply: "she is the dearest, sweetest human being" — but at the age of three Jill was sent away to a boarding school, Annesley, in Bowral. Her father is Staveley Frederick Norton Hickson, a successful businessman and real estate agent in Sydney.

An only child, she grew up with her life divided between an institution and her grandparents' Edwardian/Methodist household in Neutral Bay. She rarely saw her father, though she sees him regularly now, and when she saw her mother it intensified the sense of pain and suffering she felt. It is an experience which she is reluctant to talk about. It explains, in part, why her friends feel so protective about her, and why Neville Wran worries about her "sensitivity". It also explains a great deal about Jill Wran herself.

"It's coloured my whole life," she says hesistantly. "People ask me why I'm so *driven*, it's put me under such pressure to achieve. I just felt I had to redeem them all somehow. I've had to be very strong, to counter my mother's sense of powerlessness, of being a victim. I used to lie there in bed at night and think, 'God, what am I supposed to do with my life? Why have so many people suffered?' "

At her grandparents' home Jill acquired a heavy dose of Methodism, moral righteousness and propriety in manners. "My grandfather was a very austere Victorian fellow, never hugged me," she remembers. "They were very tough with me, I never had any money. I saw Daddy about once a year — yes, it's occurred to me that Neville is something of a father figure to me." She stops herself. "No. It's much more likely he sees something of his mother in me."

As well as this, there were recurrent family traumas involving her mother and grandparents. The young girl at the centre of it tried to make up for it all by excelling at school. "I'd done things like being the only person to win the Honour Board twice, the most accomplished Junior, I mean I was champion of most things and got the lead in the play — people hate you for that — champion in sport — in the final years I was Games Captain," she says. "It occurred to me that I was brighter than anyone else in the class, and that's a terrible burden when you're young. It was probably because I was so emotionally adult."

At the age of 15, both her grandparents died. Her grandmother first, of cancer. "She was the only one who really hugged me. Except for my mother, of course. My grandfather just adored her; he was very lonely for the next three months and died of a heart attack," she says. "In a way it's just as well it happened when it did, because otherwise I'd have turned out to be very bolshie. They were very very strict, and I was already a bit bolshie . . ."

It was an aunt, Helen Halse Rogers, who stepped into the gap and became Jill's guardian. She was secretary of the New South Wales Council of Social Services for thirty years: another achiever. The family firmly expected Jill to follow suit and become

Head Girl. She didn't. "Another girl got the guernsey; she was elected. I was in school assembly at the time and the main thought I had was *I'd let Aunt Helen down!* I'd let them all down in their expectations."

Ever since, Jill Wran has tried to outperform every expectation of her. She went from Annesley to Sydney University, got her Bachelor of Arts degree, considered staying on to do honours in Government, joined Qantas instead, and launched herself on her career as a successful businesswoman: became International Relations Manager for the airline, topped the class at the Australian Graduate School of Management at the Unviersity of NSW, and has gone on to set up her own management and literary agency with clients ranging from Ansett to Tom Keneally.

Intellectually, she was a pluralist before it was popular. Until she enrolled in the AGSM course at the university, she feared she was innumerate; she ended up taking out five awards. Golden girl.

"I keep telling myself you can stop, you don't have to prove yourself any more," she says.

Scar tissue, invisible, just behind the eyelids.

From Prude to Neville

Even at school, Jill Hickson was different. More sophisticated, a bit precocious, but somehow sheltered from brute boy/girl traumas. From about 12 years of age to 20 there was a sort of closure about her. Annesley girl, a few close friends, a bit off-putting to men.

"I didn't have much sexual experience, the most important thing was one's 'reputation' ", she says. "I don't think I'm any longer prudish, but I think I was prudish for far too long."

She went on to Sydney University, studied English literature and Government, and got involved in a long-standing relationship with a Schoolboy Hero. When that broke up, "I had a bit of a ball, went out with quite a lot of people, had two disastrous relationships in a row," she says. "When Neville wants to be unpleasant sometimes he says 'Why didn't you marry one of those King's School boys?' "

After she graduated she thought about an academic career, but decided instead to head into commerce. Her first job was in the university's Fisher library, then she joined the marketing division of Qantas and seven years later was appointed International Relations Manager, which meant hard negotiating on airline traffic rights. She was the first woman to hold such a senior position in the company, and she was appointed despite upper management reservations that a woman might not be "aggressive" enough.

Then came the night Bob Moore, the TV interviewer, rang her up and asked her to a dinner party. Neville Wran, at the time leader of the Labor opposition in New South Wales, was there. She didn't know him. "Bob sat me next to Neville and I think I must have been inestimably boring, because I'd been studying Government honours under Henry Mayer and I'd been saving up all these thoughts and ideas and ideals, and poor Neville became the repository for them all in one dinner! It was one of those nights when you know you're firing, in an intellectual sense," says Jill.

"I quickly discovered that he was not the idealist I was. He was interested but he hadn't read much of this literature, so we just talked flat out, certainly I talked all night. As he got up to leave I remember he touched my wrist gently, like that, and said 'We must see each other again' and I thought 'ooh, something's happened here, something worked!

"Then he rang me up, I had an old friend, a man, but a friend, mind, staying with me who answered the phone, and he heard somebody say 'oh hell' or something like that — it seemed Neville had got the courage to ring me and then thought, 'oh, she's already living with someone'. Then he rang me at Qantas and said 'it was a very interesting conversation, I'd like to continue it,' and I thought he must have wanted me to work for him.

"We had to put it off for two weeks because there was an absolute flood in Sydney. I couldn't open the car door, so I had to ring Neville and tell him I was marooned and couldn't make it, and he said 'never mind, I've god a dweadful cold and I can't talk anyway, . . . I was trying to make up my mind, would I leave Qantas for the highly risky prospect of a politician's band wagon? I've always been a planner and a forecaster, which I think comes from being an only child . . . and also I'm a compulsive obsessive by nature. Well, we finally had lunch at the old Marseilles, and we were taken upstairs, and I felt his eyes on the back of my legs! It's so corny . . . and I thought, 'hullo, I hadn't anticipated this!'

"The first time he came to dinner at my flat at Kirribilli, and I was trying desperately to cook the fish and the gas flame was flying up towards the cupboards — y'know, I can't think when a man is standing very close to me — he used to have this habit of standing very close to people, actually I think it's a most unattractive social habit because you crowd people out, and he said: 'I'm going to have you, Miss Jilly Hicks' and here was this beautiful bit of John Dory burning furiously . . . and I didn't believe him! And I didn't believe him until we were actually married. And when he became Premier I thought, well, that's the end of that. But it wasn't."

Living Together

Jill and Neville Wran have been married 14 years. It is a marriage that has withstood rows, rumours, intense emotional strain, elections, political scandals, Wran's tempestuous premiership, his resignation — and the constant jarring of two very different personalities. Wran can be overwhelming. Jill Wran recognises that she found a "strong, powerful man", though she is also very much in tune with Wran's need for her; it has meant subjugating a lot of what she might have done otherwise. But instead of going under, she has held out for a life of her own.

Formally, this has meant her MBA degree, Ansett, Hickson Associates, scores of different boards and organisations, and an engagement list of speeches, functions and launchings which is heavier than that of most politicians. Informally, it has meant resisting her husband's annexation of everything about her that is different to him.

"From the beginning we've been such disparate people," she says. "When I first met Neville he didn't really like people, he didn't like himself. He had few close friends. I think I can truly say I was the first person that he . . . unlocked himself to, he really trusted me.

"I don't think I'd ever come across class consciousness before. If you're a middle-class Australian, well-educated, from a genteel family like mine, you honestly didn't believe class existed in this country, and I had real difficulty trying to fathom Neville until I realised there is such a thing.

"Dad's a farmer, his family were graziers, you know — shiny shoes, clean fingernails, look at people when you speak to them, important things like sincerity . . . ah. It's only in recent times that Dad's really accepted Neville.

"Neville's fond of saying, when an argument's over, 'Jilly, you've changed my life.' If I've done anything for him I've made him feel better about himself. I think he now places more value on things for their own sake instead of for their political purposes. He's influenced me enormously. He's toughened me up, given me more fibre. I'm still extremely sensitive, but much less intense. I wonder if the best relationships he's got now aren't with people who've stood up to him — me, Gerry Gleeson, Jack Ferguson." (Gleeson was Wran's department head; Ferguson was deputy Premier.)

Has she influenced him politically? Jill Wran thinks the art of influence is not to claim it. Those who know her say she has mellowed the scholarship boy from Balmain: introduced him to classical music, opera, conservation, friendships (she lists her interests as 'music, literature, international affairs, scrabble, crosswords, conservation and animal welfare'.) And Neville Wran, who is both a rough and charming man — and can be both simultaneously — has rescued her from being the genteel, accomplished, almost typecast Miss Jilly Hickson she used to be.

"I read a lot, I was alone a lot, I was in myself a lot from the time I was a very young person until the time I married Neville," she explains. "When I was growing up, 'teens and early twenties, I was older, more adult, I knew much more than any of the fellers I went out with. I'd just had more experience of life — even thought it might not have been sexual experience. And I was impatient with them on emotional and political grounds, I couldn't get near them, I found their snobbishness suffocating and offensive in the extreme. I was radical, much more so than Neville, but then being once removed I could afford to be. For instance, the Left in the party will tell you they've usually had my support. The people I admire in the party all tend to be on the Left: Jack Ferguson, for example, and Rodney Cavalier. I hadn't met anyone who was so solid as Neville, really; I had this overwhelming sense that he would always love me.

"Do I still feel very political? No, not so much these days. Having lived politics vicariously for so many years, you're welcome to it. I'm happy he's resigned."

Will she miss being the Premier's wife?

"No. I think my life will change very little, except I rather hope it will be less complex and anxiety-ridden. I confidently expect Neville will be a very demanding, very old man. He's probably going to outlive me. He's as tough as an old sock."

Seeing the Real You at Last

There is an elusive quality to Jill Hickson Wran. Her friends say she doesn't play games, she doesn't pretend to be something she isn't. If anything she is not as self-protective as she should be. She possesses an innocence bordering on naiveté.

"I am loving, generous, and look for that in other people," she says. The statement is innocent. It is innocent of irony.

"She's always been giving, giving, giving — and not having a great sense of support," says a close woman friend. Says another: "She has never had unequivocal love".

Connected with this is her lack of scepticism of the social milieu she comes from and moves in. She seems to have accepted it without question. Because she has never rebelled against the way she was cast, has never jumped out of the demands and style of her background, she seems to lack some ineluctable core of self which she can readily communicate to others and have them respond to. And so, though she is friendly, she remains undefined. Which is why so many different people have so many different reactions to her.

But perhaps that is less important than the perception, by almost everyone who knows her well, that she is a "good" person. An old-fashioned quality out of kilter with a brutal time.

Jill Wran at Home

At her home in Wallis Street, Woollahra, Jill Wran is a graceful, somewhat isolated woman surrounded by cats and good taste. On the wall, paintings by Charles Blackman, Fred Williams, Lloyd Rees, Arthur Boyd. On the windowsill overlooking the terraced garden and lawn, perfect white cyclamens. In the kitchen, some Heather Dorrough drawings of vegetables, a stuffed wombat, and brown pears arranged in a bowl like an Art Gallery sculpture. Around the paved courtyard, post-modern columns and pedestals. In the upstairs study, a newspaper placard saying WRAN RESIGNS.

The house was designed by Epsie Dodd before the Wrans moved there from an unpretentious terrace in Victoria Street; "we haven't got much money, we really haven't," she says. The house is worth perhaps a million dollars, but it has *not* been "decorated". "Wallis Street? Terrific. It's totally unpretentious, nothing jumped up about it," she says. It's typical of her that she avoids like the plague any suggestion of nouveau riche vulgarity, but indulges her own refined sensibility with no apparent hesitation. Guilt is probably what the Alan Bonds of this world put on their picture frames.

She has help with the housework, because she's a busy career woman ("I have a wonderful woman, a retired Qantas tealady, without whom I simply couldn't cope.") But Jill does the cooking herself and thinks she's all right if she puts her mind to it. "When Neville's home I cook dinner for him. Neville's running joke is, 'Now, what's for dessert? I know you've spent all day thinking about my dessert' — and I invariably produce fresh fruit or something."

She sometimes relies on charm to get her own way, though authors say she can be a good, tough negotiator. She drops famous names like confetti, and betrays herself by saying how on her visit to New York it didn't *really* matter to her that she sat between Isaac Stern and Teddy Kennedy at a concert, or that she met Norman Mailer at a party, or that a card from one of her staff means as much to her as a card from a famous conductor. In that sense she is an ingenue: trusting, gauche, saying things that can make her listeners wince. On the other hand she is soft-hearted, very sentimental and unpretentious behind the high-gloss veneer. Guinea pigs leap into her lap. She's clumsy, always bumping into things, usually because she's in a hurry. Having to wear glasses doesn't help.

She likes the writing of, among others, Helen Garner and Kate Grenville. On the pinboard of what was her rather gloomy office in Surry Hills were postcards and snapshots from writers, a Victoria Roberts cartoon, newspaper tear-outs, theatre ads, and a Polaroid of her and Tom Keneally, both dressed in immaculate white, accepting medals at Sydney University.

At the centre of her artistic life is music: the Opera, the Sydney Symphony Orchestra, the Conservatorium, the Philharmonia Choir; she especially likes choral music, and says "some of my happiest memories are of singing in the choir, and singing around the piano on holidays". Holidays at Lord Howe Island and reading books on plane trips are about as close as she gets to a sport. "Fitness is a fiction as far as I'm concerned," she says, laughing. "I read where I cycle and jog, and I do neither. For a while I walked the dog in the park every day, but then the dog died and it's just not the same. I'm not particularly good at walking myself, my husband's not often available, and without a dog it has little appeal."

Instead, she eats selectively. She is a semi-vegetarian.

So she tells waiters.

Sex, Drugs & Rock 'N' Roll

She once admitted she had smoked marijuana. But she prefers wine and sometimes Scotch.

Her biggest achievement one year was to give up smoking on Christmas Day. She had put it off in the past because she was afraid she would have a nervous breakdown. She was dead right!

She is woman-centred rather than man-centred. She thinks women see more and they see it earlier.

She is a feminist in the sense that Jane Austen was a feminist, yes, she is very definitely a feminist — there is just no other condition, and so are her friends, in the way they lead their lives.

But they are not anti-men, they are all wholly and unutterably heterosexual.

Like she is.

She does not have affairs. But sometimes thinks she should have. In the past.

Jazz affects her like a raw nerve.

Like Mississippi Fred McDowell, she "does not like no rock 'n' roll".

A Day in the Life of the Former Premier's Wife

"OK, I'm up about seven, turn the hoses on, get the paper if Neville's not already up. Feed the cats. Get breakfast. Neville goes upstairs to have a shave and a shower, he reads the papers first, usually during breakfast, I have a quick look afterwards, then I start worrying about what bills I have to pay today.

"Phone's going, doorbell's ringing. Half a grapefruit, bowl of cereal, cup of tea . . . the big luxury at weekends is a piece of toast with plum jam for Neville and vegemite for me. Rush upstairs. Sometimes I sit on the phone for half an hour, to get my Mrs Premier's life sorted out . . . that's how it has been. Am I speaking here or there, when do I need the car? Or I might be making a speech at lunchtime, and I get that together there. Then I have very long showers, where I do all my planning for the day . . . sending telegrams, birthday presents.

"Then rush off, jump into some gear, any gear, drive to the office like a lunatic because all the way there I'm thinking of what I have to do immediately and I can't wait to do it. When I get there the phones are ringing, there's somebody waiting, and of course I don't do what I'd planned to do for hours.

"Normally Carol Serventy, who is my associate, and I exchange a few thoughts, then work furiously, usually work through lunch, the big break is when we can take time to go to the sandwich shop. No reading, not during the day; we become literary agents because we love to read, but it's a myth — once you become an agent the big struggle is to find time to read. I read books very carefully at manuscript stage but I rarely ever pick up a newly published book and re-read it, because you've done that already.

"The objective is to have the morning to think and write and do contracts; make all my telephone calls at lunchtime and immediately after, and spend the afternoon seeing clients and publishers. It never works that way; one day I'll get there.

"I never leave the office till about seven or seven-thirty, if Neville is at home; if Neville is out I work till ten o'clock. It's very bad actually, drinking coffee, having a stitch in your stomach, feeling you're never going to finish what's on your list. I spend hours in front of the computer; if it breaks down, that's when I become the ogress of Sydney!

"Then, eventually, I go home; and I try to pretend I've been home for some time when Neville walks in the door. We often talk too long and enjoy it too much and have a little too much wine because it's so nice to see each other and talk about what's happened. It's a good time, a very good time of the day; but of course it means you never have enough sleep and you're always firing, y'know, not really any *down* time. That's what Sunday mornings are for.

"We have something on almost every night, or if there isn't I work at the office. If we have one night free in the week, Saturday night perhaps, and the question is: what do we do? Do we go to the Sydney Theatre Company, do we go to the opera, a movie — and of course the five o'clock movie wins because you can get home early, have a bit of tucker, and then trip into bed."

She laughs.

She thinks.

She can be in turns girlish, facile, thoughtful.

"One of the best things about Neville's decision to retire is that you get to the point where there is so much going on around you you're almost oblivious to its true significance," she says.

The Rest of Her Life

She sometimes thinks she could do Neville's job, but then remembers she is too thin-skinned.

She might spend the latter part of her life in a major administrative job, a big job for which her experience at Qantas and Ansett has trained her.

Or she might withdraw, become very introverted and emotional, and go right off the rails.

She admits she has been very domineering, she can drive other people, she has a very strong streak. But she is not bitchy.

She hopes to remain a small but successful literary agent. She can't say what will happen after that.

She would like to write, she likes the writer's lifestyle, but she's scared stiff. She will probably write a biography of somebody else.

An autobiography would probably be far too bleeding heart.

She has known, ever since she was a very small child, that she is not ordinary. She knows she has to do something with her life. Perhaps she has done it by helping Neville Wran. But she is still quite young, and there is more to do.

In 1988 she at last achieved one of her great ambitions: she had a daughter, Harriet.

The Old Q. & A.

Q: A lot of your life has been about self-fulfilment.
A: No, I reject that, it's the fulfilment of others' expectations. I was always trying to do something for somebody else. But perhaps that's not so true now.
Q: What are you going to do for other people?
A: I don't follow you.
Q: Will you do something in which the personal falls away?
A: I thought it was immoral to be too absorbed with what you're going to do with your life, so part of the reason I became so busy, and made myself a nervous wreck, is because I've piled up things to do. I'm so damned busy I'm not achieving any one thing magnificently.
Q: What are you going to do about it?
A: I don't know.

Coda

She has good, close, loyal friends.

She is honest.

She is also vulnerable, which is an entrancing quality.

Like a Scott Fitzgerald character, she is intelligent, accomplished, highly refined. Yet for all her nervosity she has discovered no overwhelming passion to her life, and seeks it still.

We are all of us, in our private lives, metaphors for some more general condition. If we don't understand the social significance of the merely personal we will never be liberated.

Jill Wran is, of course, exquisite; yet she is also trapped, like an exotic butterfly behind glass. The glass is called Self, Success and Caste. She can hardly be blamed for any of them; but unless, like *Tommy*, she breaks the glass she will be doomed to always being inside her character, fluttering, looking out.

BRUCE DAWE

Carefully as biscuits they load the last tremulous
Anzacs on board the plane for Gallipoli.
There is more than one way in which truth can be slaughtered . . .

"On the 75th Anniversary of the Landing at Gallipoli"

This is the start of one of Bruce Dawe's latest poems. It's pretty typical: the laconic, everyday tone, the topical subject, the homely image of "biscuits", the questioning of the received wisdom about something as sacrosanct as Anzac. And it helps explain Bruce Dawe's emergence as that most astonishing of contemporary phenomena, a popular poet. Which he is.

One anthology of his work, *Sometimes Gladness*, has been reprinted eleven times. *Condolences of the Season*, an earlier collection, has sold over 60,000 copies; his total sales are well over 130,000. His poems have been set for study in schools in New South Wales, Victoria and South Australia and he is without doubt the most widely read poet in Australia. Indeed, he is now the most popular poet since C. J. Dennis and *The Songs of a Sentimental Bloke*.

Yet for all his popularity, which even a doggerel-dabbler like John Laws might envy, there is no doubting Dawe's stature. Les Murray has called him "one of the best three or four poets we have had in this country", which is high praise indeed, and even the academic critics regard him as a major contemporary writer. Dawe, in other words, is an extraordinary example of an artist who is both serious and popular, a sort of poetic equivalent, if you will, of Bob Dylan, who turned the pop song serious, and a living rebuttal of those who argue, cynically or dispiritedly, that in an age of mass-produced culture it is impossible for a "high art" such as poetry to reach the mass audience it deserves.

Dawe's publisher, Longman Cheshire, has released a cassette tape of him reading and commenting on eighteen of his own poems, which has helped him reach a wider audience than usual. In fact, he is an inveterate and effective reader of his own poetry, travelling all over Australia to give poetry readings (even though he hasn't yet learnt to drive a car). One week, for instance, he gave a reading at the University of Queensland; two days later he was off to Dalby to give another; and that was followed by another reading in Victoria. As he says in his introduction to the tape, "poetry should be heard as well as seen . . . it's an oral and public form". He adds: "Hearing a poem is a way of going back to something of the situation which brought it about in the first place. You hear the sound of a poem when you are writing one before it comes within reach . . ."

Dawe thinks that the tradition of making public your personal feelings is a new one in Australia, but one which Australians have to learn; we can't afford the old, macho "gawkiness about our feelings, this national awkwardness", so he sees his work related, somewhat surprisingly, to that of confessional poets such as Robert Lowell and Sylvia Plath and, in Australia, Bruce Beaver and Robert Adamson.

> *It seems that I have been chosen*
> *to spend what is laughingly called my life*
> *in this small city studying*
> *the totalitarianism of the banal . . .*
>
> "On Bad Days"

One of the things that makes Bruce Dawe's poetry so popular is its unique colloquial tone; he sees poetry as "just another way of speaking" and doesn't regard it as "mysteriously different to other things". This is reflected in the poetry itself, its plainness, the laconic style, the images drawn from the rich panoply of mundane existence, even the subjects: suburbia, kids, footie, antlions, Tiananmen Square, Aborigines, provincial towns, ecology,

El Salvador, bedroom conversations, love, street gangs, Bjelke-Petersen (whom I take to be the subject of his "On The Fall from Grace of a Well-Known Politician") . . . Another reason is his use of plain language in poetry; there are plenty of classical and literary and especially Biblical references, but they are embedded within an utterly familiar texture which sounds as if you are listening to the bloke next door telling you a Sunday morning yarn; the words bordering on slang, the references and phraseology as mundane as . . . well, as mundane as in his

> **To Be A Poet In Australia**
> *is to live in Echo Valley*
> *and be hard of hearing*
> *is to inhabit a Hall of Mirrors*
> *and be short-sighted*
> *is to make a long trip home*
> *and find a TO LET sign on the front lawn . . .*

Says Dawe: "I'd like to go back to writing very simple ballads. There are still things to be said in plain speech, go back to basics. I'm not a Peter Porter or a Les Murray, I tend to be much more polemical. I'd like to get some of the verities back in the scale again, taste the simple things. I like crude language, gross language, it has a life force to it."

And he's funny. In his poetry, and in real life, he says the most wry, sardonic and witty things with an absolutely straight face. Even the titles betray the flavour: "Waltzing Toyota"; "On First Being the Subject of a Question in a Late Afternoon Television Quiz Programme"; "The Best that Money Can Buy" (this last on the Queensland police force).

All this is linked, fairly obviously, to the plainsong of the ordinary people, the great vernacular tradition which stretches back to folk songs, nursery rhymes, yarns, jokes and tall tales, surfaced in the Australian bush ballads of the turn of the century and the folk poetry of Woody Guthrie (whom Dawe likes) and has been drawn upon by poets as disparate as Allen Ginsberg, Richard Tipping, Adrian Mitchell, John Forbes and Dawe himself to establish a revivified "popular" tone for contemporary poetry.

You can see the man himself in his work. He once described

himself to me as "an ordinary bloke with a difference", and that is still true. I've always come across him in varieties of suburbia: a dilapidated fibro house in Springvale, when he was a nine-to-five Lands Tax Department clerk in Melbourne, and now a weatherboard house on stilts in Toowoomba, Queensland, where he has lived for the past 20 years and is now an Associate Professor at the University College of Southern Queensland, where he lectures in English.

He is married to Gloria, a friendly Queenslander who is almost as loquacious as Bruce himself (who could talk the hind leg off a dog), has four kids, a house full of comfy furniture, a backyard full of budgies, galahs, guinea pigs, chooks, a dog called Scrappy, a sick lovebird, and a battered black spring-back folder of new poems typed on the back of roneoed sheets.

He doesn't look like a poet: he's got this big-eared, black-Cornish, sunken-mouthed skull of a face, peers at you fiercely from deep eye sockets, sucks his cheeks in like Punch, and walks like a lopsided VFL footballer, with only his funny self-satirising statements betraying the idiosyncratic intelligence with which he confronts the world.

> *I'm for the little blokes . . .*
>
> *I'm for the little fellers:*
> *green ants, sugar ants, bull-ants,*
> *even the little brown peons*
> *from the Argentine.*
>
> *I'm for the irrepressible many*
> *who pick up their dead and get on with it . . .*
>
> "The Little Blokes"

Bruce Dawe is a battler, and he likes battlers. He was born in Geelong, the son of a labourer, was in the same class at Northcote High School as John Cain, now Premier of Victoria, left school early, worked as a labourer, farm hand, copy boy, sawmill hand and office boy for years, had a spell in the RAAF, worked as a handyman, gardener and postman, got his BA part time, then his PhD, didn't publish his first book of poems until he was 32, didn't become a teacher until he was 39, and now at 60 looks like staying in Toowoomba, his wife's home town. He's a very Australian figure, in that traditional A. A. Phillips/Russell Ward sense of the no-bullshit, egalitarian working man whose allegiances are summarised on the masthead of *Overland* magazine: "Temper democratic, bias Australian". *Overland* still publishes a good bit of his poetry. "One's the fully dilapidated version of the bloke in The Australian Legend," he said to me once. "This is what he's come down to." With a straight face.

Some of his poetry is highly political; he has written very movingly about Vietnam, Asia and South America; more recently he has written about Aboriginal land rights and the conservation movement. In the charged and bitterly polarised world of Queensland politics he has been regarded as a radical and once spent a night in gaol after being arrested on a right-to-march demonstration. But there are surprises. He is a convert to Roman Catholicism, and some of his finest poems seem to embody an embittered and somewhat conservative Christianity. He is opposed to abortion, and his anti-abortion poem "The Wholly Innocent" has aroused hostility from student audiences.

Yeah, he's a political animal. "Absolutely. Politics are fascinating, it's like the circus — but as they say, you've got to be careful of the tiger with toothache or the elephant with the trots: don't sit too close to the front seats or you may regret it!" He's even got involved in university politics, resigning over an academic issue in 1982; he was reinstated three years later. He votes Labor these days and is an admirer of Wayne Goss, the Labor Queensland Premier, but he used to vote DLP. He describes himself as a conservative/democratic socialist of the European sort and adds: "I am not a pacifist. I'm a realist. You should know when the dreaming stops."

His approach to writing poetry is equally down to earth. "I don't see it as a special corduroy velvet midnight hour process," he says, and then, parodying Goering, "Whenever I heard the word *inspiration* I reach for my revolver." Instead he sees poetry as voicing the concerns of the writer and therefore connecting with the concerns of others as well.

"Unlike other people, I don't work at ambitious projects," he says, levelly. "I mightn't write a poem for months at a time.

When I do I don't spend too long over them; I don't sweat over drafts." He says he is not "overly self-critical or self-aware; I'm not shining up my soul perpetually. I don't aim to be profound, if profound means complex." His first audience is himself and, though he wants to communicate, he knows some people hate what he writes. That's all right. There's a responsibility to present your work warts and all, so often he reads out poems which he knows the audience won't like: "I don't believe in tizzying up a reading so it pleases everyone."

> *Around El Salvador*
> *the shadows close*
> *— the mighty friends*
> *reach down advising hands*
> *the helicopter gunships rise again,*
> *oiled . . .*
>
> "Around El Salvador"

Sometimes, as in his dramatic monologues, Bruce Dawe adopts an alternative tone of voice. His earlier "A Victorian Hangman Tells His Love" is one such poem. In recent years, he thinks, he has tended to write more subjectively and less formally, and has composed more (secular and religious) love poems. He still writes sonnets, and has experimented with Japanese forms like the five-line tanka and the three-line senryu. More characteristic, though, is the conversational style of "My Experience of God":

> *"Dear Father, I'm afraid I'm going to have to pass*
> *on your kind invitation to write an article on my experience*
> *of God (which is, for me, like being asked to write about*
> *what it's like to be good at maths or the world's best*
> *ocarina-player) . . ."*

He has "learnt a bit" from German poets such as Brecht and Maleko, and likes Bob Hudson's carbaret-style Oz songs: "I love that offhand, popular sort of thing." He tries to write lyrically about the very things that worry and distress him. "Yeats does it in Easter, 1916; and Auden is one of the great models for social political writing," he says, "In Australia? Well, Vin Buckley and Chris Wallace-Crabbe both shaped me; they can write very powerfully about social things." Among contemporary local poets he's particularly fond of John Forbes and Philip Neilsen: "Both are ironists, with a fine sense of wit and style." He agrees with Keats that we distrust poetry which has a palpable design on us: "We don't want to be king-hit into our seats," he says — which is a sort of lovely translation of Keats into Ozspeak.

He has watched the transmigration of poets such as David Malouf, Rodney Hall and Roger McDonald into prose without feeling any need to follow them, though a few years ago he put together a collection of comic short stories, which he wrote while still at university. Nor does he feel under any pressure to write a fashionably long poem: "It's never occurred to me what I could write about that would take so long!"

If anything, he defends his creative subconscious, like Grahame Greene, by avoiding writing criticism, or prose, or accepting the schedule imposed by grants. "I respect the novelist, because he is more hardworking, but I couldn't do it," he says, smiling. "Clearly, for a lazy person, it's easier to write poems. I'm a prolific poet, but I'm not prolific in other things."

> *Somewhere friendly*
> *the bride on whom the sun*
> *feels her eye-lids waver and open*
> *and she brushes the pebbled glass from her brow*
> *and slips out of the rusting wreckage, humming, remembering*
> *what morning it is and with whom and why . . .*
>
> "Somewhere Friendly"

Behind the laconic tone, the wry and humorous stance, lies real passion — an unfamiliar quality in Australian poetry, falling as it does between the deft academicism of an earlier generation of poets and the formal experimentation of the modernists. Surprisingly, people don't expect to find passion in the suburban lives of Australians, whether they be poets or postmen. They're just the neighbours. Bruce Dawe reminds us otherwise. He agrees he's paid a penalty living in an isolated provincial environment ("*going nowhere fast*"), but, he adds, "you have to balance that against the penalties I might have paid elsewhere". Typically, he's even written a fine poem, "Provincial City", about it.

He walks down the back verandah steps, checks the galah, kicks a stone out of the way. "I can't think of anyone who's had a better run."

Before Plato

We went, I think, in this country,
straight from the cave
to the television set.
We missed out on those civilizing
Barbarities in-between.

We put down the club
and picked up the TV guide,
tossed over our left shoulder
(for good luck)
the thigh-bone of Brontotherium,
and reached for a snack.
We switched from real-life hunger, fear, cold,
to watching them on World Vision commercials;
we let go of our enemy's throat
and lost our grip on life.

Somebody called, back there, deep in the shadows
it could have been love, or hate, or just plain
loneliness, but we were glassed-off
in a mini-series.

We stopped dreaming of falling.
And, instead,
fell.

Bruce Dawe

PETER BROCK

He looks like a God, gigantic Greek warrior's helmet, thin athlete's body, flameproof racing suit, lace-up blue suede boots, arms clasped military-style behind his back. BROCK. The white Group A race car with the black grille and the familiar big 05 painted on the roof comes snarling into the pits. BROCK. He swaps with his co-driver, who bends down like a supplicant to strap him into the cockpit. BROCK. The mechanics' arms shoot up 1-2-3-4, four wheels changed, full tank, in a fraction over twenty seconds. BROCK. Elbow resting casually outside the cockpit, he fishtails out of the pits. Blue metal showers the mechanics; there is a blast of burning high-octane gas as he powers on to the racetrack straightaway. "The Boss!" shouts the loudspeaker. BROCK BROCK BROCK . . .

Peter Brock is a spiritual man. It seems a bizarre thing for a racing car driver to be, in a sport where sheer ocker aggro and tough-as-guts bravura is the norm, until you look at his face: it's as sharply edged as a Celtic priest or a knifeblade. Black hair, black eyebrows, black face shadow, and the black unflinching gaze of the fanatic.

It's no surprise to find he comes from a strict Methodist bush background, just outside Melbourne. He started off a bit of a mug lair, the only kid game enough to take the billycart right up to the top of the hill, long hair, glamour boy, "I was a free spirit, I felt a lot of the conventions and moral codes in society didn't apply to me; I just did anything I wanted to" but as the years have gone by he's disciplined himself, controlled his cars and his emotions, shorn his hair and honed his skills and his experience down to the point where he sees racing as a high-speed game of chess, a 240 kilometre-per-hour think-match, where at last he gains absolute control of his environment.

Along the way he's won the Bathurst 1000, the most important car race in the country, nine times. It's an extraordinary achievement, considering that winning it once is a lifetime ambition for most race drivers, and it's made Brock a folk hero to literally millions of Australians. That, and the fact that there has always been something a bit up-you-Jack and idiosyncratic about Brock, a sort of larrikin insouciance which has endeared him to a mass audience which sees him enact their own aggro, and rebelliousness, and me-against-them resentment. Rightly or wrongly, the hundreds of thousands of young working-class Western Suburbs petrolheads who follow motor racing like a religion see him as one of them. He drove a Holden, the Common Man's car, until a couple of years ago. Even his much-publicised split with General Motors-Holden, and the barrage of media criticism which accompanied it, has not damaged his popularity.

After all, he's a hero.

Yet he is a strange sort of hero for Australians to have, very much a modern version, a sort of New Age updating of the traditional Aussie folk myth. He is highly intelligent, articulate, very intense, introspective, and very much into the spiritual dimension of human existence: he wants to change mankind, he wants to raise its consciousness; he thinks technology is out of control and that the human race can only save itself if it attends to the environment, and the ozone layer, and the enormous untapped potential of people to develop themselves in ways which the current social order inhibits. This is where Brock the race driver/engineer/inventor comes in. "We've got ourselves into a hole and now we have to get ourselves out of it," he says. "As an engineer you can do it very easily: improve the motor car, improve mankind's awareness . . . It's a responsibility thing. And communication, talking to people about the world they live in. I think there's a lot of people beginning to solicit New Age stuff and saying, gee, there's something in that. Collectively, mankind's consciousness is going to fix what we've done to the world. I believe we can."

When he talks like that, his voice strong and convincing, his eyes dark and direct, it's suddenly possible to see Brock as a sort of secular prophet, someone who has gained so much from his own life that he now wants to communicate it to others. He believes "young people are told too often what they can't do, the educational system limits their horizons; I think we should tell that if they have an open mind, if they set their sights somewhere they can achieve anything". That's what Brock did. He wants to "explore levels of humanness"; racing's one way, but there are many others. Brock says he can sit and watch people for hours; he loves nature. "I'm interested in everything. As you get older you realise there are a lot of things in your life which will give you a lot of satisfaction. I mean, I can sit in a rainforest, up in the Daintree, and think 'this is fantastic, there's not a place I'd rather be', and be very satisfied with your lot in life."

There is, then, this mystical, experimental side to Brock's character which he agrees could be linked to his family's Methodism (he believes in God, never occurred to him he wouldn't), and their most Aboriginal relationship with the land, and his own drive to "make high-tech development compatible with the environment". He's serious, passionate beneath his lightheartedness, and it's suddenly comprehensible why the "gigantic blue" which led to his split with Holden was due partly to his insistence on fitting a black box Energy Polariser to the Brock-modified high-performance Commodores which helped make him a household name throughout Australia. General Motors Holden engineers declared the Polarisers had no technical merit. Brock believed the Polariser was picking up an electro-magnetic loop energy generated by the engine which, by careful placing, enabled him to "dial out" a lot of the harshness and vibration of an ordinary car, make it more harmonious. "I've got a fairly radical brain, it's unfettered by scholastic impediments," explains Brock, smiling.

It was a case of footsoldier David versus The General, and The General won. It was a very traumatic time for Brock, and you get the feeling he's still absorbing it into his philosophic system. He'd been a Holden man all his life; he broke up with old friends like John Harvey, the racing driver, and the motoring media turned against him.

"It was a very emotional time, it's like a marriage breakup," he says. He is sitting in the kitchen of his house in Eltham, on the outskirts of Melbourne, with his wife Bev making coffee and his three young kids getting ready for bed. They're crawling over him, demanding attention, as he tries to sort it out in his mind. "Sour me? Never. Because what it did was teach me a very important lesson in life, which was that I was naive, I thought that everyone was like me. There's been some fantastic ideas opened there but if humanity's not ready for that, OK, we'll apply it when the time's right. I've come out of it a damn sight better than when I went in."

What makes him such a successful racing driver? Brock thinks about it.

"Quick reactions. Good eyesight. I could always look at a corner and say, oh yeah, I'll go through it that way. I'm very competitive, I like to be successful. If enough people tell you you can't do it, you turn around and prove you can. I thought I could do it, I just did anything I wanted to." He grins, sending himself up a bit. "I still do some things when people say, boy oh boy Brock, you've got big balls doing that! But from where I am, I don't think I have."

BROCK BROCK BROCK. The kids crowd shyly around him and offer anything for him to sign: photographs, portraits, programs, records, shoes and, most startling of all, there is the ritual of signing the backs of their T-shirts, in which adolescent girls and boys queue up, spin around, and present their submissive backs to be touched and graced by The Master. Transference. They have been not so much anointed as had their flesh inscribed. Outside on the Oran Park track the sports sedans are shrieking down pit straight, inside Brock's big Mobil race trailer ("the black hole, it swallows so much money") mechanics are tightening bolts with airtools that sound like machine-guns. There is a weird smell of oil, burnt rubber and tension in the camp. Raceday. Brock, cool as ever, is drinking coffee, leaning back against the transporter, talking tactics with co-driver Jim Richards. Ten minutes to the start of the Pepsi 250, the first of the endurance race warm-ups for Bathurst.

Brock's 2.3 litre M3 BMW has been outgunned by the turbocharged Ford Sierras and Nissan Skylines which have dominated the Australian touring car championship over the last couple of years. "Small motor, could do with more power," says Brock with ironic understatement; he doesn't like being beaten, he hasn't won a race all season, and today is a chance to prove that he's in there still. The classic Endurance racing sequence: Oran Park, Sandown, Bathurst. The car won't go faster but he can try to *drive* it faster, give it 10/10ths, wear the bigger cars down. "What that means," says a motoring editor, "is that they get up on top of the mountain at Bathurst and risk their lives."

Brock doesn't see it like that. "I've never thought of motor racing as some big game of dicing with death, I don't think I'm scared of dying . . . though I probably figure life's too good, I've got too many things to do right now to die, it's not in the script. I've never been injured, anywhere, anytime. Never had a serious crash, had a couple of minor ones, including one which looked pretty spectacular in Adelaide, the car broke an axle as it took off on the startline, slewed across, and half a dozen other cars piled into it!

"No, I'm not afraid. I don't go out there thinking I'm tempting fate, I think I have an inherent faith in my ability to take the necessary action at the time. What I like is the sheer thrill of driving a machine that is trying to defy the laws of gravity, and overcoming the inhibitions and perhaps even fears that you might have in controlling a car. I mean, you're master of your own destiny there for a brief period in your life. It's a mind game. You plait a car down the track, you're threading it in and out of the other cars, trying to maintain rhythm and control. Very disciplined."

Pause. His wife Bev, a friendly, glamorous and formidable woman who helps run The Brock Organisation business and sits on a high chair at the racetrack edge each meeting, scoring the laps as the Group A machines thunder past at 240 kph, comes up and massages Brock's neck and shoulder blades from behind. He leans back instantly, closes his eyes.

"I've got total faith in myself," he says, "even when things have gone wrong and you go, EEEEERRRRR, boy, that could have been interesting! I had one a few weeks ago, in Melbourne, everyone was talking about this huge save, the radiator exploded on this car coming into a corner, I was 6000 revs in top gear, which is fast, and the radiator just went BEROOOOOOM, blew water under the car as I went in there, the car went completely sideways, so I held it there for, I dunno, two or three hundred yards, y'know, just kept it on the road, drove back, and everybody said WOW! and I said, yeah, that was *very* exciting!'' Brock laughs, animated, keyed up, just remembering it. "The trouble has usually been the car, or oil spilt on the track, or a driver running you off the road because they zigged when you thought they would have zagged. The worst thing that happens to you as a driver is that your concentration lapses for a moment . . . it's not like football players, tennis players, who can look around, get themselves motivated . . . as a racing driver you can't afford that luxury, you've got to be totally committed to what you're doing at the time."

Brock began professional racing at the age of 22. He's now 45. How much racing has he left in him? "Chronologically it doesn't really interest me how old I am," he says. "I can't see any reason why I can't do things that an 18-year-old can do, I'm just as fit as most 18-year-olds. You take a lot of those American NASCAR drivers, they're old codgers, and they're unbeatable at it. I think I'm getting better. You go through phases. It's easy to win when you're on a roll, when things are going your way. But whatever anyone throws at me, I can stand it. I can do it. A lot of young guys go out there, push it harder, have an accident, yet they're going slower. And you have to ask yourself, now why is that?

"I don't drive on my feelings. I concentrate totally, but you don't employ anger to get the car down the road. I just let it happen, enjoy it. Some guys, y'know, *mash* their foot on the brakes, *reef* it through the corners, *belt* it through the gears, like 'get out of the way, I'll bash this bloke off the road, ram the car into him' . . . people do that, but I've never run a car into anyone in my life, I don't see any reason why you have to. You should go through life being more confident, more at ease, more in control of your environment . . ."

Jim Richards, Brock's co-driver, wanders up wearing his Mobil race cap. Brock stops in mid-sentence. "Mind you, at the next AUSCAR meet, if Jim Richards shuts me out once again, I'll run right into the side of him!"

Says a motoring writer: "Brock? He's a natural. Great feeling for a car, great ability to look after machinery. He was sensational in the wet a year or so ago. When he came up on the dias at Bathurst there were people, hundreds of them, crowding around chanting 'WE WANT BROCK! WE WANT BROCK!' Amazing moment. There's a real affection for him, he's the most credible sporting hero we have.''

In the marshalling yard the race cars look peaceful enough. The drivers stand around chatting, helmets under their arms or perched on the car hoods. But when they are called on to the grid everything changes: they roll out one by one, burbling and spurting, the motors revving, BLAAT, BLAAT, BLAAT, as gaudily painted and decaled as World War III budgerigars, drivers strapped into their rollcages, marshalls scurrying out of the way. Two warm-up laps. The two Brock BMWs are on rows one and three of the grid. He's decided to let Jim Richards take the first fifty laps of the race. They're up against the championship-winning Ford Sierras, a fast Mitsubishi Starion, a turbocharged Nissan Skyline which is a hot contender for Bathurst, and one of the new Holden Group A Commodores, all bulges, scoops and spoilers, which GMH developed after Brock left.

Starting flag. Lights. An enormous crescendo as they head for the first lefthander. A car spins out. No crash. The Starion pulls into the pits for a wheel change. Colin Bond's Sierra develops engine problems; so does the Holden Group A. That leaves the George Fury Nissan in front with Jim Richards in the Brock BMW a few seconds behind. For lap after lap they circulate together, locked in combat.

Brock watches from the edge of the crash barrier. Close-up, he's got short feathery hair, clean ascetic face, squared-off chin, mobile mouth, three V-shaped frown marks over the bridge of a slightly crooked nose, and a brooding intensity which is irresistible — when he was younger and carrying on as a handsome young race driver people used to think "this guy's out of control", and Bev says she still has to handle "all these women who are hot for him".

Right now, however, he's utterly alone, arms clasped behind his back, an isolated authoritative figure with the huge racing helmet making him look as though he's afflicted by some weird sort of gigantism. Sun comes humming through the Bringelly clouds on to the rain-drenched track; there are pennants in the breeze, gum trees, bare paddocks, Yokahama tyre signs, the polarised blue sky you get after a storm, and suffusing it all the throat-tightening, ugly, heart-wrenching, high-octane roar of Group A race machines as they hurtle past the spectators.

Brock is waiting.

Peter Brock is now much more than just a racing driver: he's a businessman, entrepreneur, husband, father of three kids, communicator, advertising star, and sometime evangelist for a new way of life for the world. "I don't want to waste my time just driving around a racetrack. I've got a lot of things I want to do in my life," he says. "I enjoy the racetrack, they're very relaxing days, I go there, I do what I do, and then I go, I don't play in that area; I can't think of anything more boring than discussing what I coulda done, what I shoulda done with a bunch of drivers. Racing hasn't been the main thing in my life for some time."

So what has been? "Design and manufacture, I like that. I'd like to be a consultant to the automotive industry, a bit like Porsche in Europe. Make a better car, rather than a high-powered one. You don't want a thumper. The cars I like are quiet, refined machines like Mercedes, Porsche, BMW."

Strange words for the man who is almost singlehandedly responsible for the rebirth of the Aussie muscle car. Years ago Brock began modifying Holden Commodores to turn them into high-powered street-legal versions of his race machines; the business grew so rapidly that at one stage he could claim to be the sixth largest car manufacturer in Australia. After the split with GMH he had to find a quick alternative to keep his seventy-employee business going and came up with the Lada, the Russian-built 1.3 litre sedan which he modified for the local market under contract. After that, more business deals. Later Brock confesses he'd like to free himself of any manufacturing and revert to being a designer: "I'd love to be able to come up with the ideas, give them to a lab, I'd love that. You know, sit out on the back porch, listen to music, have a beer in your hand," he says ironically.

Instead he is wandering around in a white lab coat in The Brock Organisation workshop in Bertie Street, Port Melbourne, checking on half a hundred things, with row after row of new cars parked in vast waiting bays outside, and his 05 BMW race car up on a hoist being stripped by mechanics for Bathurst, and a spare engine being tested on the dynamometer, and the red-and-white Brock/Perkins HDT Commodore he won Bathurst with in 1984 standing in the foyer, and outside the back door a fire-engine red Falcon Sports complete with skirts, spoiler, special suspension and refined motor which he is working on as a prototype package for Ford. At midday Brock jumps into the Falcon and heads for the St Kilda Travelodge, where he is to speak to a luncheon meeting of the A La Carte Club of middle-range business executives. He is running late and I have a chance to watch the famous Brock driving skills at work: he drives with one hand, fingertips only holding the bottom of the steering wheel, as he pilots the car deftly through roundabouts and along rain-slippery streets and accelerates just short of wheelspin out of the corners.

He hasn't prepared what he is going to say but improvises brilliantly, chatting about how he grew up wanting to play centre half-forward for Collingwood and how he once told the Russian Lada carmakers the magpie was a religious icon and how when he built his first race car he measured the frame up with chalk and string and won a lot of races but wondered why it always went around right-hand corners better than the left and years later found it was one inch longer on one side than the other and how he races car 05 because he took part in the Victorian government's .05 blood alcohol drink/driving campaign and how Bathurst is the greatest touring car race in the world and Sierras don't like the wet and the drivers like it even less and how Formula 1 racing is basically about melting the bitumen but Touring Car racing is about telling a car 'I know you don't want to go around this corner at 150 k but I'm going to make you' and how current race cars are too far removed from the everyday street cars that keep the motor industry going and how his own cottage industry is part of a grander design to make Australian industry less dependent on imported technology and imported automotive knowhow and thus help in nothing less than the rebirth of Australian manufacturing industry . . .

The he answers questions, calling everyone "sir", talking briskly and directly, making jokes and even talking about the polariser: "I still believe in it, if something's a fact it's a fact, but it's one of those classic situations where the time and the mood of the moment was such that it wasn't on, and really, once it became such a hot potato, I put it on the back burner. I stopped fitting them eighteen months ago. We had to bow to the way things had transpired. No, I didn't fit them to the race cars. It was designed to make something very smooth, very quiet, and a race car is not a quiet, smooth environment!''

By the time it's all over Brock has entirely captivated his audience and it's easy to agree with his wife, Bev, when she says ''he could be a communicator, he could be anything he wants to be.'' There's a charm and glamour about Brock, and a fairly conscious sincerity, which draws people to him. For lunch he's changed into a dark check suit and thin red leather tie and brushed his hair back and it's suddenly possible to discern, behind the urban sophisticate and New Age proslytiser he's become, the wide-eyed boy from the bush who took on the motor racing hierarchy in a homebuilt Austin A30 with a big red 179 Holden motor dropped into it plus some bits and pieces from a Triumph Herald — and won.

Brock puts it another way, explaining why he patiently signs so many autographs at the racetrack and talks to everyone who comes up: ''I believe those people need to be shown a level of respect. I remember as a little kid having my own sporting heroes, and then treated occasionally with a certain level of disdain by them, and I vowed and declared I would never do that to people. I have strong beliefs. I'm unwavering. You get back what you put in.''

The laps count down. Jim Richards in the Brock BMW tries to pass the turbocharged Nissan race leader, runs up the back of it, falls back to second place with a damaged mudguard and a big black tyremark up the back of the Nissan.

''He got a bit exuberant,'' *says Brock tersely. Pit stop. Near disaster: the high-pressure fuel hose won't work, the mechanics resort to petrol churns, losing precious seconds. When Brock takes over he's well behind the leader but a pit stop ahead. The Nissan pits. Brock decides to pour it on. As the Nissan charges back on to the track Brock's blue-and-white*

BMW, unbelievably, materialises on the straight. A marshall holds the Nissan back to let Brock pass — into the lead.
BROCK BROCK BROCK BROCK BROCK BROCK
For the next hour the best touring car driver in the world manages to keep a much faster car in his rear mirror. There is never more than a few seconds, a few lengths, between them. It's classic car racing, the crowd on its feet as the duel progresses. Lap 1, the last. A few years ago, at Bathurst, Brock blasted the competition, hit the front, then broke the lap record on the last lap just for the hell of it. This time he's cooler . . . but at the chequered flag he's in front.

American NASCAR race drivers, for generations, have tended to be good ole country boys: rebels, hellraisers, courage to spare. So's Brock. He comes from good Scottish farming stock who came out to Tasmania in the early 1800s and then moved to Hurstbridge, outside Melbourne. He grew up, in the main, on the family farm, "picking tomatoes, feeding chooks, milking cows, all that sort of stuff, generally being a small slave . . . it was out in the sticks, we didn't have any electric power or water till I was a teenager."

What he did have access to, however, was machinery. He learnt to drive when he was only 7 or 8 years old, starting the farm truck in gear during harvest time so the men could throw haybales on to it; then he graduated to a tractor, "an old Fergie, I found I could actually slide the tractor on dewy or frosty grass, tip the thing up in the air, get the inside wheel to spin — quite exciting! Then I bought myself a paddock bomb, an Austin 7, chopped the body off with an axe . . . a few mates, we got these paddock bombs going, raced them, Chryslers, old Chevys, the local constabulary used to smile upon us . . . we learnt to control machinery, understand it, respect it."

It's a background similar to that of another extraordinary Australian, Bruce Petty, the cartoonist and film maker: both super-intelligent farm boys who did well at school, studied art, loved Aussie Rules, went on to educate themselves — but whereas Petty's mind led him into the world of intellectuality, Brock's led him into the world of practical things, machinery, and eventually racing.

"I was always a bit of a daredevil, raced pushbikes, drove a billycart with a seatbelt, very competitive, everything was a challenge, life was a challenge . . . Why?" He thinks about it. "I grew slowly. When I was 18 I was five feet five inches. I see some of my old schoolfriends and they can't believe I'm six foot. I've probably forced myself to do things that require determination and discipline . . . an over-achiever! Then you realise there's no need to keep bolstering yourself, achieving these milestones for myself, I don't feel compelled to have to win a race!"

He was keen on football, cricket, athletics, good at running, but motor racing was always there in the background. "Dad took me to a race as a little kid and I remember him saying there was a particular car there, the Maybach Special, which Alan Jones's, father was driving, and Dad was saying: 'Watch this car, it'll win, but lo and behold another car won, a car called the Redex Special — driven by one J. Brabham! Then I got called up for National Service at Kapooka, near Wagga, and had time to go to the racetracks. I went to Bathurst in 1966 and it really inspired me. I was 20, I guess, all these Cooper Ss, and I thought to myself, this is me!"

That's when he decided to build his famous Austin A30: "It had this gun motor, stupendous power-to-weight ratio, but it was a difficult car to drive; most people couldn't drive it. I won a lot of races in it; it was a combination of being young and foolish and learning my craft with that car." By the time he was 24 Brock had won races, gymkhanas, hillclimbs, the lot. He was one of the youngest race privateers around and already a crowd-puller. Then, out of the blue, came a telephone call from Harry Firth, manager of the newly formed Holden Dealer Team; would he like a drive with them? "I thought it was one of my mates putting on a Harry Firth voice, I couldn't believe it," he remembers. The career of Peter Brock, King of the Bathurst Mountain, Peter Perfect, The Boss, was on its way . . .

These days Brock and his family live in a rambling mudbrick villa designed by Alistair Knox, the famous "alternative" architect, in the outer Melbourne suburb of Eltham; they have a farm nearby at Doreen which they are going to reafforest and build another Alistair Knox house on ("all circles and curves to harmonise with the landscape", says Bev Brock) plus another five-acre farm in the scrub outside Port Douglas — "an oasis", Brock calls it. He loves snorkelling: "I dive down and forget to come up for air."

They have friends like John and Rasa Bertram, of America's Cup fame, and Trish and Ranald Macdonald, of the *Age*, and Ric and Pauline Dowker, Ric being the chiropractor who helped Brock get his body together three or four years ago and, says Brock, "is very very good, it allows me to operate without pain, without fatigue". Dowker helped Brock design the Energy Polariser and many motoring critics see him as the man who has turned Brock on to the New Age ethos. But Brock sees it as all beginning much earlier than that and links it with meeting Bev.

"She helped me look at myself," he says unselfconsciously. "I looked at this guy who didn't know what he was, holes in his shoes, life is a ball, no thought for the future . . ." And now? "I never worry. I'm on a learning curve. Many people are afraid of change but I'm on the side of those who stand up and say 'let's make this a better world'. I'm satisfied with myself, who I am. I don't feel as if I have to prove anything."

He says, yes, he wants to make a lot of money, "but only because it allows me to do what I want to do". He's got projects, ideas, ideals he wants to put into practice. Three or four years ago he decided he wasn't up to scratch physically, so he gave up smoking and goes for natural health remedies. He's working flat out but swears "it has to stop; it's not fair on my friends, or the family, or my employees". He used to rage around but, once again, has learnt to channel this enormous energy and ambition of his elsewhere. "People say you're this wild-eyed kid from Hurstbridge, just into motor racing," he says. "But they don't know me."

Brock completes a victory lap, rumbles back to the grid, takes off his helmet, takes out his earplugs, and leans back against race-hot car, drinking soda. He's sweating badly, he loses up to three kilos a race, and his hair is soaked. Bev comes up, holds his cheek with her hand, gives him a kiss. BROCK BROCK BROCK. On the winner's dias he thanks his sponsors, gaudy gold-plated Pepsi 250 trophy cradled in his arm, and poses for the TV cameras. As he strides down the edge of the track people crowd up and shout "Good on yer, Brocky!" He stops, turns, waits to let them snap him with their cameras.

Back in the Mobil trailer he strips to his underpants and sits with his towelled head in his hand, exhausted. He looks suddenly thin and vulnerable. He dresses slowly in white Racing Team windcheater, white pants, white shoes, donning the glamorous patina of success, of superstardom, but his movements are slow motion, drugged. For half an hour he walks and talks like an automaton.

Endurance racing.

When Colin Bond, race rival, comes up to congratulate him, laughing and joking, Brock slowly recovers his *joie de vivre*. They swap insults, jibes, stories. For the first time since the race Peter Brock smiles. One down, Bathurst to go. Turning, he says to me: "I don't ever limit myself. I always believe you can do anything you want to do. Look, I really am a free spirit. And where I want to be is where I want to be."

PAUL KEATING

The crucial thing to understand about Paul Keating is that he is a man of passion. He is many other things as well, of course: the best postwar Treasurer Australia has had, a brilliant and instinctive politician, the likely next leader of the Labor Party. Unless something goes drastically wrong, he will probably end up Prime Minister.

Keating and the present Prime Minister, Bob Hawke, have had an on-off relationship for years. They were rivals in the early 1980s, grew close during the first three years of this Labor government, then moved away from each other after a public argument over some economic initiatives Keating took while Hawke was away in China and Keating's failed attempt in 1989 to lever Hawke out of the Prime Ministership. Throughout that time, however, Hawke has always regarded Keating as his logical successor . . . and he is right to. Keating has manoeuvred himself into the position of heir apparent and there isn't much Hawke or anyone else can do about it anyhow. The only question mark over Paul John Keating is whether his temperament may stop him short of his ultimate goal.

Keating's capacity for passion may come as a surprise to anyone who doesn't know him very well, and to the media people who have labelled him Mister Cool. They have been beguiled, perhaps, by Keating's famous self-possession, his dark tailored suits and monkish jesuitical air. Smiling his way gravely through a rack of financiers, bankers and businessmen come to hear The World's Best Treasurer address them on economic policy, he is often hard to distinguish from the corporate heavies around him; he can seem the very essence of well-balanced reserve.

But I know of very few politicians, either in federal Parliament or elsewhere, who have anything like Keating's deep-seated capacity for emotion, anger and diatribe. Strip away the gravitas he seems to have adopted in the past few years as a fitting model for a man who is Treasurer and would-be Prime Minister, and what you are left with is a naked Boy From Bankstown who has had to fight and kick his way to the top of the Labor scrum and is still handing it out to those around him.

Keating's passionate nature is one of the most endearing things about him. There is a warmth and spirit to the man, an intensity somewhat akin to the "fire in the belly" Aneuran Bevan was said to have had, which sets him apart from some of the dullards, self-servers, ego trippers and Ghengis Khan antediluvians who manage to get into Parliament.

The first time I ever met Keating was in 1975, a few weeks after that ugly relic of a Governor-General, John Kerr, had sacked the Whitlam Labor government. Whitlam had admonished the nation to "maintain the rage" and I was doing my part by speaking at rallies during the feverish election campaign that followed. At one meeting on the North Shore, the Labor speaker was Keating, then a virtually unknown young politician in a baggy brown suit and Frank Zappa brown shoes.

Keating spoke with such fire and conviction that I was immediately impressed. He seemed powered by a genuine outrage at the way Fraser had "stolen" government from Labor, and at the "filthy conservatives" who had engineered the coup; you could be cynical and say that part of his chagrin was due to the fact that after years of politicking, dealing and struggling he had been made the youngest Minister in the Whitlam government just a few weeks before it was dismissed, but Keating's anger was more general, more deeply political than that. In fact, knowing nothing about him, I half-assumed he was a radical in the ALP — he kept talking bitterly about what had happened to Jack Lang, one of his lifetime heroes — and it was only later that I learnt he was in fact part of the New South Wales Right machine and had an awesome reputation as a numbers man, head kicker and kneecapper . . . a reputation he still possesses.

There is a weird paradox there, between Keating's personal passion and his political conservatism, that provides a key to the man and the controversies he is continually embroiled in, including the famous one early in 1986 when he threatened publicly to "crucify" John Howard and "obliterate" him from the Liberal leadership — all because of some slurs in Parliament by "Iron Bar" Tuckey, the Opposition muckraker and malcontent, about a breach-of-promise suit brought against Keating years ago by a woman called Kristine.

It is a paradox explained partly by his background. He grew up in a fairly typical Irish-Catholic family in Bankstown, soaked up Labor politics over the kitchen table, never finished school, joined the party at the age of 14, took over the presidency of the ALP Youth Council in New South Wales, and by the time he was 25 had so manipulated the party branches in Blaxland that he won pre-selection and went straight to Canberra. Keating was determined to claw his way out of his environment and it wasn't too long before he was living in an opulent house furnished with striped wallpaper and wasp-waisted chairs on the only hill in Bankstown. (These days he owns two or three houses and has deserted Bankstown for Elizabeth Bay and Canberra.)

"It's no good pretending we're working class now . . . I've made the move up which a lot of Australians have," he told me years ago. "Isn't that what we're all after?"

But you never sever your roots quite as easily as that, and in his talk and style and many of his attitudes he's still a rough-and-tough Catholic brawler from the gritty underside of Australian political life. "I'm a tyke," he says, half-proud, half-parodic, reaching into his subconscious, using Biblical imagery to scarify Howard.

Keating is a brilliant talker, fast on his feet, witty and an absolute master of vulgar invective. "Criminal", "stupid foul-mouthed grub", "loopy crim" and "piece of criminal garbage" are some of the epithets the Treasurer has heaped upon his opponents. Most of his favourite phrases are unprintable, though "in and out of the cat's arse" and "like shitting in the ocean" are perennials; at one stage the Press Gallery began compiling a dictionary of extravagant Keating phrases and dictums but abandoned it because they couldn't keep up with him.

Most of the time Paul Keating is funny with it. He's got a quick-silver sense of humour and is so deft at repartee you can only admire him. He also has a saving capacity to send himself up. At a Press Gallery dinner, Keating, who was the only invited speaker (he is, of course, a gallery favourite) delivered himself of a hilarious parody of the various correspondents and ended with a satirical account of how much, despite his own leadership ambitions, he and Bob loved each other: "I get off the plane from Europe, clock under each arm, and Bob comes up and gives me a big kiss on each cheek . . . 'So pleased to have you back, Paul, mate.' "

Behind all that badinage, however, is a real edge of seriousness. Keating has more than one major passion in his life, but the overriding drive is his goal to become Prime Minister of Australia. He has pursued that relentlessly ever since he went into politics; in fact, I doubt I have ever met anyone so single-mindedly ambitious as Keating. Now that he is within reach of it, he is not going to let anyone — John Hewson, Bob Hawke or anyone else — stand in his way.

Though I have heard various Stop Keating scenarios in the past few years, I haven't come across one yet that sounds feasible. Keating once boasted that he had got John Dawkins, a possible rival, "exactly where I want him, at the end of a gun barrel". He has such a palpable lust for power that others pale beside him; whereas Hawke shillyshallied over whether to make the move from the ACTU to Parliament, and Hayden agonised Hamlet-like as to his own worthiness for the job, Keating is driven forward by a remorseless self-confidence. Years ago Maximilian Walsh told me that he knew only two Labor men who weren't a bit scared of power: Whitlam and Keating. Paul, he said, was prepared to grab the naked flame and hold on. He was right.

A second great passion of Keating's is money. He has virtually no background in economics — in fact he is less equipped with economic theory than any Treasurer for decades — but he has always had an intense interest in money and how to make it. Under his old house he used to have a beautiful burgundy-coloured 1960

Mercedes SL Sports "as an investment"; since then he has dealt in houses, teamed up with other businessmen and become a wealthy man. Malcolm Fraser used to taunt him about owning a villa in Italy; Keating's own taste these days runs more to a mansion in the Champs Elysées (perhaps in retirement?).

He has an auctioneer's nose for a bargain and a real estate agent's flair for a deal. When he went for a Sydney Harbour cruise with a bunch of businessmen not long ago, they were astonished to find that Keating knew every house which was for sale on the salubrious waterfront of Point Piper and Darling Point and could offer a nice assessment of their value. Real professional. Keating knows that if he ever abandoned politics, out of disillusionment or failed ambition, he could command enormous sums of money in the corporate arena. He has developed an extremely close relationship with the Sydney business community since becoming Treasurer and during the furore over his tax reforms, including the taxing of fringe benefits, threatened to quit the government if he didn't get his own way. It wasn't the first time he'd mentioned it: he knows what he's worth and it's a bloody sight more than the lousy bucks he gets in Parliament (he says).

So, in a funny sort of way, it's only appropriate that Keating should end up as Treasurer of the nation. For a money-hungry kid from the sticks, dealing in billions of other people's dollars is sheer delight (though nerve-wracking too). He has a real feel for money: he likes it, and he's good at it. Hence his continual taunts at Howard that he was a failure as a Treasurer. Keating genuinely believes that the last Liberal government stuffed up the economy, that Howard covered up about the deficit he and Fraser ran up before the 1983 election, and that he (Keating) would never be so stupid.

There are other, though less consuming, passions in Paul Keating's life. He loves antique furniture, especially from the French First Empire period, and goes on trips through Europe collecting it. What began, perhaps, as just another "investment" and a way of legitimising his ascent up the class ladder of taste has grown to the point where he is now a connoisseur and even went into partnership with a friend in an antique shop in Sydney. Doesn't do anything by halves, does Paul.

And in recent years he seems to have turned himself, somewhat unexpectedly, into a family man. He didn't get married until late, in fact he lived at home with his parents until he was in his thirties, which is pretty unusual. He met his wife, Anita, who is a lovely woman, when she was a KLM air hostess and pursued her with typical Keating single-mindedness around the world.

For a while there Anita seemed to take a poor second place to politics. Keating used to call her "Dutchy" in his offhand, chauvinistic way (Keating has not only inherited the old Labor tradition, he's inherited most of the old Aussie biases that go with it), but now he has four children and spends a lot of time with them. While other Ministers may go in to work in their offices on Sunday, he stays at home. He's become protective of his family, too, which may partly explain why he over-reacted to Tuckey's "Kristine" slur. When one of his Labor colleagues got involved in a sexual affair, Keating delivered himself of a now famous and much-quoted line: "If you want to be in power, you can't afford to fuck around."

Keating's straightened out his personal life. He's got power, and he wants more, and if the Liberal leaders think they can derail him, they can, to quote another favourite Keating phrase, "stuff it".

So there he is — mercurial, abrasive, immensely talented, charming, a knife-edge of a man whom even his opponents respect. An absolute original.

So what's wrong with him? The trouble with Paul John Keating is that, for all his extraordinary gifts, there is a blindness about the man. Politicially he is so narrow as to be one-dimensional. Raised among the knife-fighters and bloody-minded pragmatists of the New South Wales Right, he has never doubted that that is what politics is really about: power, getting it, holding on to it at any cost and worrying later about what to do with it and why the hell you want it anyhow.

He's intolerant. Keating seems to have an inexhaustible reservoir of bile and savage enmity which he is ready to spill over on to any opponents, whether within the Labor Party or without. It makes him formidable, as his Parliamentary performances show, but it also makes him incapable of much subtlety, or openness to other people and their ideas, or even dispassionate judgement. Hawke's a listener, Keating's not. Trying to argue with him is like trying to talk sense into a chaffcutter — he's all mouth and no ears. Hence the common perception that he is arrogant. He's got something to be arrogant about, of course, but people have mistaken that for the one-eyed, one-track tunnel vision which is characteristic of him.

John Button, one of the most perceptive people in Parliament, once told me that he agreed about Keating's narrowness, and went on to say about his drive for the Prime Ministership: "The attractive thing about Keating is that he's pretty open about it all. Keating is a very intelligent man, that's the first thing to be understood about him. And he's got some sort of style about him, sort of like a bullfighter's style. He's got a bit of flair; he'll kick a head, but he does it with finesse. From my standpoint I would like to see someone broader, a more comprehensive figure, intellectually, as a future leader. But I must say he's developed a lot."

And that, of course, is the ultimate reservation which many Labor people have about Keating: his dedication to his own ambition rather than the broader purposes of the ALP, and his life-long willingness to play the internal power game to the exclusion of political principle.

Keating's no idealist — he gave all that up, if he ever had it, years ago. He despises the Left ("They're the epitome of irrelevance . . . if I could get rid of them we might get somewhere," he told me with typical candour years ago) and dimisses the Centre Left as woolly-minded softies, though he is prepared to do deals with them and has lately inched away from the New South Wales Labor machine. Though he is passionately committed to the Labor Party and has held up Jack Lang and Francis Xavier Connor, the rough-as-guts Energy Minister in the Whitlam government, as his mentors, he has lost any sense of Labor being dedicated to what is fair; for him it's all about success. That's why Keating was originally able to embrace the idea of a consumption tax, which would have been the most regressive bit of Labor legislation for decades, with such fervour: OK, so it would have hit the blokes in Blacktown and Bankstown (where's that again?) but it would have been efficient, it would have been a fail-safe revenue raiser for the government, and it would have cut the political ground from under the Libs. He lost that particular battle and seems to have changed his mind since — but that's not typical of him.

Similarly with a capital gains tax. Keating opposed it for years, despite its manifest equity, and was only brought around to it because of its potential to raise revenue and diminish tax avoidance. He believes the welfare bag of policies is finished and the future lies with the technocrats, the administrators and the private sector. Maybe for his bumper sticker: "Pragmatist, and Proud of it." Keating doesn't see it like that, of course. But he has little political theory to back him up, few general ideas, scorns the intellectual content of politics, relies on his instincts and trusts to his ferocity of purpose to get him through.

And there, at the heart of it, is the essential Keating paradox. Anger without ideology breeds reaction. Keating, for all his extraordinary talents and Labor loyalty, has ended up a reactionary, and the political fire which once fuelled him is reduced to the white ash of the personal. It's a shame, and a waste. All the man's teeming passion, which could have been bent towards the great humane ideals of the Labor movement and the task of turning them into a reality, has dribbled away into personal invective, and the numbers game, and partisanship for its own sake, and threats on the steps of Parliament House. Trivial pursuits.

I like Keating. There is a spirit and honesty to the man which I respond to instantly. He is tough, courageous, and one of the current Labor government's greatest assets. He has been the driving force behind the government's economic policy, which these days dominates the political agenda. But unless he grows — and he has shown in the past that he is capable of it — and transcends that narrowness Button talks of, that wounding blindness, he may never end up the sort of Prime Minister that many Labor people hope he will become.

LEONIE KRAMER

Leonie Kramer and Patrick White are wrestling in Desolation Row, the *Titanic* sails at dawn, there are masks on the onlookers with the heart attack machine; as the contestants separate, each recognises his/her own face in the other. Sceptics. Refugees from the death of God. Sexual transgressors. Critics entrammelled by the society they berate. At such times the distance between them is illusory.

Patrick White calls her Killer Kramer. She is talked about as the Dragon Lady. "It's the silliest thing ever. I haven't seen him for ages," says Dame Leonie of the notorious quarrel between Australia's most renowned writer and the nation's most formidable critic. But in a book review in *Quadrant* magazine Dame Leonie writes of White's latest novel, *Memories of Many in One*: "it raises real doubts about White's seriousness as a novelist."

She explains: "The curious thing about it is it's a send-up of some of his own central preoccupations and methods. It sends up the transcendentalism, what I think of as Patrick's particular brand of spooks . . . the Mysteries suddenly appear in the form of chariots or whatever." She pauses. "It could be sad. It could be an exhausted sigh."

Such judgements hardly endear Leonie Kramer, the nation's only Professor of Australian Literatuwre, to the writers she criticises. In his autobiography *Flaws in the Glass* Patrick White writes about "those who are unequivocally male or female — and Professor Leonie Kramer". Dame Leonie takes it to mean she is sexually neuter . . . or, as some feminists argue, that she has acquired her considerable success at the cost of turning herself into a man-in-drag. The male sex gains its revenge by giving women balls. She thinks that's silly too. But if there is any truth in it, it is perhaps parallelled by what she calls White's "haunting sexual ambivalence", which she sees expressed in many of his novels . . . and which is confirmed by White's revelation, in his autobiography, of his homosexuality.

The wrestle continues. In a famous diatribe in the 1950s, and in his earlier plays, White lashes out at Australian suburbia . . . but returned from England to live in it. Dame Leonie says she herself is out of sympathy with the tenor of Australian life, particularly its intellectual life, yet "I feel very at home in my own society".

Patrick White, she thinks, is "at heart a real sceptic". Days later she says of herself: "I'm a sceptic." Indeed, the more you listen to her talk about White, the more astonishing the parallel between the two becomes. Trying to explain, at one stage, her own "great respect for religious belief", she resorts to using White as an example:

"I don't know what I am. I'm certainly not an atheist; an agnostic is a silly thing to be. I'm a leftover. Patrick keeps raising . . . he keeps grappling with this . . . what happens if God is dead? It's the question Dostoevsky asked. What are the sanctions? It's very important for people to recognise they didn't make the world, man is not the measure of all things, there is something beyond . . . You have to hold on to the belief that God isn't dead in order to provide that dimension which is non-material . . ."

It became clear, slowly, that though she was explicating Patrick White's position, she was in fact talking about herself. "The need I feel to *do something* is a consequence of the moral training I got from the church," she says. *Do something*? She's been doing things all her life: Professor of Australian Literature at Sydney University, former chairman of the ABC, on the boards of the ANZ Bank, Western Mining and the NRMA; a powerful conservative voice in everything from the Institute of Public Affairs to *Quadrant* magazine to dozens of groups, movements and advisory bodies. She is undoubtedly one of the most successful women in Australia.

Right now, at age 64, she's biding her time. "I would like to think I would move on to some public position," she says. University vice chancellorships? "Well, I've been offered several of those and turned them down," she says briskly. "That sounds like a terribly upmarket, flippant remark but it's not meant to be. They were interstate. There's no way I'd expect Harry, my husband, to uproot himself just because of that. It would have to be something to do with education or the media. I suppose things like arts councils or bodies of that kind. I have no doubt I fell foul of the Labor Party over the ABC. Would I have to wait for a change of government? I would hope not. That's one of the things that makes party politics very distasteful to me."

For all her reputation as an arch conservative, Kramer doesn't see herself like that. She's never belonged to any political party; she votes Liberal quite often but not always; no, she won't say who else she has voted for. "I was asked to go to the Liberal Senate ticket in 1983 and I was very flattered by that" — but she turned it down. She has a New Right bulletin on her university desk but disclaims it. "I'm not a member of the H.R. Nicholls Society, I don't know anything about it — I don't even know who H.R. Nicholls was. I'm a terrible dumbhead about this; I have no idea what the New Right is, who they are; I can't stand labels or slogans, all those things that try to make it simple for you not to think. I believe in private enterprise but I'm not an absolute free market forces person; I don't believe in the Moral Majority. I'm not a extremist. I don't like the exercise of power. I found that when you are at the top of the hierarchy what you acquire is enormous responsibility, but your capacitiy to exercise power is absolutely limited. Australians are obsessed with power. Yes, I do express firm views but there's no way I'm going to try to force that on anyone."

Which is all very surprising, considering her formidable image. Critic John Docker has analysed her at length as a baleful and authoritarian influence on Australian literature; at the ABC she was regarded as the Maggie Thatcher of the airwaves. Part of the problem is the distance between her personal manner, which is witty and quite beguiling, and what she actually says. You have to watch her: she slides rapidly from an impeccably liberal defence of a humanities-based education to extolling Western Australian entrepreneurs; starts off with the angels and ends up with Alan Bond! And when her secretary politely refuses to bring her a cup of tea Dame Leonie remarks, without malice: "Every now and then she asserts her authority and I get the tea. This is the way the world is. This is egalitarianism."

What Dame Leonie Kramer is, basically, is a traditionalist. She believes in preserving what is best in the liberal/conservative tradition she has inherited, whether in education or politics or society, and doesn't want that "chopped out because of some ideology". And though she doesn't think of herself as a crusader — "I see myself as a disseminator, an explicator" — she has spent much of her life defending those values against the barbarians.

At first her personal style seems to confirm her public persona. I remember her, when I was an English graduate at Sydney University, as a young woman with her hair pulled back in a tight bun, a brusque manner, enthusing about Les Murray and scorning the vernacular satire of Bruce Dawe; now she seems almost a dowager, hair cut back to a mannish shortness, spectacles dangling around her neck, a Victorian cloak over her shoulders as she sips from a teacup, little finger of her left hand sticking out, a slow teardrop forming in the corner of her eye as she talks briskly and purposively about public policy, the galloping consumption of progressive education, the need to be intellectually rigorous, the unresponsiveness to large ideas in Australian life . . . conventional stuff.

After a while you realise she is not as straight as she appears. She has a lighthearted, playful way of talking which she uses dextrously to poke fun at others and herself; that and her sardonic sense of humour makes her a lot of fun to be with. She sprinkles her conversation with a lot of phrases such as *absolutely* and *enormously* and *no, certainly not* so that even her most moderate pronouncements tend to sound extreme. She writes in the same way. Everything in Leonie Kramer's world seems projected by her intelligence into a clear light of certainty.

She likes to throw a bit of slang and exaggeration around, accusing John Docker of being "bad tempered" and of portraying her as "some ghastly Fascist with a whip", describing herself as "very boring" with no crises or dramas in her life; she's just worked "damned hard" and been "very tenacious" and was "lucky enough to have a good family, a good education, a lot of luck and a lot of accidents" and no, she doesn't feel any guilt, "I am not privileged, I'm sorry for people who don't make it, but I don't think people should have equality of reward — I'm concerned with quality, not equality."

She is saying this in a three-storey house in Vaucluse Road, Vaucluse, with a swimming pool foregrounding the Harbour view, in an old-fashioned, rather gloomy drawing room of Chippendale furniture, gilt-framed watercolors, china plates, floral carpet, a lace tablecloth loaded with Scotch, books on Mountbatten and Slessor, a recent copy of the *Institute of Public Affairs Review*, ("Australia's journal of free enterprise opinion") and mementos of the housekeeper who "was a member of the family". In this hushed ambience the loudest sound is the ticking of the grandfather clock.

Upstairs, in the corridor, is a portrait by Harley Griffiths, a minor Melbourne impressionist, of Dame Leonie as a child of three: a tubby, doleful girl in a blue dress, pants drooping below the hem, one leg up, one leg down. Three decades later she can still remember posing for it: "I felt very bored." A few years ago she annoyed feminists by saying she found a lot of Australian women "very boring". It's her way of dismissing people and things that are not as sharp and idiosyncratic as she is.

She had a very happy childhood. Father in the bank, a lay Church of Christ preacher; mother wanted to do medicine but was channelled into music. A cultivated household in Kew, Melbourne. Encouraged to read books. Educated at the Presbyterian Ladies College. Which one? "There is only one," she says, smiling. Strong training in moral obligation and responsibilities; "it was taken for granted that we would go out to university, take leadership roles."

Strangely enough, she was very rebellious at school. One of her reports accused her of *a wilful waste of opportunity*. "It happens to be true," she says now. "Absolutely. I was very restless. It went on for several years. I was nuisance in class. It's all silly, schoolgirlish stuff. I was threatened with expulsion by the headmaster, told I'd go the way of Henry Handel Richardson and

Dame Nellie Melba; they were both thrown out. I thought he was a silly old man.

"I used to walk out of class when I couldn't be bothered being there any more. Once I actually went away from school altogether, I was sick of it, went to see a friend. Just feeling totally rebellious. Then later on I got myself into trouble because I got very cross with a couple of girls, prefects, who were frightful snobs. They were fiddling around with the duty roster and I got stuck into them. I had a burning sense of injustice. That rebelliousness is still there, I think. As an undercurrent. The reason I won't wear the dour conservative label is because I'm constantly dissatisfied with the status quo."

Dame Leonie is herself unfailingly polite, and she is proud of the fact that PLC was "very firm in its inculcation of proper social attitudes; snobbery, of course, you can never completely eliminate, but it was dealt with." And adds, with some passion: "I really cannot bear people treating other people as inferior beings. Education should bring out someone's abilities, whether it be dressmaking or Ancient Greek; there's no difference in value, only in doing them well or badly. Hence my emphasis on excellence." And later, leaning up against the wall near her girl-in-blue portrait: "Equality has to do with style, how you treat people."

And there, of course, is the trouble. Behind Dame Leonie Kramer's lack of snobbery and personal commitment to civility lies an absolutely patrician acceptance of the inequality which surrounds her and the society which produces it. She argues for scholarships — but accepts the profound educational inequalities which makes scholarships necessary. She espouses equal opportunity — but for grossly unequal rewards. The notion that equality has to do with "personal style", not real social justice, befits an eighteenth century philanthropist or a Mississippi plantation owner. No wonder that in a public lecture (in honour, ironically, of socialist Dr Nugget Coombs) she delivered a blast at "education policy which panders to our sacred cow, egalitarianism".

"I'm anti-Socialist," she says. "I'm opposed to the notion that planners can bring about some social Utopia. Equal opportunity legislation is planning gone mad! I don't regard myself as a whale, or a fossil." But, as she said when accepting the $15,000 Encyclopaedia Britannica award, she is opposed to "the tyranny of revelance".

Such narrowness in someone so intelligent as Leonie Kramer is genuinely surprising. It's as though, all her life, she has had to exercise her mind rather than her imagination.

She half-agrees. She succeeded at school, university and in her academic career, but "didn't question it". "Yes, I've gone straight ahead from my family, my school." Oxford University was tough, but "I was very tenacious. The tougher things get, the more obstinate I get. I won't give up." She met and married her husband, Harry, then a South African student, now a pathologist, came back to Australia, had two daughters, Josephine, now 35, who still lives at home, and Hilary, married with a baby ("now I'm a grandmother — I thought I'd never make it"), made a career decision to specialise in Australian literature because her original choice, seventeenth century English poetry, was too esoteric, and moved remorselessly up the academic ladder: tutor, lecturer, professor, Chair, Dame. No worries. Never any need to rethink the direction in which she had been pointed since, at the age of six, she was delivered to the PLC Kindergarten, Melbourne.

The straightness of the trajectory she confirms herself. "I don't think I've changed much. I do believe in order. I didn't even think about these things — educational policy, the media, all that — till the last decade. It's been an intellectual process. I'm not governed by my emotions. I try to be cool; I'm calm and detatched. I don't panic easily." Her literary taste tends to reflect that cool: Martin Boyd, Shirley Hazzard, Christopher Koch in the novel; James McAuley (she has written a preface to a new edition of his poems), Les Murray, David Campbell (she is editing his collected poems) among the poets. But she says she likes the new women writers too: Helen Garner, Blanche d'Alpuget, Kate Grenville. Occasionally she seems out of touch, confusing Moorhouse with Moorhead . . .

Does she regret having spent her life as a critic of books, that she wasn't a writer herself? "No, I've got no creative talent at all," she replies disarmingly. "I think I wrote one poem in my life; I've never tried writing since school magazine days. And I'm an . . . what's the word? . . . unregenerate sceptic about criticism by people who are not themselves creative writers. Criticism is enormously important but essentially secondary, transient." Later, however, a somewhat different regret surfaces. "I wish I'd had more time to write; write a great long book as all my colleagues do. I regret not having several books on the shelf. But those sound like blemishes on an ideal Austen tea party. It would have meant sacrificing family life."

These days her interest in cultural history and critical theory has tended to take over from fiction and poetry. She's started to shudder at the prospect of reading yet another batch of new novels. "I continue to read it because I have to, but not many good novels are published," she says.

She doesn't believe there are schools of Australian writing, nor of Australian criticism. She is not a structuralist and scorns the notion "that you abolish the author and look at the linguistic relations within the text"; the context of literature is important. Nor, she argues, did the *Oxford History of Australian Literature*, which she edited, "run an anti-social realist line" — though she doesn't think you get particularly good writing out of social realism. To the argument that Helen Garner and perhaps even Frank Moorhouse represent a sort of Revised Realism, a fiction of the mundane, she replies that she notices more the fashion for the Gothic: "It's part of Patrick's influence, I suspect."

When she's not reading, or speaking in public, Leonie Kramer is gardening. She's developed a passion for natives and has planted what amounts to a native forest on her and Harry's farm at Colo. She likes classic New Orleans jazz — Louis Armstrong, Jelly Roll Morton — and included a Fats Waller in her recent program for the ABC's desert island discs show, but that's partly because she can't stand modern "serious" music. She reads in French and German, she has a "scatty" acquaintance with Italian, and "I've sworn that before I kick the bucket I'm going to read one text in Russian."

Again she returns to Patrick White, arguing that he is a major novelist, but accusing him of "intellectual snobbery" because of his "apparent condemnation of the common people — I won't wear that". Yet it is White who has committed himself to populist causes — marching in the streets for Citizens for Democracy, conservation, the anti-nuclear movement — while Dame Leonie has kept herself aloof from the apocalypse which Yeats predicted. It's as though White represents some alternative persona, some illicit strain in herself which she recognises but rejects. They are both aristocrats in a common-place; it is not themselves but their reactions which differ. Outside the walls a twenty-first century of Third World poverty, revolution and nuclear threat awaits them.

The past? "I have no memory for things that have gone wrong. The nasties." She muses about that. "Maybe I've had nothing go wrong?" The future? "I'd like to give more time to it," she replies wryly. "The story of my life has been people asking me to do things and my doing them. I suppose I'm going to go on doing a good deal of public speaking; I seem to be on the merry-go-round. I want to do some writing but I've always been reluctant to dig my essays out and stick them in a book, because I don't want them to become a kind of orthodoxy." Instead, the public life. Speeches, admiration, some "very nasty criticism" and some high office still to come. She looks around her islanded drawing room. Images of comfort and stability. "I accept it, I don't question it, because it works."

She could be talking about our entire society. It works . . . for her. As she talks another slow bead forms in the corner of her eye; she removes her spectacles wipes it away. In the corridor the girl-in-blue, aged three. One up, one down. Pleasant. Responsible. Doleful. Sixty years later she is manifest, unchanged, in a drawing room in Vaucluse, overlooking the Harbour, as the future slouches towards her.

ALLAN BORDER

Allan Border is one of those blokes who never smiles. Well, hardly ever. The man is like his cricket: gritty, shitty, highly competitive, narrow, a streetfighter who battled his way to the top at a time when Australian cricket was in a state of crisis and Border, more often than not, had to rescue it through sheer personal will.

He's one of the moodiest men in world sport, as his nicknames show: Grumpy, Ragsy, Angry Anderson. Someone who knows him likens him to a Queensland blue heeler: you never know whether he's going to bite you or bark. As captain of the Australian XI he's respected rather than liked.

Border is the oldest player in what is basically a team of youngsters, a former contemporary of Lillee, Marsh and Chappell, and as such, represents the old Aussie culture in a new generation of cricketers: a man's man, bit of a chauvinist, honest, good to his wife and kids but likes a beer with the boys, a steady bloke who's come up the hard way, likes the "old values", and has built his life and cricket around the sort of mental toughness which can take a bowling attack apart or which he can turn on others (and himself) with equal abrasiveness.

And he's got courage. As a professional sportsman he's "broken all my fingers apart from one thumb . . . ribs . . . jaw, that was playing baseball . . . numerous cuts and abrasions, a couple over the eyes, and on the back of me head . . . ear . . . that sort of thing . . . it's not a big deal". He admits to "physical fear" when facing fast bowling, but says "you need a bit of guts and determination to get in line, steel yourself, be prepared to get hit a few times if you're going to score runs. If anyone says they enjoy facing real quick bowlers they're having themselves on."

The result: two years ago, ten years to the day since he first played Test cricket, Allan Border became the first Australian cricketer ever to play in a hundred Test matches. He's already scored more Test runs than Bradman, Greg Chappell or any of the other Australian cricketing greats. He's taken over a hundred Test catches and over twenty wickets as well. Richie Benaud says he would have been a great player in any era; he's generally regarded as one of the finest batsman in the world today.

Yet Border has his critics. As a batsman he's aggressive and tries to dominate the bowlers, but as a leader he can be negative and uncommunicative. Greg Chappell, who was Border's captain, says: "He's excellent as a team man and team mate, always had good ideas, knows what's going on; he should be a better captain than he is. He doesn't take the pressure of having the ultimate responsibility very well; when he does make a decision it's often too late; he gets the blinkers on. When he's under pressure he goes right inside himself. He should talk more to his players."

Border virtually confirms that himself: "I have a pretty short fuse, I know I get a bit too intense about things. I sit there, I get the shits, and I find it hard to break the cycle, you just can't get over it; you expect guys to be 100 per cent, you expect yourself to be perfect all the time, and it doesn't work out that way. Sometimes I find that hard to accept. I can snap into that intense, critical thing . . . if I'm angry I sit in a corner by myself and that's not ideal . . . you've got to be a bit more aware, y'know, of the other guys. I really have to fight with myself to get out of that."

His father, who was in the wool trade, says that if anyone crossed young Allan when he was a boy, "he was just as likely to have a cricket bat between the eyes". The family used to say it "brought out the Irish in him" — in fact he's quarter Jewish, half-Irish, and quarter English. His mother, Sheila, describes him as "stubborn, doesn't like failing". His wife Jane, a glamorous and intelligent woman who was a school friend, says he is "very determined, cricket has always been No. 1. If we lose badly he takes it badly. He should take things less seriously. He's the most introverted, untypical Leo that ever was." Benaud: "I like him." A fellow cricketer: "Moody bugger. Selfish."

And Border himself?

It is the day before the First Test against the West Indies at the Gabba, Brisbane, a couple of years ago and Border is sitting cross-legged in his white-tiled, open-plan, patio-and-bougainvillea house set in two hectares of bush at Chapel Hill. He's just come in from a swim in the pool, wearing purple boxer shorts, and is trying to work out, in his painstakingly honest way, just what makes him so bloody-minded and competitive. He was one of five brothers in a "battling" family in Mosman before it become "a yuppie suburb" and used to play constant backyard games against them, first with a cricket stmp and ping pong ball and later with the real thing — they broke so many neighbours' windows that his Dad finally had to agree to take out insurance for them! "I always liked to do well when I was growing up," he remembers, "I dunno, just born with it I suppose. I don't like to be just an also-ran, even if I play golf I like to do as well as I can . . ." If he won the backyard games, says his Mum, he would burst in through the door and announce: "I AM THE CHAMPION!"

He was good at baseball, too, and for a while played A grade in both cricket and baseball. But he was small: he's still a somewhat short, stocky figure, 175 centimetres (five feet, nine inches) tall, weighing 80 kilograms (twelve and a half stone) and in his under-12 days "I was about kneehigh to a grasshopper, and we'd come across these teenage giants, you know 10-year-olds who were six foot (1.5 metres) tall or more . . . Jesus! We were the Midgets from Mosman! Sometimes you wish you could play in the First XV Rugby team, as a kid it matters to you . . . you thought, 'that guy's been picked for a rep team because he's big' . . . they stood out, and you were this little fellow . . . bigger kids used to get the recognition more than the smaller kid." Sometimes he wasn't selected for a local cricket team because of favouritism. He developed what another cricketer describes as "the famous Border chip-on-the-shoulder", though his wife says he doesn't have that at all.

What counts, anyhow, is Border's reaction: it was, says his parents, *I am going to prove to you that I am better than you are.* He's been doing it ever since.

It is the morning of the First Test at the 'Gabba. There are beery shouters already in front of the scoreboard, stripped and sweltering in the sun, wolf-whistling the girls that go past; Queensland police in short sleeves and widebrimmed hats; a line of long-distance cameramen with their grey gunbarrels trained at the wicket; camera crews perched like watchtower guards above the media box; mown grass; an ocker voice over the PA system; and that steady excited hum of crowd banter and laughter as the stands fill up.

Border is out on the ground practising with his team, hitting low catches to a crouching semi-circle of players. He is an incongruous budgie figure in gold-and-red XXXX beer visor, old T-shirt, white shorts, grey socks, dirty shoes. He's got bad skin for a cricketer, burns easily, so he coats his lips with pinkish cream and wears this bloody visor everywhere and has this all-over-the-face beard which helps keep the sun off. He's not smiling. He reckons this young Aussie team is emerging from its low point and he wants to prove it. Stuff the looks. He's his own man, to the point of being a loner: "To be quite honest . . . I've got a circle of friends, but not a huge amount, I'm not a real social butterfly . . . keep a bit to myself."

He talks in a slightly uncouth, dressing-shed way, barely tolerates the media, gives speeches when he has to, keeps everyone, even his mates, at a bit of an arm's length. Professional cricketer. Became captain, reluctantly, when Kim Hughes sold out to South Africa, now says: "I enjoy my role, it's rewarding to a point." Bit worried about what he'll do when he leaves the game, because he doesn't know much about anything else . . . and isn't interested, except in his kids. What you see, says Jane, is what you get.

The ground clears, leaving the stumps glistening, solitary in the sun. There is a west wind blowing across the Gabba, flags erect, swallows swooping over the pitch. Border and Viv Richards, the West Indies captain, stride out to take the toss. The crowd applauds. The two greatest batsmen in the world watch the coin spin against that blue Queensland sky. Richards calls "heads"; it's tails. Border says instantly: "We'll bat."

Then follows one of those bits of byplay which help make cricket such an enduringly fascinating game. The two captains shake hands for the cameramen, and Viv Richards puts a big, expansive hand around the back of Border's neck. It's friendly, but it's also got built into it a suggestion, a code, the faintest signal of dominance. Border tolerates it for barely an instant, shakes free, then stands alone with hands on hips. Richards picked the wrong man: if ever there was a snarly, gritty, blue heeler of a man who refuses to be dominated by anything, it's Allan Border.

Border belongs, psychologically and historically, to an earlier era of cricket, when Australia had a fast bowling attack which included Dennis Lillee and Jeff Thompson, captains/batsmen like the Chappells, wicketkeeper Rod Marsh . . . famous names that Border was a bit in awe of when, as a young ex-Colts cricketer, he found himself being promoted to Sheffield Shield and then to Test cricket while still in his early twenties. Now that he's the senior figure in a young team Border can see that there's been a generational change and it rankles a bit. "They're pretty confident, these younger people; in my day we were't as outgoing. A young bloke comes out and he doesn't care whether it's me or Viv Richards . . . I dunno if I'm explainin' it right . . . they just seem a lot more . . . cocky," he says.

"Sometimes I like the old values. Like the young bloke comin' and sittin' in the corner and observin' and speakin' up when he's spoken to, earning his stripes if you like; these days this doesn't happen. That was my attitude when I first got into the Test team, especially with the likes of Lillee, Marsh, Chappell, I just sort of sat without saying too much. These days that doesn't happen. Young bloke comes into the side, he's part of the side straight away. Everyone equal attitude. I'm distanced because they've got different attitudes; they like different music, different movies, different food, but we have a lot of common ground. I don't think they're critical of me; they look at me as a senior player who has justifiably earned respect."

Border is old-fashioned in all sorts of other ways as well. He knows one-day cricket is all the go: "Society has dictated that, all sport has become faster, more razzamatazz, more action-packed. People demand it because it's a faster way of life these days.

We've had to keep pace with it, people just love the one-day game, coloured gear, playing at nights; that's the changing face of cricket. But I prefer the traditional game, that means a lot more to me; I'm a bit more of a purist. I think we've got to keep that traditional type of cricket very much in the forefront because you can't teach kids just to play one-day cricket; you need that good strong solid base.

"I've adapted reasonably well, I enjoy the game. I'm a bit inconsistent, I'd like to have a few more big shots, bowl a little better. I'm very negative about my bowling, I'm loathe to use myself because I don't think I'm ever going to get anyone out! Tests . . . there you play at your own pace; you can build an innings. It's a *test*, y' know, mental, physical, skills, it suits my style. I'm not an outgoing, outlandish sort of person, I'm a bit more of a, y' know, wait-and-see, build it up, slowly and surely, and that's reflected I suppose in the way I bat. One-day doesn't suit my character; it's a bit hit and miss."

Border is also very much a traditional Aussie sporting bloke who spends most of his time in male company, likes drinking and horsing around, and in his earlier days developed a great admiration for Rodney Marsh, the Test wicketkeeper, because he was such a clown and practical joker. "I enjoy the mateship and all that goes with it . . . it's an important part of the game," he admits, and justifies it by arguing that the beer-after-the-game ritual helps sort everything out — "it's not just buddy-buddy".

He's opposed to wives and families going with Australian cricketers on tour even though other teams allow it: "That's still very much a bugbear, I personally think it's better when the side is totally committed to what they're doing and don't have wives and children to worry about. It's more ideal if the girls aren't there. I get into a lot of trouble about that. Sometimes it's hard when you're overseas; you miss them a lot. If they're with you you're consistently worried about where they are, what they're doing; sometimes on the morning of a Test match you don't want to be waking up at six o'clock playing horsy horsy with the kids, you want to relax a bit."

Says Jane: "He probably is a bit of a chauvinist. He's useless in the house, useless when it comes to being tidy or putting things away, doesn't wash or wipe up; he's learnt to make himself a cup of tea. Al thinks when the wives turn up, things go wrong. Theoretically it's nonsense, goes into the Book of Superstitions. But he's good with the kids; if he says anything they jump. He loves their stupid sayings, stupid answers. That's Al — he's as big a kid as any of them.

"He's very old-fashioned, his morals and ethics are very old-fashioned; he's got a strong sense of family, of responsibility. His Mum and Dad gave him responsibility when he was young. He's a lot more serious now, a lot more grey hairs, more on his mind. He's had a very rough go of it, the first two years after he became captain were very, very tough. Home is a retreat for him."

Border himself says much the same, though in his usual understated, low-key way: "Oh yeah, I love the family atmosphere, I'm very lucky, Jane's been very tolerant of all the cricket intrusion, kids are great. I enjoy that side of my life, great." He even learnt to change the kids' nappies when they were younger: Dean's now 6, Nicole 4. He's bought a Range Rover so they'll be safer when they drive down to Port Macquarie, where Border's parents now live, or to Sydney, where Jane's family lives. When he was a teenager he used to bum around with his mates, do a lot of bush camping and surfing, but he doesn't have time for that now. He doesn't read, he's not interested in politics, watching sport on TV or wrestling with the kids are his main diversions at home. What he's narrowed himself down to, basically, is being a professional cricketer.

It is the Benson & Hedges lunch which formally launches the cricket season and all the heavies are there at the Brisbane Hilton: officials, selectors, sponsors, businessmen, the entire West Indies and Australian teams. Border looks distinctly uncomfortable in unfamiliar suit and tie, short curly hair brushed back, chatting to media types and promoters. The night before he was at a bat-signing ceremony. He bears it all as best he can, knowing it comes with the captaincy, but he acts a bit like Crocodile Dundee wrestling with a bidet. It's a long way from backyard bashes and broken windows in Mosman.

After the speeches, the Chardonnay, the chicken chasseur and

B & H ballyhoo, Border gets up at the microphone to introduce the Aussie test team: "Geoff Swampy Marsh from Western Australia; his partner in crime, the keg on legs, David Boon; Dino Jones from Victoria; the West Australian godfather, Mike Veletta; the master of disaster, Tim May; Tony Dodemaide, the quiet achiever, Chris Mathews, a welcome return to the Australian team . . . The guys are all permed up, as you can see, very rare . . . tough task ahead of us . . . West Indies the Number 1 team in the world . . . it's going to be one hell of a summer . . . these are the guys we are hoping will do it for us. Thank you."

Afterwards he gets wheeled before the TV cameras and has to say it all again. He does it well, stumbling a bit over the words, trying to be sensible and even-handed, answering "aw, yeah" and "aw, well" to all manner of questions; it's a relief when it's all over and he can get back to a beer with the "guys". He drinks it, Queensland style, straight out of the stubby. He transferred to Queensland for a big fee, but still hasn't managed to win the Sheffield Shield for his adopted state: "that's one of my ambitions, I'd like to do that," he says. He reckons he's become a Queenslander: "No, don't miss Sydney. Friends maybe, a little bit of family, but generally we've found a pretty good niche up here, great lifestyle. Crickets been good to me, you get paid to do something you enjoy doing."

Yet he seems so uptight, so edgy and turned inwards most of the time that you begin to wonder just how deep a satisfaction Border gets from it all. A cricketer who respects him fears "if you promote someone above their ability you do them a disservice. He would be the perfect vice-captain, not captain." Another wonders if "Allan's shitty because he's been playing at a time when Australian cricket has not been at its best." He has been criticised for batting at No.5 instead of further up the batting list, which might stop him having to rescue the side so often.

For a while there he led the Australian Test team to a series of humiliating defeats; it wasn't until the tour of England in 1989 that the tide turned and Border began to achieve the same success as a captain that he had long before achieved as an individual.

Mike Coward, the *Sydney Morning Herald* cricketing writer, believes Border had to survive the two great revolutions of modern cricket — the Packer World Series upheaval and the South Africa incursion — and had to painfully rebuild the traditional game after its key players had been suborned, destroyed or retired. Whatever the reason, Border acts like a man under enormous stress. And stress is the one thing in his life he doesn't handle well.

He's an asthmatic. Has been since the age of 12. He carries a squirter around with him in his coat pocket in case he gets a sudden, disabling attack, and takes medication as well. His moodiness is legendary, and both older and younger players tell of when he has "cracked a blacky" and retired into himself in fury, refusing to talk to anyone, cancelling engagements, swearing at everyone and everything. In his biography of Greg Chappell, my brother Adrian McGregor refers to "Border's dark, implacable alter ego" and recounts one incident in which Border, after a run of batting failures, refused point blank to talk to some kids in a coaching class and spent the next thirty minutes shouting and arguing with Chappell, storming up and down the 'Gabba dogtrack, back into the changing room, refusing to budge. At any moment, thought Chappell, who is not the easiest-going of characters himself, this man is going to buckle to my will. Border never did. The relationship between the two has never been the same since.

The same sort of bloodyminded, pigheaded, surly faced obstinancy is what helps make Border a formidable batsman. He won't give up. He can get beaten three times by a bowler and then play the next ball as though nothing had happened. He's not a stylist; he has a short backlift and often seems to be scrabbling around, but the runs keep coming. One Test bowler told me Border can punish any ball which is even an inch off length; he's bowled at him, he knows. Bobby Simpson, the Australian team coach, talks about "the magnitude of the bloke" and says: "Allan would never be regarded as a pretty player, he's a player's player, a performer; technically he's very good, and he's also a very positive person, very sure of his talents. He gets runs, and he doesn't let the team down."

Says Allan Border himself: "Mental toughness is my big plus as a cricketer. Technique's important, ball skills . . . but sheer talent isn't the answer, there's a lot of people with talent to burn but they don't use it properly. It's your attitude more than anything; you use your skills as much as possible, recognise your limitations, and mentally you're tougher than the guy next to you. I've tried to become a more consistent player than a flamboyant player, I think I could go out there and play like a David Gower, maybe with not the same finesse, but I don't think I'd be consistent. You avoid high-risk shots . . . which ones? Hook shot. Taking the ball off the stumps through the onside. I dunno, I still get out doing those things!'' Swig of XXXX. He gazes across the Gabba: sharp nose, pale grey-green eyes, freckles, chipped-bone thumb strapped up. No smile.

Whether Allan Border is the right sort of person to lead Australia is something cricket buffs argue about. He gets extremely tense before a big match; he can turn a rough tongue on the younger cricketers — but who else is there? Border says: "I identify with the team because I'm captain. If you do well individually it's always nice, but it's not quite the same kick. Generally I'm pretty satisfied with myself, especially with captaincy; I've slotted into that role pretty well, because it's a difficult thing." Has it affected his batting? "If anything I've batted better . . . I'm a little bit more selective, don't thrash it around as much as I used to. Bit more responsible."

For a stocky bloke, Border hits the ball hard. Gary Sobers was a boyhood hero but, he says, "I don't try and be a clone of anyone. In my early days people used to compare me to Neil Harvey but that was just because we were both smallish lefthanders. I don't think we had any great similarity of style." He sees being a lefthander as something of an advantage, because some bowlers don't like bowling at a lefthander, but "at other times it can be awkward because wickets tend to get rough outside the lefthander's off stump, which allows bowlers to bowl at the roughage."

He's not a terribly physical bloke: doesn't work out in the gym, dislikes going on training runs ("I'll go if I'm told to"), prefers to graft away at his technique in the nets; yet there is an undeniable sense of purpose and strength about Border, he's the sort of bloke you'd think twice about before crossing, he won't and can't be intimidated, and in these days of attack bowlers he's one of the first batsmen you'd pick to stand up and retaliate.

"The accent these days is on strike bowling, knocking sides over with that," he says. "That's why the West Indies have been so powerful over the last ten years; they've had a quartet of fast bowlers who could knock a side over twice for reasonable scores and allow their batsmen to bat without a great deal of pressure on them. That's the way to win Test matches these days.

"The really fast bowler, they do have that physical fear weaponry. There are moments when you think, this bloke's bowled quick, if it hits me it's gonna bloody hurt. But if you want to be fair dinkum you've got to be prepared to wear him down, show you're not scared of him. The most ferocious bowler I've faced? Aw, different bowlers on different days: Malcolm Marshall, Joel Garner — greater fear factor there — Michael Holding, Andy Roberts. Richard Hadlee had his moments, made you jump around. And Lillee and Thompson, though I didn't face them as much."

Border's approach to most things is fairly pragmatic. He thinks some of his mates retired before they really wanted to. "I hope to play for a while yet, I feel I'm still very competitive. I don't want to retire and think, gee, I wish I'd played for a little bit longer; you're a long time retired." What might he go into? "That's the million dollar question, I've spent so much time making sure I play good cricket I've neglected other areas. There's not many things that really grab me." He could probably stay with the XXXX brewery, maybe do some cricket coaching, help kids with "kangaroo cricket": "It'd seem a shame to play the game for so long and then neglect it completely. Yes, it worries me, cricket's not going to go on forever."

South Africa? Border says he's caught between the pro and anti views on that; the cricket authority has made every effort to make the game multi-racial, he says, but because of the regime it looks as though their efforts will be in vain. "As a cricketer I don't see black/white," he says. No, he's never been approached to go to South Africa. "If I were I don't think I would go. It would have to be something extra, but even financially speaking you've still got to live with it, and I wouldn't be prepared to do that."

That's the flip side of Border's general conservatism, his belief in "discipline" and team sports. "Too many kids don't like sport, I dunno, they're brought up differently, that part of schooling's gone out the window. I think it's character building, teaches you to watch out for your mate rather than just the individual. Y'know I get amused with that late night bloke, Clive Robertson, he says sportsmen are absolute jerkoffs, he can't understand why anyone bothers with sport, and look what sort of a person he is, the biggest cynic of all time!"

Drugs? Border thinks about it. No, it's not prevalent in the cricket scene, he decides, not like, say, cocaine in the United States. "This current bunch are fairly responsible, they're a hell of a lot quieter than some other Aussie teams I've been involved with, nowhere near as boozy. I'm not saying we're angels, I suppose everyone's been subjected to drugs over a lifetime, you go to parties . . . you could take an upper to get you through a session . . . I personally would be a bit scared to do that sort of thing because you don't know what the effects are." So has he ever got into drugs himself? For the first time, Border hesitates. "I couldn't admit to it," he says. And smiles. Almost.

Allan Border is essentially a transition figure: someone who is old enough to have grown up through the years of the larrikin strike attack of Lillee and Thompson and the batting battery of the Chappells and the wicketkeeping of Rod Marsh, and to absorb the cricketing culture they represented, and is now still young enough to try to pass the heritage on. Sometimes it's worked — as in the triumphant tour of England in 1989 when Border's team began as underdogs yet won the Ashes — and sometimes it hasn't. Border, who is nothing if not dogged, has simply battled on. Greg Chappell, after his famous confrontation with Border, came to some firm conclusions about Allan Border's character and decided: "He'll make more runs and knock my record over and go so far past it won't matter. He'll play 120 Tests and make 8000-9000 runs. He's a very rare breed."

Allan Border is now on the way to making all those forecasts come true. When he was a kid, says his Mum, he used to let his elder brother Johnno take the lead in the backyard cricket game, to see if he made a mess of it, before going out to prove *he* was better.

If he won he would come back and make the claim he has been enforcing on himself ever since: "I AM THE CHAMPION!" Just so.

JOHN CAIN

"John Cain is his father writ small." It's a harsh judgment to make of the man who has been the most successful Labor Premier in the history of Victoria but it's one of the crosses John Cain has to bear — always being compared with his father, Jack Cain Sr, the turbulent, passionate figure who dominated Victorian politics when his son John was still a kid who liked to memorise Test cricket scores and deserted (ran away from?) Geelong Grammar because, one suspects, the bullyboys there branded him a "Commo's son".

Cain, by common consent, was the great Labor survivor of the 1980s, the man who displayed all of Hawke's pragmatism and ability to win elections but kept to a mildly reformist program and retained enough Labor principles to halt the mass desertion of voters which happened elsewhere. Until 1990, that was, when a series of political disasters — the tramway strike, the ill-fated state government adventures into financial entrepreneurship, the collapse of the Pyramid building society — suddenly made Labor unpopular with Victorian voters and jeopardised Cain's position as Premier. Now there is a lot of suspicion of him as well as the usual party rivalry. And as the strain of being a politician in the economic and social quicksands of the last decade has begun to show on Cain's deeply scarred and furrowed face, so a different man has begun to emerge from the protective reserve with which he has guarded himself in the past.

For much of his life Cain has had the reputation of being a dull, humourless, boring plodder. The jokes about him are legion; an acquaintance describes him as "even more dull than he seems!"; an editor who had regular lunches with him says "I can't remember a single thing he said." Even his ultra-loyal wife, Nancye, has been heard to call him "dreary". When Cain was defending his government against the charge of "running out of steam" and "hitting a flat spot" one media commentator described the Cain government as "one unending series of flat spots". There's also a lot of petty personal criticism of Cain as being "mean" and "small-minded", as though he isn't quite classy enough to lead a state like Victoria. To anyone familiar with the corrupt bearpit of New South Wales politics, such charges are absurd: Cain is that comparative rarity on the contemporary political scene, a man of integrity.

Yet the wariness of him persists. One Cain-watcher points out that Cain distrusts people, won't meet strangers halfway, alienates people who approach him as they would any politician. He views a lot of Melbourne behaviour with distaste, dislikes much of the media. He can be incredibly patronising; he has the irritating manner of someone who feels he is never dealing with equals — he is always talking down, patiently explaining, like an uncle to naughty children. (In fact children love him, they set up that high-pitched shriek "Mr Cain! Mr Cain!" when he visits playgrounds; there's something about that heavily creased, avuncular face they respond to). Over-riding it all is the myth that Cain is an utterly suburban, unexceptional character, Mr Average Family Solicitor, who seems to have become Premier by accident.

Myth and anti-myth

It takes a while to realise that John Cain has virtually created the mythology himself. Here is an immensely self-repressed, self-controlled, consciously manipulative man who has decided Victoria is an innately conservative state with an irredeemably conservative electorate and that the only way to win and keep power is to reflect that in his political style.

Thus the widespread myth that Cain is a wowser. *Just perfect* for a wowser state! Cain, like the prune, a Joyless Puritan! In fact Cain doesn't seem to be a real wowser at all; indeed it's something of a relief to find he drinks, gambles on the horses and the trots, loses his temper, and swears quite a lot — just like any other red-blooded Aussie Male. As he says himself:

"What's a wowser? I have a glass of wine at dinner, I've got nothing against drinking. I guess because I don't drink a lot they decided I was a wowser. I read all that crap about me being a wowser, it's so superficial and boring . . . bloody stupid nonsense . . . I used to smoke. Smoked a pipe a bit too. Yeah. When I was at uni we used to have all-night card schools, thought it was terribly smart . . . every other bugger smoked so you smoked . . . I was told it would ruin my wind for footie, but I felt 'I'm such a bloody good footballer it doesn't matter!' (laughing). Nah, I wasn't a good footballer, but I thought I was terrific! I gave it away . . .

"You've probably read I don't travel on freeways: the bloody lies people tell! I travel economy on domestic flights, yeah. Waste of money. The only people who travel first class are public servants and trade union officials and any other bugger who can get somebody else to pay for it. It's just barmy.

"Yeah, I don't wear a morning suit to the races. To the ballet tonight? Dinner suit. I've had a dinner suit since I was 17! Listen: people wear suits and dinner suits for social occasions. That's enough, right. That's all it is. Simple as that. Why would I go and buy a bloody morning suit? Wear it once a year. I'm not going to do it! Nonconformist? I don't think so. They're not conforming when they go to the bloody races; every other bugger's got a suit on! *I don't make no waves*, as Mayor Daley might say."

Cain laughs, takes a gulp of minestrone, looks around. He's a quick, chirpy, lighthearted brat of a man, as bright and beady-eyed as a marsupial rat or a chipmunk, with a fine sardonic sense of humour and a delight in matching wits with anyone around him. No wonder he and John Button are such good mates: they are both small, irreverent, jokey sort of blokes. Button, indeed, once described Cain to me as "one of the most self-assured people I have ever met". But even that confidence gets up people's noses, especially when they think he's got nothing to be confident about. Says a leading Melbourne political correspondent: "He's a bit like Bjelke-Petersen was, once he is out of the Premier's role, and the respect accorded to that role, he has nothing to say. You wouldn't want to cross the room to talk to him. He can't be bothered with anything much non-governmental. He's Premier or he's nothing.''

In one sense it's an important insight into Cain, who is an intensely and almost myopically political animal. But once you tune into his sardonic, bantering, crackerjack personal style, which he rarely allows to come through during those three-times-a-week TV press conferences he gives, he is quite fun to be with. He's not the only person in the world to combine a fundamental seriousness with a lighthearted surface demeanour.

What slowly emerges, after you spend some time with him, is that John Cain isn't a passionless character at all. He is, on the contrary, a man of fierce moral convictions and nervy energy, and enough contradictions to make someone who knows him to describe Cain, half-seriously, as ''a torn human being . . . he needs constant reassurance that he is a significant figure . . . that's why he is such an over-achiever.''

Cain comes from a classic Labor background, the son of Jack Cain Sr, a self-educated working-class revolutionary who worked his way up to become Premier; the mark of Cain is upon John, indelibly inscribed by a powerful father and the ill-starred career he had. (Jack Cain Sr was thrown out of office twice, once by a reactionary Upper House, once by the great Labor split.) But John was a boy with a difference: sensitive, intelligent, on the way to discarding his class culture. Later John Cain's parents shoved him upstairs to Geelong and Scotch, to get an education and a better life. But Cain was rejected by that upper-class culture too; they despised him, just as they still sneer behind their begloved hands at Plain John and Nancye. Cain was turned back upon himself, culturally deracinated, unaligned with both the class he had left behind and the class he had been pushed into. Enter the familiar John Cain of today: a very private person, an Independent, no really close friends, guarded to the point of paranoia, and always always always under control.

Where does he get his emotional support from? ''My wife,'' he says simply. ''She's tolerant, she's wonderful.'' He is incredibly protective of Nancye in a way that is obviously self-protective as well. But on a trip to London he could hardly bear to go window-shopping with her; his government role came first. "She would never pressure me to give up politics," he says. The Cains have three kids. One lives at home, others still close. The nuclear family support system for one ambitious man.

Says someone who likes Cain, analysing his political manner: "It has involved a conscious repression of everything natural about him, his native wit and style. If only he'd let go . . ." Conscious repression. Cain as control freak. The paradox is: if he let go, people would like him more — but would they vote for him?

Cain the red-ragger

Sometimes a less artificial Cain breaks through. It comes out in the acerbic, combative exchanges he has with his press inquisitors; "if he doesn't like the question he lampoons the questioner," says one journalist. There's a lot of bile and resentment in the way he slashes at "those conservative bastards; they make the rules that suit them . . . I get very bitter about this . . . yet they're the people who always break the rules. You don't need much of substance to be a Liberal or conservative politician. You're not about anything at all really. Just a pay packet and a motor car and the prestige."

There is no ambiguity about the tone: it's the authentic old Labor disgust at the "rich drones" in our midst, something he could have learnt at his father's elbow. ("We used to talk over the dinner table a lot," he says. "We were close at mealtimes".) Cain still thinks of himself as a radical, though he believes "you've got to temper your radicalism with what's attainable". He acts like a man who has never forgiven the conservatives for what they did to his father, how they destroyed his government in much the same way as another Upper House (the Senate) was used to destroy Whitlam generations later. It was Cain who sacked the former Governor-General of Victoria, Sir Brian Murray, before he could do a Kerr and try to sack Cain.

In Parliament, even before he became Premier, Cain was famous for his snarling, sneering attacks on the Liberal/National Party coalition. He still does it. *"Here we go!"* shouts a Liberal backbencher as Cain, bent forward at the waist, head stuck out, hands slicing the air, starts hectoring the Opposition about their dishonesty and accusing them of trying to buy people off with dollars . . .

This disjunction between what Cain *feels* ("I am emotional, I feel keenly about lots of things . . . injustice, greed, waste . . . I get angry, I lose my temper sometimes though I don't shout at people") and how he thinks he has to *act* is the explanation of the most common criticism made of Cain in Victoria: that he is a hypocrite.

He isn't. Cain acts on clear moral principles most of the time. But it means people have picked up, almost instinctively, an unresolved inner conflict between what John Cain feels and what he does. They detect his dual nature, call him two-faced.

Anti-Cain

Also, if Cain is as characterless as he's made out to be, it's hard to understand why he arouses such antagonism — which he does. Indeed, there is a surprising amount of criticism of Cain — within the Victorian ALP — for being too autocratic, for having drifted so far to the Right, for imposing his own brand of snail-pace gradualism upon a government which has been in power for several years and which should have achieved more in that time than it has.

A key member of the Melbourne City Council, which is controlled by Labor, lists Cain's faults thus: no central values or philosophy except staying in power; no understanding of the *city* of Melbourne, its people, its special character; arrogant, undemocratic, a centraliser who has turned his back on community participation; an artistic and cultural philistine who poured money and land into the Tennis Centre but is insensitive to artistic and cultural needs; and a marketeer who knows how to sell but not how to create.

Lest this seem too fierce, it should be understood that Cain has conducted a running battle with the council and ripped their planning powers away from them in a way which parallels what happened earlier in Sydney. Cain reckons he's done a good thing there, got some good planning going "without being dominated by the rednecks", not realising that to others he's a redneck himself. He defends what his government has managed to achieve without any "dramatic social upheaval": better workers' compensation and motor insurance, more generous superannuation and long service leave and new appointments (including workers and trade unionists) to government boards and corporate bodies. "The Establishment doesn't just dominate these things any longer," he says.

And he's proud of turning Victoria into what he calls "a small 'l' liberal State" by liberalising drinking and shopping hours, legalising brothels, allowing nude bathing, relaxing the old puritan culture for which Victoria was famous. "We've probably done more than Don Dunstan in terms of social change," he says. Adds one of Cain's mates: "Look, on Sunday now you can get a fuck and get pissed. That's not bad, is it?"

Cain the developer

Mid-week. Melbourne is humming away, stylishly dressed businessmen and women picking their way around the roadworks. "Honestly, you take a stroll around the city on a late afternoon and sometimes the sun is blotted out by cranes!" boasts Cain, forgetting, perhaps, that that was the favourite line of another great moderniser/developer, Joh Bjelke-Petersen.

The cranes, of course, are merely a semiotic code for what Cain sees as his greatest achievement as Premier: the painful, incremental overhaul of the Victorian economy. "We've turned this place around," says Cain earnestly. "I'm enormously proud and satisfied with what we've done. There are so many areas where change is needed, where you have to unscramble what goes back to last century. You can't do it overnight. There are still areas of great hardship out there. If we had more resources we could do more. I'd have loved to have been in government in the sixties or early seventies when it was pouring out your ears, you could do what you liked, but I've got to proceed with what I've got. We missed our chance in the sixties, bloody Menzies and Bolte just squandered those years.

"It'll be a long haul. It's no good being in office for three years, or four, or five; I want to see long-term change. The reformist zeal of some of our comrades is interesting, but they do lose track of the real world."

Cain the conservative

John Button told me once about Cain: "I regard him as a conservative, in his style and much else. He drives a car conservatively, he has conservative habits of thought; ideologically he's in the mainstream. Yet he has a lot of compassion, he has certain fundamental beliefs about fair shares, giving everyone a fair go . . ."

There's no doubting Cain's idealism; despite his years in power, learning to stroke the media, compromise compromise compromise, he retains an edgy up-you-Jack commitment to Labor principles which makes him by far the most Left of any current Labor Premier; he hardly ever talks to Hawke or Keating, he heads the most reformist political machine in the country, and he takes notice of all the Victorian factions — including the Socialist Left. He knows machine politics can turn rotten and compares New South Wales with Mayor Daley's Democrat machine in Chicago: "Machine politics in NSW is that sort of thing, not necessarily corrupt, but may be," he says. It won't happen in Victoria while he is leader.

Cain, however, may have suffered a different sort of corruption. At the core of his political approach is the belief that Victoria "is a most difficult and conservative state. There *is* an establishment here. Labor has never won large majorities in Victoria. Look, my father was in politics for forty years, and in Parliament for twenty qyears, and only five years in a Ministry, in government. The risk Labor governments run in Victoria more than anywhere else is scaring people off."

Hence the famous moderation of the Cain government. His favourite phrase: "Don't scare the horses." But it has led Cain to be even more cautious than he need be; he has become a prisoner of his own history, in exactly the same way as he has imposed a carapace of conformity upon his personal image. As Button characterised him years ago, he has become, cruelly, a conservative.

Thus, when I asked Cain what was on his political agenda, there was a palpable silence. Agenda? Er . . . well, no doubt the policy committees would be working one up . . . One of his advisers was equally nonplussed. Agenda? Er, well . . . probably lighten off in an election year . . . get your people out a bit . . . don't put anything on the table to have the guts kicked out of it . . .

John Cain: "I can't see what the alternative is. Every politician has to display some balance and caution, a degree of moderation. You know what the checks and balances are: the party system, interest groups, pressure groups, all that. You can't get too far out in front of public opinion. You've got to reflect what's happening."

More of the same. For year after year. For as long as he manages to hold on to his position as Premier. When I mentioned this to a Labor stalwart in a Melbourne branch he put his head in his hands. "Jesus!"

Cain the Irishman

You ask Cain who he is, what he is, and he says "I dunno". Never looks in the identity-mirror. Not interested. No background! Self-created human! The Man Without Qualities again. No wonder he's regarded as characterless. But you press him further, ask him what tradition he springs from, and the answer is a surprise.

"Irish. Irish in Australia — I came out of that lot, I think. Ever read that book by Patrick O'Farrell? My father's parents came from Ireland. Irish father, Welsh mother. My father was Catholic but he rejected the Church. Do I feel Irish? No. I don't feel identity with any ethnic group. If anything I'm a WASP."

Cain the Nationalist

OK, does he feel identity with *anything*? Cain laughs. "Yeah, this great country. I feel part of it. Yeah, I'm a nationalist. I feel very Victorian. And not just because of Shield cricket! I feel proud of Victoria; most of what we've been doing here is about Victoria. When you go overseas you don't just talk about being Australian, you talk about where you come from. I think we should exhibit much more national pride, be more like the Americans. It's developing — more people know the national anthem now, for a start. I sang it seven times on Australia Day, at the Bicentenary celebrations and I felt better each time! (laughing) The Governor-General didn't know the first verse; he had the Princess holding the bloody thing up for him. I said to him afterwards, 'You should know it'. Patriotism is a negative thing, national pride is a positive thing. Y'know, we're good because of this and this, and you go out and sell it.''

A bit parochial?

''You can argue we're all a bit too parochial. The states have become more parochial, the national government will never be influenced much by what happens in one state — even if Victoria is a model. I don't accept Sydney has taken the lead over Melbourne. We're the intellectual, sporting and financial capital of Australia. You Sydney lot are all the same . . . look, we've got the best restaurants in the world, certainly the best Chinese, I go to a few of 'em. Darling Harbour? Yeah, I drove past it. I wouldn't want a monorail running through the heart of the city. I think we reflect the strengths that are exhibited by Mediterranean, robust cities.

''More radical political culture? Yeah. I'm not just the beneficiary, I'm to some extent the creator. Melbourne wants a monument? I never said that! That's a throwback to the Hamer days, when the Hamer government was seen as wallowing around and not standing for anything. Yeah, the Opera House is a landmark. Some say the Tennis Centre, by default, has become the same for Melbourne.'' He pauses to take a breath. Once Cain starts talking it's hard to stop him. ''It's a pet project of mine. They call it Cain's Cathedral! Yeah, they can't copy our Tennis Centre. It's a bloody beauty!''

Cain the tennis player

Cain plays tennis most weekends, on his own tennis court. Invites friends around. Some have been coming for twenty years. He has tennis friends, and political friends, and other friends.

Now he is sitting in the white sunblasted concrete concourse of the huge tennis stadium which his government has built near the Melbourne Cricket Ground and which doubles as an entertainment centre (TONIGHT: PINK FLOYD). He is enjoying the time off paperwork; tonight he goes with Bob Hawke to open the Australian Ballet Centre and attend a gala performance of *Sleeping Beauty*. Not his cup of tea.

Cain is a philistine. He was the despair of Patrick McCaughey, the former director of the Victorian National Gallery. Didn't even like the Heidelberg School of landscape painters much. He lent Cain four to hang in his Premier's office. They're still there, but Cain doesn't even know who painted them. Who's this? M-C-C-U-B-B-I-N? He doesn't read much now, no political theory, though he did read John Pilger's *Heroes*. Hasn't finished *The Fatal Shore*. Seen a few more films lately. Occasional dinner party, old friends from the law, when he was a suburban solicitor.

Gets up about 5.50 a.m. most mornings, goes for a run around the local streets. Headband. Two-and-a-half miles. "I'm gettin' slower, have a walk in the middle. I miss a few mornings." Used to go waterskiing, pulled a hamstring muscle, gave it up. "But I'm a great beachcomber, like to wander along the beach at Carrum. Got a weekender there, just a few yards from where my family had one when I was a kid." He likes the footie, hasn't missed a Grand Final for 46 years, but he's not a footie fanatic. "For sheer satisfaction and enjoyment I like to sit in the sun at the cricket. Used to play, not very well. I love it."

Right now, however, he's at the Centre he's so proud of, patiently posing for photographs. He takes a comb out of his pocket, smiles sheepishly, runs it through his thinning hair. Button told him after he became Premier: "You have to understand that this game is all about the media these days." He is wearing, again, a grey suit, grey tie. Greying hair. Cupid's bow mouth. He is almost 60 years old. He spends a lot of life doing things he doesn't want to do because he thinks it's important. "Yes, I'm a socialist," he says quietly. "I'm not running away from the term. But I go up to the bush and I'm told it's all a socialist plot to require people to be more responsible with guns."

Cain was visibly upset after the Hoddle Street massacre, swore he'd do anything necessary to try to stop it ever happening again, and introduced the toughest gun laws in Australia. It turned into an issue which blew up in his face, but he persevered and won the next election.

Now he's at the Tennis Centre — after all Pat Cash was here a few weeks ago, and then AC/DC. He's a stubborn man ("a lot of it is persistence in politics, I reckon; stick at something"), he's absolutely sure of what's right and wrong, and he's not going to be deflected by people who jeer at him and bang on his car with placards. Could he defuse all that hostility by not calling himself a socialist? *"You don't call yourself anything, that's the way you defuse it, Craig,"* he says.

Cain on Cain

The Cain stigma goes back a long way. Jack Cain, his father, was the son of an immigrant Irish labourer who drowned himself in a river near Bacchus Marsh in 1890. Jack changed his name from Cane to Cain, left home as a child, falsified his background, and ended up three times Premier of Victoria. He was a powerful, strongly-built figure and obviously had a profound impact upon John Cain, who was born when his father was already 49 years old. Says Cain now:

"I admired him immensely, oh yeah. I mean, he was a bloke without any formal education . . . they talk about Mick Young . . . my father battled his way through the trade union movement, the Socialist Party, the anti-conscription movement . . . came into Parliament in 1917. No, not uncouth. The bookshelves were littered with books that were part of his self-learning: we had *Das Kapital*, R.G. Ingersolls, the great Rationalist . . . for birthday and Christmas presents I used to buy him political books."

Cain grew up in a household dominated by day-to-day politics. He and his elder sister Joan became "de facto local member's secretaries . . . we used to answer the door, talk to people out of jobs . . . that's influenced me, I'm a product of the post-Depression years, I went to school with kids whose Dads were on the "susso", they came to school without shoes, without food . . . we grew up in very hard times, that's why I'm accused of being a bit mean, conscious of a dollar. Times were tough, you had to husband your resources carefully, I was always very impressed by that." Cain talked to his father a lot, went on country trips with him, took part in his political meetings. But he doesn't agree he was overawed by him. "He was just a friendly bloke. We went to the cricket in summer, the football in winter. And the beach, we spent a lot of time at Carrum, he was a great beach cricketer. My main memory of childhood? Very happy."

Cain's mother, Dorothea Grindrod, was a milliner, very professional, ran a chain of shops, and Cain was very close to her; because his father was away from home a lot she played "a father role" to him, he says. But he rejects the idea that she was more genteel than his father. "They were both achievers," he says, trying to explain where his own drive for achievement originated. To suggestions that he is more the product of his mother than his father, and was influenced more by the women in his household, Cain says forthrightly: "That's absolute bullshit! You're a product of your entire environment. I wasn't a lonely child; if anything I was a bit of a know-all as a kid." He could rattle off cricket scores from past Tests, knew a lot about politics; a "nice polite boy", as a neighbour described him, from a good house in Northcote, whose father at least had a job. Premier.

Nevertheless, his parents were worried that he was on his own a lot and decided to send him to boarding school. It was a crucial and symbolic act, the start of Cain's gentrification and what you could call his class confusion. "The family was out a lot, dad was Premier, my sister was a lot older, my mother was working at the job of being the Premier's wife . . . the little wife did this, did that, that sort of sexist syndrome . . . I'm glad my own wife, Nancye, doesn't have to go through that."

They sent him to the most upper-class, most prestigious boarding school in the nation: Geelong Grammar. Cain hated it. He lasted only a few weeks, fled home. Even now he is defensive when he talks about it. "It's not relevant, I just wasn't happy, that's the end of it, full stop, finish." The only good thing about what was a traumatic episode was that he met Rupert Murdoch there: "He was the friendliest bloke I met there, we were good mates, have been since. Rupert was the Comm of Geelong Grammar at the time!", he remembers, laughing.

He went back to Northcote High School, but the next year ended up a boarder at Scotch College, which he says he liked though "I was given a rough time because my father was the Premier . . . it was the time of Chifley's attempt to nationalise the banks; there was a lot of bitterness on Scotch College hill . . . those kids reflected their parents' attitudes, many of 'em had country parents . . . I took some delight in being the Opposition,

I was just about the *only* Opposition. I knew I had right on my side, I didn't have any trouble, it was easy."

Cain got his matriculation and wanted to stay an extra year at school, but "Dad said, 'you're bloody mad, go out and get an education, do law, make up your mind what you want to do in the future.' " He did just that: worked as a porter at Chelsea railway station, "cleaned the dunny, swept the platform", got his law degree; his Scotch peers went on to golden legal careers, he became a suburban solicitor.

When John was 26, Jack Cain died. "No, I never felt I had to live up to my father," Cain says quietly. He stood for preselection for his father's seat because Labor kingmaker Pat Kennelly wanted him to, but lost to Frank Wilkes — the same man Cain deposed as Labor leader twenty-four years later. It wasn't until the 1960s, when Cain and some other Labor professional people organised a group called the Participants, that his political career took off. "That's when I got my political fire," he says. The Participants included John Button, Dick McGarvie, Xavier Connor, Frank Costigan and Michael Duffy, and formed the nucleus of what now is the Independent faction in the federal Labor party; Cain was their first chairman. The Victorian ALP, he says, had become "a nark party" after the great Labor split; the Participants helped organise federal ALP intervention in the Left-controlled party machine on behalf of the "moderates" like themselves, and in 1976 Cain reaped the benefit: he at last got into Parliament.

He turned himself, unexpectedly, into a dirt-digger and Parliamentary actor, hammering the Hamer government over its land scandals, reading and researching everything he could lay his hands on. In Parliament he still winds himself up into half-hour diatribes against "the other mob" who don't give a damn about jobs for ordinary people: "it's just incidental to them, to the rich man getting what he or she wants." Five years after entering Parliament, Cain, in a typical consensual manoeuvre, got Wilkes to resign as leader. No blood, but he got there all the same. Seven months later, in April 1982, he became Premier — the first Labor Premier since his own father. In 1986 he outstripped Jack Cain's record as the longest serving Labor Premier in Victorian history.

It's a dynasty, of sorts. If ever Cain was under his father's shadow, he has stepped out of it. He is his own man.

Knees bent, Cain is combing his hair in a mirror. Again. He straightens, turns, smiles his bright, chirpy smile. Outside the Tennis Centre the security guard didn't recognise this nondescript character and refused him entry. Now the TV cameras wait. "OK, let's see how we go," he orders. Time for another "bit of theatre". *"Mr Premier . . ."*

Future Cain

It's a sunny, lyrical day in Melbourne's CBD. Cain is strolling along Spring Street opposite Parliament House, heading for the Society restaurant. Three builders' labourers in hardhats and singlets shout at him as they approach from the opposite direction:

"G'day, John!"

"Good on yer, Johnny!"

Cain replies instantly: "G'day. How are ya?"

The paperseller recognises him, smiles at him. Someone in a car waves. People trust him, even if he distrusts them. It's said he has the common touch, but it's something much more profound than that: Cain *is* common, dirt common, and it's one of the most likeable things about him. If there was anything phony about it people would pick it up instantly. "His heart's in the right place," says a friend. Says a politician: "He has a feel for what ordinary people think about an issue." On his wall in his Premier's office is a pictureboard of family snaps: barbecue, family party, holiday, Nancye and John and the kids. A Goode Plaine Man. Chaucer would have approved.

He's worried about mortality, political mortality. What sort of person is he? "I never take that overview of myself, I haven't got time. I try on a free weekend, I try and reflect on where we're going, but you don't really have the opportunity to just sit back and assess what's been done, what hasn't. Bob Menzies used to go to the cricket, go to London for three months. My father, when he was Premier, sat in the boat for four weeks. That doesn't happen now," he says. "Politicians get used up. Did you ever read that book by . . . who was it? . . . yes, Toffler . . . *Future Shock*. You're quickly shopsoiled and chucked out. It's happening to all of us." He stops, forks fish cutlet into his mouth, takes a drink of mineral water. "I just take every year as it comes."

Later, almost with wistfulness: "I don't regret the way politics has taken over my life. I've given it my all."

A last question: has he felt under pressure, all his life, to exceed his dad? "That's quite wrong," he says abruptly. "I resent that. It trivialises what I have been trying to do. It's not just beating my father's record! My job has been different . . . We're very fragile here."

The fear is, he has been suborned by the very system he opposes. You start off pretending to be "one of them", for camouflage, and end up acting like one; you hold on to power and forget what to do with it. The last words he said to me, as I left the office of the Premier of Victoria, 1 Treasury Place, Melbourne were: "It's all a game, isn't it?"

It isn't a game. Too many people's lives are at stake. *"John Cain is his father writ small."* When he goes, will John Cain have proved the judgment wrong?

On 7 August 1990 John Cain resigned as Premier of Victoria, blaming the "disloyalty" of those around him. He was more the victim of the peculiar circumstances of his time: deregulation, greed, the fast-bucks culture that grew up around Australia's high-flying entrepreneurs, plus the sheer financial mismanagement of his own government and the business institutions it became involved with. John Cain tried to beat the conservatives at their own game — and failed. It raises a crucial issue, precisely the one which destroyed Gough Whitlam: can any politician confront the profoundly conservative power structure of Australian society and hope to survive?

HARRY SEIDLER

I remember the shooting at the Karl Marx Hof. It was a large housing scheme built in the late 1920s, incredible social housing built by the Social Democrats. It had just been finished. It was about two kilometres long with large vaulted openings in it. Its blocks were full of workers, and they were being machine-gunned . . .

Every now and then Australian culture gets confronted by someone who is grand enough to challenge just about everything it believes in. An iconoclast, a rebel, an extremist, a passionate believer — if you like, a hero. A Patrick White, a Ned Kelly, a Bea Miles, maybe a Gough Whitlam. Someone you love or hate, but can't ignore.

Such a one is Harry Seidler. He is probably the most significant architect in Australian history since the convict Francis Greenway. His impact on our cities has been enormous, first as the fiery young revolutionary who broke through the old council restrictions on "modern" architecture, and later as the designer of some of the most overpowering skyscrapers in our central business districts: Australia Square, the MLC building, Grosvenor Place, Capita in Sydney, Riverside in Brisbane, QV1 in Perth, Shell HQ in Melbourne, with still more to come. "I'm gonna work till I drop," says Seidler.

And he has paid a terrible price. Seidler is now commonly regarded, especially among younger architects, as old-fashioned, domineering, out of step with his time and place. His Blues Point Tower is (unfairly) on many a hit list of buildings people would like to see torn down and his attempt to raze the old Johnson's building next to Grosvenor Place alienated even his supporters. Fairly or unfairly, he has come to be a symbol of everything people hate about contemporary architecture. What Seidler confronts them with is Modernism in its purest, most rigorous form; he is one of the few architects practising anywhere in the world today to have studied under the old Bauhaus masters (Gropius, Breuer) who revolutionised twentieth century design and he has never rejected the social and aesthetic idealism of his teachers that architects can create a better world for people to live in and thus transform them: "If I had a religion, that is it," he says.

And thus what we find ourselves beholding, in Seidler and in his work, is the achievement of a supremely passionate and cultivated ideologue, a transplanted European, who has attained an international reputation as an architect and who has made it his lifelong task to transform the Australian manmade environment. No wonder we feel uncomfortable with him. What we have here, inexplicably, on the wilder shores of the cultural universe, is The Last Modernist Hero.

Every building didn't just have a flag but a banner hanging its full height, from the top of the roof all the way down — big, red banners and white fields with swastikas on them . . . There were shootings going on.

At first glance, Harry Seidler seems an unlikely candidate for such a grandiloquent role. He is short, unprepossessing, with grey curly hair plastered across his scalp, gold-rimmed oval spectacles, a big smile, compulsory Gropius-derived bow tie, a pronounced Canadian/American accent, a quick, chirpy articulate man who, when you get to know him, is a charming companion but who is also so socially awkward and work-obsessed he can seem unbearably rude. "He's a wonderful man, I mean that irritable, high-handed public image of his is only one facet, if you can get behind that you find this warm, lovable human being who cares passionately about his work and much else too," says Andrew Andersons, a close friend who headed the New South Wales Government Architect's Office design team during its best work for the Bicentenary. "He's been a great inspiration to me."

Other architects are not so kind. They dislike Seidler's egotism, his self-promotion, the books he helps produce about himself. Philip Cox thinks he is "undeviating" but is "disappointed most in his un-national viewpoint; he doesn't understand the poetic force of Australia, he's a particularly cold man in this respect". Still others grant him a grudging respect. He's a bit like his buildings: you mightn't like them, but you'd miss them if they weren't there.

Part of Seidler's problem with the outside world is his unflinching dedication to what he sees as "the best", his unwillingness to compromise the "total work of art" which he believes each building to be; he insists on controlling the design of everything from the sculpture outside to the colour scheme inside, and stays involved in everything until, as he says, "the ashtrays are on the table". There is a firm belief among the cognoscenti that if you move a vase in Seidler's own home in Killara, the whole house seems lopsided. His perfectionism extends even to how his work is communicated: he commissions only Max Dupain and John Gollings to photograph his buildings, Harry Williamson for his graphics. To hear Seidler ripping apart some shoddy PR brochure on one of his projects is indeed to witness The Master in full furious flight.

Seidler is aware of all this, of course, and over the years he has mellowed . . . a bit. Marginally. "I'm not domineering. I'm a very humble person. I simply want to be allowed to paint my canvases as I see fit," he says. So why are his buildings so domineering?

"So what great cathedral in the cities of Europe is *not* domineering?" Seidler explodes. "I mean, what's wrong with architecture that is domineering; a work of art is domineering by definition, there's nothing wrong with being domineering as long as it's beautiful. I believe skyscrapers can be very beautiful; it is the language of our time. People are excited about skylines, they are incredibly marvellous to look at, preferably from a distance; they can be a magnificent expression in architecture." Seidler says he feels no "sense of authority", he doesn't believe in "standover tactics", but admits he feels incredibly fierce if he is crossed by what he considers stupid planning edicts. "And I have a good right to be, because I find it to be interference with my work, my *art*," he says. "I consider it a personal affront. I want freedom to practise my art, and I don't like to be stood over by people who are not artists."

Now, this sounds like the familiar public-image Seidler, but it is precisely this intransigence which enabled him to force through a flat roof on the first house he ever built here, for his mother, Rose Seidler (he has since given the house to the nation), thus freeing up the entire generation of architects who followed him. And it has enabled Seidler to build some of the most formal, sculptural and highly refined structures in our cities — structures which are widely admired, here and overseas, as brilliant expressions of Late Modernism. But they have also been heavily criticised as monolithic, inhuman, overscaled, "the buildings everyone loves to hate".

To get things straight: Seidler is sometimes pilloried as a "glass box" architect and his buildings lumped in with work which he detests but, as he says, "I've never built a glass box in my life! It gets my back up a bit, I'm accused of something I've never done at all." In fact Seidler regards glass curtain walls as totally unsuited to the Australian climate and typically builds out of concrete with massive sunshading, which helps give his buildings their highly sculptured shapes; he argues it's "not very bright" to simply import a North American idiom here and has taken photographs (he's a keen photographer — it's one of his few hobbies) of a local glass skyscraper which has venetian blinds to keep the sun out. As for boxes: in his towers Seidler has designed circles (Australia Square), octagonals (MLC), quadrants (Grosvenor Place) and triangles (Riverside) but scarcely a box; somewhat to the bemusement of his peers he feels he has entered a "baroque" period in his architecture and now makes deliberate use of curves and flowing lines.

Still, it's true that in a Postmodern era, Seidler remains a defiant Modernist, absolutely out of sympathy with the attempt of a new wave of architects to create buildings which are humane, decorative, lighthearted, even popular. If the Postmodernists believe in giving people what they like, Seidler believes in given them what they *should* like. He abuses the new metaphor-laden architecture as "licentious decorative caprice" and "the tantrums of a rich, spoilt child delighting in being contrary and shocking us with corny stylistic idioms, not to say ludicrous bad taste". Awash in a sea of reflector glass, icing-cake colours, illusions and allusions, Seidler's buildings remain stark, uncompromising and somewhat dated. When I was writing the text for a recent catalogue/book on Australian architecture, Bill Corker, of Denton, Corker, Marshall, the award-winning Melbourne firm (and one of the few Seidler responds to) said to me: "The whole *ism* is postmodern. Modern is dead." Corker may be interested to learn that, in Sydney, the Modern is alive and well and living in Killara.

We skied for 10 days, and during those 10 days Hitler marched into Vienna. The one recollection I have is that the teacher who was with us knew all about it, and he gave us a little speech. He said, 'You, you and you stay inside' — and they were the Jews in the class — 'and all the others outside'. The Nazi flag was being hoisted . . . I, at the age of 15 . . . sensed enough to know that this was the end.

To understand Seidler you have to understand that here is a man who has been traumatised by one of the terrible events of twentieth century history. He is the classic emigre, one of the generation of gifted European Jews who fled the Holocaust and made an enormous impact on the New World societies where they took refuge.

He was born in 1923 into a prosperous middle-class business family in Vienna and until the Nazi movement gained momentum lived a typical Central European life of plays, maids, holidays at lakeside resorts such as Lake Bled (he still visits them, rediscovering his boyhood) and a strict academic schooling at a *gymnasium* which "was run like a military academy . . . the way they got you to perform generated a deep resentment in me". His mother was involved in avant garde art and both parents gave Harry and his elder brother Marcell a strong sense of right and wrong: "It is morally right to do the decent thing; they gave me a social . . . What's the word? . . . conscience. Social conscience." Watching the big May Day parades down the Karl Marx Hof, red flags everywhere, excited by the Spanish Civil War, he became a socialist and committed to its "fairness". "I'm an old Leftie," he says. He responded enthusiastically to the Whitlam era in Australia; in 1990 he went back to Vienna and was awarded the city's Gold Medal by its Leftist government.

But 1938 was not a good time to be in Vienna, and a Socialist, and a Jew. One day he was picked up in the street by SS men in black uniforms and told *"Jude?* Come with us," and forced to scrub a commandeered house down from top to bottom.

> *The minute I thought I had it clean one of them came in with his jackboots and walked all over it and stepped on my hands: "That's not clean enough. Start again." Real bully stuff . . . People were being picked up all the time. Anyone politically active, or anyone who had been a member of the socialist party or a communist, just disappeared.*

Seidler decided to escape to England.

I was put on the train, alone, one day. They all came to the train to say goodbye — cousins and aunts came too. I never saw them again. Most of them died.

In England he lived for two years under the protection of "this old, aristocratic family . . . very kind, civilised, educated people . . . they had a blue Armstrong-Sidley . . . the chauffeur addressed me as 'sir', I thought that was absurd . . . it just didn't fit . . . I liked the gardener." He tried to enrol in engineering in a local technical school but it was full, so he was asked if he would be interested in studying building instead because there were openings. "I said, 'Oh, that sounds all right.' And that was the beginning of my architecture career. A fluke like that."

Then Seidler suffered another traumatic experience: along with several thousand other German refugees he was arrested and interned by the British government in case they were "spies" and finally shipped off to a barbed-wire internment camp in Canada — along with Spanish War freedom fighters, anti-Nazi activists and refugees from concentration camps. Seidler still gets angry when he talks about it. "There was one guy there who had not been free since 1933, he was at Dachau for five years. They locked him up, which was the most idiotic thing in the world. Some people went off their rocker. One guy tried to escape and was shot." He pauses. "At the age of 17, to find that's what governments do, that's what bureaucrats think is intelligent; to sit in gaol, for no reason at all, for an indefinite period: that really hurts. So maybe I can't be blamed for ever since maintaining a suspicious mentality towards the powers-that-be. I just won't accept edicts that I know to be not reasonable."

Ever since, Seidler has been waging a one-man battle against bureaucracy, planning edicts, council restrictions, anything he sees as "stupid". He quickly resorts to legal action. It's brought him some famous victories and some famous losses. It's also been largely responsible for his public image as irascible, intransigent — as he puts it himself, the "Bad Boy" of Australian architecture.

Bad Boy? During his two years of internment, Seidler kept a secret diary, in German, which he finally published in 1986. It is a moving, very Seidleresque account of what he suffered; on the cover is a picture of young Harry with pencil moustache, brushed back dark hair, prison shirt and internment number printed across his chest: 273. Seidler still speaks German. "Perfectly," he says. He gives lectures in German at European universities. No, he doesn't feel Jewish. "I never felt anything religious. My parents were non-believers and so am I. As far as Jewishness was concerned, I never had any. I don't know what the hell it was supposed to be!"

So what is he? Seidler thinks about it. He is sitting in his Breuer-designed chair in his house in Killara, which is hung about with paintings by Stella, Calder, Albers and other artists of the Modernist era, surrounded by the artefacts of a cultivated, well-travelled European. When he answers it is with a curious mixture of commitment and ambivalence:

"I feel totally Australian now. I mean, I wouldn't live anywhere else in the world. This is my home, this is where I belong. It's given me the most unbelievable opportunities, fertile ground to develop, such as I don't think would have been possible anywhere. Culturally I'm a mixture between a European upbringing and North American by training . . . but it's all right here. Nothing wrong with it." Doesn't he miss the world arena, the global scene with which he constantly compares himself? Once again, the same ambivalence: "Look, Vienna is a provincial place, God forbid to have to be an architect in Austria, architects design shopfronts there. Canada's too damned cold, people shouldn't live more than 35 degrees from the equator! America? An immensely competitive and vicious society . . . I've looked at the centre, I've worked there, I used to commute to Paris; I didn't find it all that remarkable . . .'' He stops. ''Yes, I'm rationalising. I'd drop everything if somebody said to me: 'build me a big building in Boston, New York . . . on the double'.''

Says Penelope Seidler, his wife, one of the Evatt family: ''He's a loner. It's his background. He's a European, though not unAustralian. He regards himself as an international person; his world is the whole world. I don't think he feels he was ever accepted here, he feels an alien. Underneath it all he regrets it.''

Paolo Totaro: ''when you are uprooted there is always that thing that lingers on, that you are not quite yourself, that somewhere else is the real you.''

At the border, in Aachen, between Belgium and Germany, ''All Jews out of the train, including your luggage''. The train left and the thugs came around with jackboots . . . beat up a few people. I got hit a bit.

After he was released from internment Seidler studied at the University of Manitoba, Canada and then went to Harvard at one of the great moments in architectural education, when Gropius, Breuer and other masters of the Modern movement — like Seidler himself, refugees from Nazi Germany — were teaching there. For Seidler, it was a revelation: he embraced the idealism and philosophies of the Bauhaus with a passion which has never deserted him, and which still provides much of the driving force behind his life and his work.

He found himself, he says, ''fitting perfectly into the teaching and personalities I came across at Harvard. They spoke the same language. Gropius brought all his mates from Europe; he and I used to play ping pong . . . he was a social philosopher, an aesthetic philosopher, but behind all that the question of the actual choice of form still remained: why this, not that? So I went to study with Albers. Then Breuer. He wasn't a theorist. You do it because you do it. Which was terrific too, because he had a fabulous way of doing things. I used to be a terrific draftsman: fast, accurate . . .''

When Seidler talks about this time his face lights up, he smiles, he becomes animated: it was obviously a time of great intellectual excitement for him. He travelled briefly down to South America and worked with Oscar Niemeyer, designer of the city of Brasilia. All the time he was absorbing the tenets of High Modernism: purity, minimalism, restraint, truth to materials, functionalism, the search for appropriate form.

Says Andrew Andersons: "Harry is totally faithful to the ideology of Modernism, that's his strength, that's why he can be so unswerving and consistent — and irritating to those who aren't committed to that ethic. He was among the avant garde even until the late sixties, a leader, but now he's out on a limb. To be ideologically and philosophically old-fashioned, that really hurts!"

Seidler could have stayed in North America; he came to Australia in 1948 because his parents, who had fled here from Germany and knew their ambitious son well, offered him his first major architectural commission: design a house for them in Turramurra. He did so, found himself with more commissions, and exploded on to the local scene like a prophet of the Modernist revolution. Notoriety and antagonism have followed him ever since.

Today Harry Seidler is as single-minded, one-eyed, dedicated, intolerant, obdurate and infuriating as ever. I find him a curious combination of intelligence and blindness. In 1989, as co-judge with him of the annual Royal Australian Institute of Architects (NSW) awards, I resolutely decided to spend the four hours for which we were incarcerated in a hire car Falcon between Sydney and Newcastle arguing for the significance of Postmodernism as not just an architectural style, but a profound cultural shift in twentieth century late-capitalist ideology. Seidler listened, perhaps understood, but budged not a millimeter. Postmodernism, for him, is simply Jazz Age pastiche, an architectural fashion industry: "They're really dead-end streets that people walk into blindfolded, these things go up and down like the hems in ladies' dresses."

So who are his peers? They are all overseas: Richard Meier; "My classmate, I. M. Pei; Gropius always said he was terrific and nothing's changed, he's still the best. Ed Barnes. There must be somebody somewhere else . . . Hans Hollein, in Vienna; Foster and Rogers in England; I have regard for the Pompidou Centre but I have so many quarrels with it on a practical level, to be really nasty one could call it a rusting tin can, it's impossible to maintain. I compete with them right here; they know what I do, and I know every damn thing they do." Doesn't he like any local architects at all?

"I was particularly friendly with Robin Boyd, who was a significant fellow," he says. "Daryl Jackson, he's a force to be reckoned with. Murcutt, there's no doubt about the fact that he's a very sensitive and unique fellow, he's found a formula for doing buildings that have an unmistakable local character and visually there's a lot of desirable attributes, but I wouldn't consider him a *competitor*."

What about the criticism that his buildings are unAustralian? "I've been labelled, crassly, International Style but I'm an architect who produces unmistakably Australian buildings. You can't build such buildings, nor would you try, anywhere else. They should look appropriate to the place: that involves the way of life, technology, climate, materials, an aesthetic, what is in the air, what people want to look at. Then a building will be distinctive and I believe my buildings are terribly distinctive, very Australian."

Not everybody agrees with him. Critic Philip Drew, who is part-author of a forthcoming book on Seidler, believes his work shows little regional awareness. Seidler has set his face resolutely against any local reference or allusion, any Aussie metaphor, in his designs; he finds that "really pitiful", a "misplaced localism". As a child in Vienna he used to see an early Modern building with the inscription over the portal: TO EACH ERA ITS ART. If that means concrete-and-steel corporate towers in Australian cities, so be it.

In Australia, in his personal life, Seidler has created a copy of the European life he left behind: cultivated, the best of everything, but because he is a stranger in a foreign land it is quite an isolated life. Penelope, his wife, who also manages the practice, acts as a sort of lightning conductor for Seidler's idiosyncracy. They have a close relationship; their two children, Tim and Polly, have left home; they are left with this spacy, architectonic house in the bush and torrential creeks of the North Shore, and a pool in which Harry swims a few desolutory laps each morning, and a Citroen Pallas with a French sticker parked in the raw concrete garage — no pretence, wealthy, a bit sterile, the calm ambience of a man for whom work is everything.

Penelope met Seidler at a party. "He was certainly unlike anyone else I'd ever met," she says. "He had so much to say; knew exactly what he wanted, what he was going to do; full of ideology and philosophy. It was something you can hang on to." He doesn't care much about wine or food, doesn't play much sport (except skiing), can't even work the video; they go to a few openings, don't entertain much; no yacht, no weekender, no life in the fast lane. He is too ambitious a man to waste time on trivia.

People react to Seidler in wildly differing ways. The wife of one architect regards him as a "cuddly little koala". Another architect regards him as ruthless, ultra-competitive, yet someone who has never pushed architecture to its possible edge: "He designs safe, competent buildings." A lawyer describes Seidler's buildings as monuments to "his urge for immortality — I wish he wouldn't let his ego get in the way". Among some of his peers, Seidler has an unenviable reputation for moving in on projects which other architects have initiated. But Paolo Totaro, who taught Seidler to play Bach on the piano, regards him as warm, orderly, bruised, a bit melancholy and a great artist. Penelope says he is shy, not pushy — except in getting his own way with the design of a building. Seidler: "I give my clients what they think they want, but only if it turns into architecture! I don't compromise. I'm in control."

That narrow, unidirectional approach is typical of Seidler. He has no small talk; he tends to dismiss people who don't share his passions. To get his attention you have to harangue him about something he's interested in. He's a bit self-concerned, combs his hair in lifts, has an unabashed and feisty ego. To like Seidler you have to keep making allowances for him: some people are prepared to, some are not. In his office, for instance, his draftspeople are asked to wear the drab grey regulation Chinese jackets Seidler picked up in Hong Kong. What a man! In this day and age you'd hardly think it possible.

They had a little ceremony of pulling up the swastika flag outside while we were told to stay inside and watch through the window. That was really quite a demoralising thing ... Suddenly I'm different from them.

Seidler has been enormously successful. Next to his office at Milsons Point he has built a luxurious flat which looks like a glitzy Hollywood film set. Yet at the core of his career is a cruel irony, one which afflicts the entire Modernist ethos: what began as a revolutionary, socially idealistic movement has ended as part of the Establishment, the Power Bloc — the revolution become reactionary. In architecture Modernism has created the very emblem of contemporary corporate capitalism, the high-rise tower, which has turned popular opinion against the entire Modern movement.

Seidler, who began as a political radical, now works primarily for big developers like Lend Lease, who have financed most of his recent city towers (including the ones he has designed for the former casino site at Darling Harbour). His life is almost a metaphor for what happened to Modernism itself: a Germanic start, forced translation to the United States, incorporation into the mainstream of High Capitalism, and now on the defensive against a new wave of rebels who regard him/it as incurably conservative.

Seidler is aware of the situation and has some answers. First, he tries to preserve open space and public plazas around the base of his towers, even if it means the buildings go higher. Architect Christine Vadasz believes Seidler is one of the few who can make those plazas work, whereas others criticise his towers as overscaled and say they destroy the normal streetfront. Seidler says he would prefer plot/site ratios to be lower, so the buildings would be lower, but argues "that's not for me to be responsible for". Couldn't he refuse to do it? "Well, so somebody down the street will do a terrible job," he answers, shrugging.

In his heart Seidler still believes in urban planning, medium-to-high density development, and the sort of plan he put up years ago to raze McMahon's Point and replace what's there with towers like Blues Point. The alternative, he points out, is for Australians to "have the privilege of living out past Penrith, or in walk-up flats lining the expressways. Those barracks! You've seen them? No wonder people hate flats! I still believe the community is entitled to a fair deal, and when I see that not happening

I get very upset. When I see the hopelessness of people trying to find a decent place to live, I lash out. The status quo is producing an unmitigated hell."

"I mean, I would do anything to do something that goes beyond the individual building," he muses one late afternoon. "I'd be available instantly. Not enough money? That would never concern me, not in the slightest. Absolutely. The idea of making money doesn't turn me on. Other things are far closer to my heart. To have the results I seek, that's the reward I'm after."

Over the years Harry Seidler has had his rewards. He has dominated Australian architecture, changed the shape of Australian cities. He has pursued his principles with a fierce intensity which a middle-of-the-road culture finds an affront. He has never lost his idealism, his sense of destiny; as his old teacher, Sigfried Giedion, wrote: *"to be destined as a fighter for his and our Generation"* — but he has become the victim of a system which even his energy can't overcome.

Now, at the age of 66, he is an emigre in his own land, a man swimming against the tide, a visionary misunderstood. "He's a quiet, lonely man," says Penelope Seidler. The Last Modernist Hero is a grand but painful thing to be.

BOBBI SYKES

"I was the oldest of three black children. All-white town. A very weird situation happened. I lived in this white area. My sisters and I used to walk home from the school and the white kids used to throw stones at us, they used to stone us every afternoon. So I used to walk backwards and send my two sisters running on ahead of me, and I used to stay there till they were safe, and then I used to exchange stones with all these white kids who thought it was great sport to stone us. These kids split my head open so many times. One time I was layin' on the ground and my mother raced up, she's picked me up and ran all the way to the hospital with me with blood pourin' out of my head . . ." She stops. *"I still don't understand those sorts of people."*

It's Bobbi Sykes. In some ways she hasn't changed since a decade ago, when she became a national figure as a militant Aboriginal activist: the same Afro hairdo, the same cool, tough gaze, the same finely moulded, quite beautiful face, the same passionate commitment to the Aboriginal movement she showed when she was arrested at the Aboriginal Embassy confrontation in Canberra.

But in other ways she's different. She's older, and though she jokes about it she seems worried that she's approaching the average age of death for Aboriginal women in Australia: 47. She's got a degree, a doctorate in education from Harvard, where she studied for four years. She seems frailer, and warier, and less outspoken than she used to be. She's even started thinking about "the development of me!"

"People like me, after a demo we're supposed to go back in a box till the next demo. They don't want to know how ordinary you are," she says. "I've grown older, that's about all. You can't walk around being angry twenty-four hours a day. I have other things to do. I argue about who's going to cook the potatoes, same things other people argue about. I'm angry sometimes, if you run into somebody who's really stupid about racism here. Australia became British by over-running the local population, killing them if you have to, and then outnumbering them; same thing has happened to native Americans . . . Shit! If you hadn't brought up the topic, I'd be talkin' about something else.

"I was never as angry as newspapers would have painted me. I never tried to live up to that angry image of myself. According to that I was walkin' around with a machine gun under each arm, grenades, all sorts of stupid stuff. Why would I carry a gun? Guns don't protect people. If you carry a gun, people *know* you carry a gun, and if they come to do some talking with you, *they* carry a gun." She reaches down to the handbag against her chairleg, moves something around inside. "It's still ticking," she says. What is? "The bomb," she says, laughing.

"Psychological violence is much more terrible. And white people wage a terrible war of psychological violence against black people all the time. In my heart there are these incredible contradictions. Like, if you want to know where is my place, my place today, where *is* my place? Where is Mum Shirl's place? Where is *our* place?"

She talks quietly, calmly, every statement full of questions which she asks of herself and the world. Her accent is broad Australian, fairly Aboriginal, with a faint trace of the four years spent in the United States. Since coming back from there in 1983 she has done a lot of writing: journalism, government reports, a book on the Aboriginal movement in the last twenty-one years called *Black Majority*, a book of short stories. University of Queensland Press has also republished her *Love Poems and Other Revolutionary Actions*:

> *My Warden-in-Charge*
> *Why do you lock me*
> *Into a room*

> *A locked room in a locked block*
> *A locked block in a locked prison complex*
> *Heavily guarded*
> *To visit with people*
> *through mesh net grills*
> *Who are also locked*
> *away from me?*
> *I won't run away*
> *I live on the outside*
> *And that's a prison*
> *too*

At the centre of her consciousness, her experience, is her blackness. She says she isn't anti-white, meaning individuals; she has white friends. "Sure. Stacks of 'em. Some of my best friends," she says, straightfaced. But she's against white institutions, "their old people's homes, their orphanages" (she grew up for a while in one). She talks bitterly about "white folks", white society, Mr White Man, the reality of racism in contemporary White Australia.

"Y'know, white males don't have to have any of this consciousness of themselves, they float around saying things like 'we're all people' . . . that's a load of bullshit, because women are always aware and conscious of the fact that they're a woman . . . well, with the black, you're always conscious of the fact that you're black. You get attacked far more for being a black than for being a woman, though they attack black women in a different way . . . they're more likely to rape a woman than a man. I don't think I understood that until I was in the Embassy and I saw the police. I saw them come over and start punching out the black women. I mean, the police force at that time was all male, they walked over to this predominantly female group, and they started sockin' our people, hittin' 'em with truncheons, punching 'em on the jaw and everything, and I thought, I just can't believe this. The people they attacked turned into being *blacks*, not *women*."

She stops, lights a cigarette. Long fingernails. Gold wedding rings. She is thin, graceful, in dark blue sweater, dark blue pants, sneakers. There is about her this constant sense of disjunction, of dissonance, of surprising and jarring contradiction between the

Townsville Aborigine and the Harvard sophisticate ("I think I'm a chameleon. I have the ability to mirror back to people what they are. I'm on the executive of the Harvard Club in Sydney but I'm happy to go out and live in a creek at Alice Springs and the people regard me as one of theirs. Everybody regards me as one of them, but not quite."

"I can remember precisely when I knew I was black. I was in school. Some visitors to the class come in, and we were all standin' there in a semi-circle around the teacher, and these visitors come in and one woman said to the teacher: 'And who's the dear little coloured girl?' I looked around to see who she was. And I realised everybody was lookin' at me. Because, y'see, you don't see yourself. So your idea of yourself is to a large extent defined by what other people see when they look at you."

That blackness has defined Bobbi Sykes's life. It forced her out of school early, pushed her into factories and domestic service in North Queensland, turned her into an activist — "any black with drive, till the mid seventies, could only be an activist" — and today has made her the sort of person who can say: "I think blacks reach a point of desperation. Yeah, I think it's gathering in the wind somewhere. I think they're running out of patience. I'm runnin' out of patience. The blacks are after justice. It's got to be sorted out; it can't keep going from generation to generation. If land rights aren't recognised, then it doesn't matter what they appease the people with, Commission homes or that other bullshit sort of stuff, y'know, the next generation will rise up in their anger. What's important? The establishment of power in the black community. I have nothing against Black Power — except that we don't have any."

Is she a revolutionary? "I don't think of myself as a revolutionary. I don't think you can be a revolutionary unless there's a revolution; otherwise it's fairly sad. But I have revolutionary ideas — about race, about women's issues, about the whole political system. I believe the environment is designed to make people feel impotent, make them feel they should limit the areas they hope to change. Stuff like that. Now I feel: why shouldn't I change the system if I don't like it? Why shouldn't I change the political process, or the relationship between blacks and whites, or men and women, if I don't like it? We should all be working for that."

In the multi-faceted Aboriginal movement her stance puts her close to Gary Foley, who is a good friend, and Michael Mansell. She supported the visit of Mansell and others to Libya, an attempt to bring international pressure to bear upon Australia. "The first step is an acknowledgment by the white Australian people of the just struggle of Aborigines. We don't have this acknowledgment yet."

She supports, therefore, Prime Minister Hawke's move for an Aboriginal Treaty. But it has to be negotiated, just as personal relationships between whites and blacks in a racist society like Australia have to be negotiated: "it can't be a treaty that Bob Hawke brings out readymade and says here you are, Aborigines, sign it," she says. "There's a large portion of the Australian people have to be educated to agree with that concept. That's the next problem."

Sykes says she is not a Marxist because "I assume if you're a Marxist you have to read Marx," which she hasn't. "I've never been a member of the Communist Party. I don't think of myself in those terms."

In the 1970s she identified with the struggle of black Americans and in the media was described as a sort of Oz Angela Davis, but she explains now: "I don't model myself on her. My hair grows out of my head like this; like, I have pictures of myself as a baby wearing this Angela Davis haircut! Afro? Well, I prefer to have it described as that to having it described as . . . y'know, when I was arrested in Canberra, the policewoman wrote, for your description: 'HAIR: FRIZZY'!" She bursts out laughing. "Oh, wild!"

She went to England on a wave of notoriety, to enlist support for the Aboriginal cause. But the movement was divided and there were problems; Bobbi Sykes was educated, glamorous, and resented. In her book of poems she writes:

> *The trip to England is a mighty success,*
>   *rah, rah, rah,*
> *Militant Black Leader ARRIVES screams the Press . . .*
> *Talk, doll; rage, doll; rant, doll;*
> *Horrors in Australia,*

> *rah, rah, rah,*
> *Tell it like it is, tell it like it is.*
>
> *From home the news —*
> > *'Police are out to get you'*
> > *'Blacks are out to get you'*
> > *'Whore, prostitute, deserter of children'*
> > *'Wealthy, posing as poor'*
> > *'Left-wing Communist extremist'*
> > *'Counter-revolutionary, opportunist, elitist'*
>
> *Quietly now —*
> > *Bobbi Sykes is not as black as us . . .*

She doesn't like talking about her background. "There's a huge tide of people involved in making changes," she says. The movement, the community, counts. Yet, pieced together, her life acquires a symbolic dimension. She was born in Townsville, in North Queensland. Her father was black, but she hardly knew him; her mother, who is still living "up the coast", is white and raised Bobbi and her two younger sisters. When quite young she went to St Joseph's orphanage in Rockhampton.

"It wasn't one of the happiest periods of my life; I haven't been back," she says. "It wasn't awful, I wasn't flogged. As a matter of fact I was happier in the orphanage than I was in Townsville. I've thought about that a lot and the reason was, being the oldest of the three girls, I was always responsible, so when people called us names I had to do the fighting. When I was in the orphanage I wasn't the oldest and I wasn't the youngest. And there were a lot of blacks there so I was hidden."

Back at Townsville, she remembers that "there wasn't much of it, you could ride around it five times in one afternoon. I used to do that, on my pushbike. If you rode in a straight line you'd end up in Charters Towers or Ingham or somewhere!" She went briefly to high school, studied fourteen subjects, including Latin and all the prerequisites for a science or medicine degree. "But they didn't have blacks at school after your fourteenth birthday. The teachers told me there was no way I could do medicine, that I had to go into domestic science. So I thought: I'm not going to do that either, so I did typing, bookkeeping and shorthand, just to have all the bases covered."

She laughs, a harsh, ironic, laugh. "In a lot of ways I'm pretty bright, in other ways I'm not. I know now that many teachers speak two languages at the same time so the whites get one message and the blacks get another. The whites would be encouraged to proceed and the blacks would be discouraged. They were saying 'You can do anything you want to do' and I thought they were talking to me! They're very clever at the double message now, aren't they? There's so few black kids doing their HSC and thousands and thousands of white kids. Then you know the teachers have got a hand in that. The white kids' parents tell them they can succeed, the black kids' parents tell them they can succeed, so the dual message is obviously coming from the schools. Some gets in from outside, like the media."

She'd have liked to have been a surgeon, maybe doing heart and lung transplants by now. "I don't doubt I had the brains." Instead she became a trainee nurse at Charters Towers hospital, didn't finish the course, and worked in factories in Townsville and Brisbane. "I regret that options weren't open," she says. "Y'know, I have thought it would be nice if white people treated black people as equals; if we had equality I could have done something else with my life. I suppose everybody has these 'what ifs'. But most people's 'what ifs' come back to some choice that they make. Like, what if I didn't get married, I'd be runnin' around like a bachelor stud. But what I'm talking about is people's lives being otherwise, *not* out of a choice they made. I didn't have that choice.

"No, I don't feel sour. Or cynical. What's the point in nurturing all those useless emotions? But I have regrets; I think there are a lot of blacks who, because of lack of opportunity, have had their potential to make a contribution to this society minimised."

Sykes worked her way down to New South Wales and soon got involved in the activist movement. She read and read, educated herself, started writing for newspapers and magazines and became the first secretary of the Aboriginal tent embassy set up on the lawns outside Parliament House in Canberra. She was fierce and articulate and there was a personal edge to her anger; in her book of poetry she writes "I underwent some traumatic experiences that were beyond words". She surfaced from a nervous breakdown, but found time to write the autobiography of Mum Shirl Smith, the Aboriginal "elder" who could neither read nor write. In her poetry book, Bobbi Sykes thanks Mum Shirl and others for "pushing" her and dedicates it:

> For my mother
>> Who knows a lot about children
>>> But not so much about Blacks
> For my sisters
>> Della and Lee
>>> Who didn't let me grow up lonely.

In 1978, a visiting black academic from Harvard, Professor Chester Pierce, Professor of Education and Psychiatry, saw some of her writing on social issues and asked her to send more to him; the following year she got a cable inviting her to be a postgraduate student at Harvard. "He's a brilliant man, he's had a great influence on me," she says. She wrote her thesis on Aboriginal education issues, got her doctorate, returned to Australia in 1983 as Dr Roberta Sykes, began lecturing at the School of Medicine at the University of NSW and wrote discussion papers and reports for government authorities such as the Commonwealth Office for the Aged. She also got involved in Black Women's Action, an unfunded organisation which has begun sending other Aboriginal women to the United States for higher education.

Sykes had married young and had two children, Russell, now 29, a psychologist who sits on the Social Security Appeals Tribunal, and Naomi, now 22 and living in Sydney. After a few years her marriage broke up; she lives now in a quiet cottage near bushland in North Sydney, and spends most of her time by herself, "working, and thinking . . . thinking's very important . . . I want to develop my sense of freedom." Now her son's left home she has the chance, for the first time in her life, to spend some time on . . . herself.

It's a remarkable career for someone born in North Queensland, a few miles from the Aboriginal encampment of Black River. "I've done the best I could with what I have," she says quietly. "I mean that in the sense of opportunities rather than brains." The pot-bellied stove warms up. She has a tortoiseshell cat, family snaps on the wall, racks of books, a study with her own photocopier, keeps her phone number and address private, and has a bitser puppy. "My sister has a Doberman, for protection; but who's gonna protect me from the dog?" she says, grinning.

Does she feel very Aboriginal? She thinks about that a long time, chewing gum, her face lined and a bit weary and vulnerable suddenly, and her answer is suitably complex: "I never feel white. When I go out into the desert I feel part of traditional Aboriginal culture, but it's very hard to feel that in Sydney. When I'm in the city I feel part of urban culture. The situation we're in today we have to be able to move very rapidly into different cultural situations, but you have to make sure you don't fragment, lose your identity, particularly when you're spending a lot of time in white institutions. It's not a problem for me now, not like it was some time ago. Before the 1970s, most blacks living in white society believed themselves to be ugly just because they were black. It's more complex than just conforming. You know you can't *be* white, so sometimes you reject everything that *is* white. What's the point of any of these white aspirations, or anything white gonna tell ya? You tend to throw the baby out with the bathwater. And if you don't have a sound grounding in very positive black things, you don't have anything to replace it with.

"Since then I have developed a whole lot of ideology of my own about what I consider are black things. And I don't think . . . ummm . . . like people used to say to me . . . ummm . . . *the more educated you get the more white you get*, as if education was a province of white people only. Well, I dispute that. I think blacks were more educated before whites came here than they ever have been since. So to aspire towards education is a *black* aspiration."

> *Food for the soul*
> *enters not*
> *through the vagina*
> *nor the ears*
> *twitching still*
> *from psychedelia,*
> *but through the pores*
> *as they open*

> under the heat
> of sun,
> sun which turns
> after a million years
> the wearers' skin
> to black,
> proud Black.

She believes Australia is still an appallingly racist country, and spins off story after story to prove it: the Pryor boy who "suicided", the daily evidence which was uncovered by the Black Deaths in Custody inquiry. "In Townsville things haven't changed that much. Do I feel as strongly as when I was in the protest demos in the seventies? Why would I feel anything less? Has anything changed?

"The Liberals sent me a copy of their bloody policy. The basis of their policy is justification of the denial of land rights. Aboriginals have to get the land rights they want. But we have gone back to a terrible situation because of Hawke's retreat from a national land rights policy, we're now operating on a state-by-state basis. That's dreadful. We thought we were on the verge of getting it sorted out in the early seventies and we've gone full cycle back to exactly where we were then. I was part of all that." Would she be prepared to become part of it again? "Sure."

She has plans to push changes through. When she was at Harvard she met black executives who were appalled that the big transnational corporations didn't have black people in important positions in Australia. But are many Aboriginal Australians educated to the necessary level?

"I've heard that!" she replies sharply. "I think it's racism. People use other things to justify it, like 'they don't have any education'. That's been used to keep blacks out of work for 200 years."

She agrees, however, that the number of Aboriginal students who drop out of school is "a big problem". Reasons? "Inappropriate nature of the school curriculum, the racism of some white teachers, some white educational environments, ill health . . . that still plays a major role . . . stress . . . blacks at high school are under much more stress than white kids." A part-solution, she thinks, is separate black high schools such as the one at Healesville in Victoria. "That's a good thing. There should be more separate institutions. There has to be options. A school doesn't have to be an all-black school, as long as it's under the control of blacks. All the teachers don't have to be black, as long as they answer to blacks."

She says she is not a feminist because she sees the women's movement as a struggle for power and control in the white culture: "This struggle is between white men and white women." In a chapter in a recent book she argues in detail that "black women realise that black community priorities will not become priorities of the white women's movement" and points to the resistance of black women to the pro-abortion push because "forced and coerced abortions and sterilizations were commonly practised on the black community". Her phrase: "attempted genocide".

In her own life Bobbi Sykes confronts racism all the time. "I'm not scared by it," she says, then adds: "There have been times when I have been scared by it. There's crazy people out there! My mother, she's worried about the potential for violence in the white community; she thinks people might try to kill me, like Martin Luther King. As a white male you couldn't possibly know, because the people who are into terrifying blacks don't terrify other white males . . . they consider you're the club.

Y'know Kamahl, the singer? He offered to buy a man a drink on the plane and the man said 'I don't drink with blacks'. I have to deal with those contradictions all the time. Unlike Kamahl, I haven't made millions to insulate me, right? He probably gets his groceries delivered so he doesn't have to go into the supermarket. When I got to the supermarket I'm occasionally assaulted by people, they race up and say 'Are you Bobbi Sykes?' and they want to have pieces of me right there and then in the supermarket. Excuse me! Let me get my Drive and my steel wool and get out of here! When you get rich enough like Kamahl you don't have to confront that shit. Y'know? Now, I'm not rich enough. More than that, I'm a female, so the men find it easier; they can send a woman out to do the buying, I'm in charge of the food, therefore I have to go to the supermarket, and so do a lot of hostiles who watch TV and read the newspaper. For many years I didn't mention the children because I wanted to protect the children till they're big enough to protect themselves . . ."

So what does the future hold for Bobbi Sykes? She's done a lot of lecturing, and has been offered academic positions which she says "I've turned down because somebody else has limited their role". She has begun to find lecturing very unsatisfying because she can't tell whether she's changed anyone's attitudes; writing is more accessible.

Has she ever felt she'd like to leave off being an Aboriginal, be something else? No, she replies thoughtfully. It's given her life a focus: "*You* don't have a revolution to organise, the education of an entire nation to organise!" She works away, refines her ideas, writes, organises, maps out strategies of change. And tries, in all that, to find time for herself. At the heart of it all, a sense of immemorial hurt and a sense of resistance.

"You get people who say, you, Mr White Man, you can do anything you like to our community and I'm not going to be violent . . . right? Y'understand? You got a lot of blacks have that attitude. White people can come along, blow their kids away, hang them in gaols, do whatever they want, and they keep sayin' 'I can't be violent'. You've played your last card when you say you not going to be violent, because everybody knows when the going gets tough you gonna burst into tears. I'm not going to burst into tears."

JOHN HOWARD

20 June 1987

John Howard is a man staring at political death. In a few weeks he'll be history — either as the most unlikely Prime Minister in modern Australian politics or as the man who had a once-in-a-lifetime chance at the most glittering prize in the nation, failed and disappeared. What is happening now in this 1987 election is as brutal as that.

Right now things don't look good for Howard. He has presided over the break-up of the Liberal-National Party coalition; he has watched a destructive old man from Queensland, Joh Bjelke-Petersen, wreck his political timetable; he is facing, in Bob Hawke, a popular and opportunistic Prime Minister; and the media reaction to his tax and economic policies has been unremittingly hostile. Yet, if the basis of Hemingway's famous code of the hero is "grace under pressure", then John Winston Howard qualifies as something like that. Over the past fortnight, staring at the shotgun barrel threat that finally destroyed Papa Ernest himself, he has responded with the sort of cool grace that is the mark of a man who believes in himself and who retains a sort of gritty integrity to the end.

A few times, symptoms of the ordeal to which he has subjected himself have broken through. Before one of his TV interviews, Howard went into a paroxysm of mouth-stretching exercises that made him look like Kermit the Frog. Another time, after a particularly gruelling interview, he fell back in a chair, his face caked in makeup, and tried vainly to will himself to sleep. And once, before appearing on the Terry Willesee Show, I saw a sudden grimace of panic seize his face and just as quickly pass away. It was the day he launched the Liberal Party's tax policy at Box Hill in outer Melbourne and, in the blaze of TV lights and critical questions about the GET IN FRONT AGAIN economic package, he gained the first whiff of just how hostile the media reaction was going to be.

For most of the time, though, he retained the chirpy, light-hearted, almost self-deprecating insouciance which is at once the most surprising and appealing characteristic of Howard, one which he (unfortunately) rarely reveals on television or in the theatrical rhetoric which he uses in Parliament and which is his Plain Dulwich Hill Man's substitute for charisma.

"I'm an issues man," explains Howard, strolling down the back of the RAAF BAC-111 jet which is his election Zoo Plane. "He's like a very smart 12-year-old," says an acerbic cartoonist. "He hasn't got enough imagination to understand the trajectory of anyone but himself," says a social worker from from the Western Suburbs. "God help us if he gets in."

On the day Howard launched his tax policy in Melbourne, the Anita Cobby trial came to an end in Sydney. John Travers, the three Murphy brothers and Michael Murdoch were found guilty of repeatedly assaulting and raping and then murdering the young nurse. Her naked body was found in a cow paddock at Prospect, near Blacktown. This territory is classic Western Suburbs: high unemployment, high crime rate, low income, working and sub-working class, high levels of social violence and distress. It's the half-settled Aussie version of Thatcher's urban Liverpool and Birmingham ghettos. The horrific Anita Cobby case is a parable.

The Box Hill Town Hall is packed with flags, camera crews, boom mikes, SLRs, video cables, photographers, economists and media correspondents: Ken Davidson, Laurie Oakes, Paul Kelly, Mike Stekete, Michelle Grattan, Greg Hywood, a hundred others. They are staring at the fifty-page packets of tax policies, tables and Liberal Party slogans which have just been distributed. "Unbelievable," says one. Says another, scanning the tax scales: "I'm definitely going to vote Liberal, stuff the other people . . ."

Howard's front bench of shadow economic Ministry walks in — Carlton, Chaney, Brown, Short — and take up seats behind the rostrum. Ian Macphee, sacked from the shadow Ministry as too "wet", sidles into the audience: "I wasn't invited but I decided to come along." A slow hush descends on the throng; the photographers kneel expectantly like supplicants, the TV lamps switch on. John Howard, in grey-striped suit, red-dotted tie and red pocket handkerchief, strides in, faces the crowd, asks: "Are we ready?" and launches into what is virtually the Liberal Party policy speech for the election:

"A Liberal government will abolish the capital gains tax, the assets test, the fringe benefits tax . . . reduce corporate tax rate from 49 per cent to 38 per cent . . . work harder . . . reductions in government spending . . . must wait six months to receive unemployment benefit . . . decisive change in the economic direction of Australia." Says one of the Canberra correspondents, listening: "It's a good policy: bash the unemployed and the sick."

The questions start up and Howard handles them with his usual civility; what with the fringe of greying hair at the back of his head and dark eyebrows and balding pate he looks like a neighbourhood bank manager, stern but friendly. However, as the questions become more hostile and include phrases such as "rubbery" and "Is it equitable?" he stiffens and becomes curter and exasperated in his replies; his spectacles gleam, his white shirt gleams, his capped teeth gleam. "The Australian public is being presented with a clear choice . . . we are presenting an option, if you give incentives you must have program cuts . . . some of them will have an effect on people living in this community . . ."

To be abolished: Medibank Private, four government departments, the Schools Commission, the Human Rights and Equal Opportunities Commission and a dozen other social programs. Cutbacks in all government areas, including welfare, education, health care. Cutbacks to the states which fund community services. "The Australian people want bold, imaginative reforms," says Howard in peroration. When he finishes, nobody claps. Except his shadow Ministers.

Next day at Penrith, in Sydney's Western Suburbs, 31 bikies face up to 217 murder charges relating to the massacre at Milperra, also in the West, when a girl passer-by and several bike riders were killed in a hotel yard shoot-up. The West has its own sub-culture, an "underclass" syndrome of unemployment, petty crime, drugs, factory fodder aggro and sexual violence. Thatcher's "two nations", in which one part of the community is concreted into poverty and social repression, is already becoming a reality in these urban flatlands. Another parable . . .

What sort of Prime Minister would John Howard be?

He would be an activist: if Howard has his way he will radically change the face of government in Australia and push the political ground so far to the Right that it would take years, maybe a decade, to bring it back. He has promised to hit the ground running and means it. In an interview he told me: "Politics is about momentum; you accomplish most in your first six months. It's because of the natural goodwill and support people give you in the first six months; then they start to become less tolerant. Look what Reagan accomplished in his first six to twelve months, I admire that. Hawke squandered that time. I won't. The abolition of departments and the restructuring of government will commence straight away. We'll abolish the capital gains tax and the fringe benefits tax in the first session of parliament.

"We'll make immediate changes to industrial relations; the bill's been drafted already. The health care system, the new higher education and schools system . . . we're ready to go on those. A lot of it will have to do with what we announced when we launched our tax policy: new tax rates, more incentive, cuts in government spending, abolition of various bodies and grants, asset sales and privatisation . . ." As Howard says, all this is only three weeks away — if he wins. His very first acts? Choose his Cabinet . . . "I assume we'll be in coalition with the Nationals." After talking to Treasury and the Reserve Bank, he will "take decisions quickly on the economy, that's what I'll do. I'll also talk to leaders of business groups and interest groups." Next, a televised Talk To The Nation "about our situation and our program".

To formalise all this, Howard intends to set up a completely new Cabinet office "of people from the private sector, plus public servants, a group of people around me who give good advice", which would be responsible to him personally. This means a deliberate downgrading of the Prime Minister's Department in terms of policy input, though Howard would retain it. His plan is not quite the American system of unelected Cabinet members, but a sort of Australian substitute for it.

The model for a Howard government? Not exactly Ronald Reagan, though he admires a lot of what Reagan has done. It is probably closer to Margaret Thatcher, whom he likes personally and whose policies are closer to Howard's. (He also likes the way she has won three consecutive electoral victories.)

An early symbolic act, like Gough Whitlam's abolition of conscription? "At the foreign-policy level, I'd make some significant moves to improve our relationship with Indonesia, first through orthodox diplomatic channels . . . and later a Prime Ministerial visit to Jakarta." He thinks about it, how to dramatise the Howard takeover. "I'd have thought abolishing a sizeable percentage of the public sector and the fringe benefits tax would be symbolic enough!"

Howard says he is going to have a "broad-based" Ministry, with nobody (and no factions) excluded; this may mean a return by Peacock and Macphee to the front bench in the interests of party unity. He doesn't believe the present disunity will last in government; a Liberal Prime Minister has much more authority than a Labor one — he chooses his own Ministry for a start. He intends to group some Ministers under one senior Minister; for example, there would be three junior Ministers under the Treasurer: "one for Tax, one for Expenditure and one for odds and ends". Would he keep the Treasurer's position for himself? "Oh Lord, no; been there, done that! Never again." He laughs. "A Prime Minister who has been a Treasurer has a certain understanding of it all."

Howard says he feels "excellent" about the election and the Prime Ministership: "I can't wait to get there." He thinks the Liberal campaign has got off to a good start, although he describes some of the media reaction as "quite bizarre", adding: "I mean, I've certainly not had a supportive media for thirteen months; I'm rather used to it." What style would a Howard government have? "There'd be less of a fetish about consensus. People expect governments to take decisions and implement them," he replies immediately. "We'd be less interventionist; I would take some of the approaches Margaret Thatcher has taken in allowing some industrial disputes to be settled between the companies and the unions, rather than the government feeling it had to get involved. I certainly wouldn't be seeking to run an ostentatious style of government, because I'm not by nature an ostenatious person. It's just going to be . . . er, well, what you might call Average Australian. Because that's what I am. I think I have more empathy with people who live in the suburbs of Australia than any political leader in the last twenty years."

This points to a crucial fact about Howard: his plainness. He lives in a somewhat swept-up house in Wollstonecraft on the near North Shore, with antique furniture in the sitting room and an extra storey added recently, making it the tallest house in the street, but it's very much an ordinary family home with three kids (Richard, Tim, and Melanie) running riot everywhere and wanting to be taken to the park. He and Janette don't go out much except to political functions; it's a luxury to stay at home and eat takeaway. They never go to the movies, don't read much and go for holidays each year to the same old lodge at Hawks Nest near Port Stephens, because John likes to tramp through the bush a bit though he's hopeless at water sports. He plays tennis sometimes, used to play golf, loves watching cricket and footie. Just got around to putting a small pool for the kids in the backyard. It's all very Barry Humphries humdrum, Mister Normal, a marginally more affluent version of the small business stratum which is Howard's (and the Liberal Party's) basic constituency; it's ironic that the high flyers who hobnob with Packer and Bondy are the Labor Party leaders such as Hawke and Keating, while the Liberal Party is led by a small, mousy man who is very much a homebody, argues endlessly with his kids and wife and is quite friendly and unpretentious.

His wife Janette describes him as someone who "likes a joke, parties, people situations"; he used to throw the best parties in Parliament House. "But being the Treasurer, the hard guy, and then leader of the Opposition toughens you," she says. "You have to learn to be able to say the unpleasant things. He's been wearied; he's thought sometimes it would never end. You look seriously at it and you think, do I really want to do this?" But, she says, Howard hasn't become soured or disillusioned, it has simply strengthened his resolve. He's been training himself for this chance at the top ever since he was a schoolboy and told his classmates he was going to be Prime Minister, and he isn't going to stop now. There's a dogged persistence about Howard that everyone recognises, even his enemies. If anything, Hawke's announcement of the early election came as a relief. Says Janette: "He was all sparky, rushing around the house saying, 'Wow, here it is!' This family loves elections. The Dog and Pony Show, John calls it. He loves it."

So where does it all come from, this sense of purpose that drives John Howard? Basically it's lower middle-class Methodism, a strong sense of community responsibility and doing something worthwhile with your life. This can split two ways, into the radical/Labor Methodism of someone like Brian Howe, Minister for Health in the Labor government and leader of the parliamentary Left, or into the individualistic self-help Methodism of Howard's father, a Dulwich Hill garage proprietor who was a member of the Liberal Party, supported Menzies and welcomed the end of petrol rationing with a fervour young Johnnie can still remember.

Even within the Howard family the same split exists: brother Stan is a senior partner in Stephen, Jacques & Stephen, the law firm, and a Liberal functionary; brother Wally is a Burwood bookseller and Liberal; but brother Bob is a university lecturer in political science and an ALP member who opposed the Liberals (and his family) over Vietnam. He told me once: "John's a rather serious-minded fellow, a conservative . . . he really does believe that every man is his own fortune, the free market system works best of all . . . there's a lot of our mother's character about him. He's a very strong person, very conscientious . . . he believes in all the old values like duty, loyalty . . . he's not at all sceptical, he doesn't realise those values and symbols can be used by particular interests for their own ends."

Throughout his career, in law and politics, Howard has conformed utterly to the more conventional side of his background. Joined the Sydney University Liberal Club after leaving school, president of the Young Liberals, met his wife Janette at a party for Liberal scrutineers, cultivated NSW Liberal machine man John Carrick ("very much a father figure," says a friend), stood for the NSW seat of Drummoyne, got beaten, moved deliberately to Wollstonecraft because he knew the sitting member, Sir John Cramer, was old and likely to retire, and in 1974 won the seat. Became Fraser's Treasurer, first as a stand-in for Phillip Lynch, then in his own right. Became leader of the "dries" in the Opposition, and was finally elected leader of the Liberal Party when he refused to pledge the allegiance Andrew Peacock demanded.

Straight.

Today Howard comes across as a highly controlled, wound-up but integrated man who doesn't seem to be disturbed by any internal conflicts, despite that furrowed-brow worriedness which Tandberg catches so well; he doesn't ever feel the need to unburden himself to anyone, like Hawke used to, because the distance between his interior and exterior is nil. He is also a narrow, scrabbly, fox-terrier of a man who pushes on no matter what defeats he suffers and has shown an amazing capacity to endure and survive — qualities which may yet carry him through to the Prime Ministership. The strain of the past year — leading the Opposition, watching his popularity plummet, the coalition breaking up, and now the election — has taken its toll. He doesn't smile much any more and he's often on guard, though he throws away a self-parodic line every now and then; the other day, rushing from one TV interview to another, he decided to leave the makeup on his face. "I'll save the public sector some expenditure," he said, "I'll privatise the make-up industry." At such times he's at his most likeable. But then you find that he is on the phone to Charles Copeman and Bruce Shepherd, and is praising John Stone to the media, and is telling the parchment-faced old ladies of the Salvation Army retirement village at the Brisbane working-class suburb of Inala: "I can't promise you . . .", while pushing through a ruthless Economic Rationalist/New Right program of public welfare amputation in order to transfer wealth to the most privileged and exploitative groups in the community.

"He's not a fanatic," says his wife. "But he acts like one," says someone else. There's an arrogant, intolerant side to Howard that comes out in the snarling, hectoring tone he uses in Parliament. A national Press Gallery correspondent told me once he thought there was "a dark side" to Howard; others detect a whiff of moral puritanism about him. Howard was a hawk on Vietnam, antiabortion and, compared with Fraser, is a reactionary on South Africa; his illiberalism shows in the way he sacked Macphee. He likes the adrenalin in politics, but it is invariably channelled towards narrow ideological ends.

It is a crisp, wintry Sunday morning; in Wollstonecraft, the houses stand like English picture books in the sun, unopened papers on the doorsteps. Plane tree leaves are scattered across the nature strip. The Howard kids are doing a Tom Sawyer on the back paling fence, painting it (and themselves) timberstain brown. It is so quiet, so absolutely peaceful, it seems like nothing could possibly go wrong with the world.

Near Blacktown, in the outer Western Suburbs, the House Commission bungalows and spec houses stretch for kilometre after kilometre and dwindle away into empty paddocks, sagging barbed wire fences, shacks and trailer homes. The unemployment rate for 15-19-year-olds is 18.6 per cent, almost three times the national average. Over 100,000 people on welfare. A fifth of households earn under $8,000 a year.

In Penrith on Saturday night, the local hoons in black T-shirts cruise down the street, drop a howlie at the traffic lights, chuck a U-turn, cruise back down again. On the outskirts of Blacktown, in a cow paddock called the Boiler paddock between Prospect Reservoir and the F-4 Freeway, Anita Cobby's body was found.

What Howard proposes to do, by chopping back on welfare, education and community services, is to tear the extremes further and further apart — and hope "law and order" will handle the consequences. 1984 is over; the Clockwork Orange nightmare awaits.

Wednesday. Howard is hurried by his minders into a cavernous room in the front of the Box Hill Town Hall; security men turn the media throng back at the glass doors. He has to record an interview with the Ray Martin Midday Show in Sydney. Very important. All those housewives.

Howard is plonked down on a chair at the far end of the room in front of the camera crew. He has a small TV monitor he can look into so he can see Ray Martin on the screen. He stares into the monitor, gestures for a glass of water, practises smiling. "I can't hear anything yet," he says, adjusting his earpiece; he used to wear a hearing aid years ago and started going deaf again last year; an operation in an Adelaide hospital (complete with Howard in striped flannel pyjamas) fixed it. The cameraman shouts: "Straight down the barrel!" Howard wipes the sweat off his lip, crosses his ankles, clasps his hands nervously between his knees. "I can't move, can I? No. I can't do a thing," he says. Kneeling in front of him, whispering in his ear, is Senator Jim Short, the shadow Finance Minister, a pale bulky man in a blue suit; he is talking Howard up — or down. Around the edge of the hushed room other Liberal shadow Ministers, press officers and Hugh Curnow, head of Masius, the Liberals' advertising agency, are watching.

"Stand by!" Senator Short scurries away. There is a deathly silence. Howard is transfixed, like a stuffed mannequin, staring a the monitor. When Ray Martin finally comes on, a surreal scene ensues: nobody can hear what he is saying, only Howard, who seems to be talking like a robot into a machine that isn't listening. Only Howard's words, as disconnected as in an absurdist play, drift into the sepulchral room:

"Pleasure, Ray . . . mmm . . . a pity . . . good . . . scare campaign . . . for you and me? . . . $26-a-week tax break . . . stop the smarties doing that . . . bayside mansion . . . Medicare has broken down . . . I stopped a lot of rorts when I was Treasurer . . . you've got to remember, Ray, you have to pay for tax cuts somehow . . . (pause) . . . I am trustworthy."

Cut. The interview's over. Howard gets to his feet, takes the audio bug out of his ear, looks around. Nobody says anything. I watch the strain go out of his body. "Don't know how you do it,"

I mutter. Howard stares back, eyes wide open, as though shell-shocked. "I sometimes wonder why," he says.

And so it goes on, all day. Radio 6PR interview, Town Hall. Radio 2GB interview, Melbourne office. Sandwiches. Pre-tape Terry Willesee interview, Channel 7. "I'd be delighted to debate Mr Hawke. He's Prime Minister, I want to be Prime Minister. Sure. On this program? Sure." Out by white Commonwealth car to Channel 2, Elsternwick, his security men scurrying into the back-up car. He arrives early, slumps into a chair, throws his head back, closes his eyes. Five seconds. Phone call. Mark Day, live. Drive-time. "Hello there! How are you? I'm fit!" Someone is shouting abuse over the ABC intercom. Grahame Morris, his senior private secretary, tries to throttle it with a cushion. Howard is shouting into the telephone, leaning against a sideboard: "Sack 'em? Look, 12,000 public servants retire a year."

He returns to the hospitality room for a glass of orange juice and a corn chip, as chirpy as ever. "We've taken over the agenda, Labor's running after us," he says. Any more big guns after the tax package? "This is our only 25-pounder." As Prime Minister would he move even further Right economically, towards the Monash think-tank extreme? "They don't believe you need make any allowance for people having families. Well, I don't agree with that. I'm still a bit damp. I never said I was bone dry." He smiles. "Yes, I'm the most ideological leader the Liberals have had. Er, but couldn't we have a less harsh word? Committed?"

Next, the ABC's 7.30 Report. More make-up: "You're starting to shine, Mr Howard." It's a mixture of tension and sweat. Howard's been at it since dawn. Richard Carleton arrives for the Carleton/Walsh interview. Howard asks for a different chair: "This is a very uncomfortable one, it doesn't move!" He settles into a new chair, facing Carleton: "I'd like to be an elegant leader of the Opposition." Halfway through the interview the floor producer changes Howard's jacket. "I didn't know Max was going to be as tough as that," quips Howard. Max is. He hardly lets Howard get a word in edgewise. "YES!" says Howard towards the end, "we CAN make these expenditure cuts." His voice rises to a falsetto, cracks momentarily like a nervous tic. Silence. Howard listens. "Pleasure."

Howard takes a comb out of his inside coat pocket, scrapes it through his thinning hair. By 7.00 p.m. he's on the RAAF jet to Brisbane. Then the Gold Coast, Jupiter's Casino, Sydney, Hobart, across to Perth. It goes on and on.

Pleasure, Ray.
Pleasure, John.
Pleasure, Prue.
Is it?

> Saturday night, in the main street kerb,
> the angle-parked cars are full of watchers,
> their feet on invisible accelerators,
> going nowhere, fast.
>
> Bruce Dawe, "Provincial City"

In Queensland, Joh Bjelke-Petersen is advocating a flat tax so that millionaires will only pay the same tax rate as poor people. In Penrith, nine Commancheros and Bandidos are found guilty of murder, another 21 convicted of manslaughter. In Canberra, Keating is telling the Press Gallery that Howard is flaky, he's stumbling, because he's basically guilty; he knows the figures are rubbery, he needed a consumption tax to pay for it all but backed down, because of Joh, just like he backed down to Fraser in '82, when he should have resigned. In Sydney, Janette Howard says: "He's one of the most honest people I've met in my life. He's softer than me. But I don't think I could match his courage."

And Howard himself?

It's the close of the weekend; he's been filming TV ads for the Liberal Party for two days but managed to squeeze in a visit to Concord Oval for the Australia versus France Rugby test; now it's back to the campaign trail. He kisses the kids and Janette goodbye — "See you next week" — lugs his inevitable suitcases into the white Ford LTD and settles back for the night drive to the airport, coloured reflections flashing across his face. On, off, on, off.

In summary: "I am not some sort of heartless automaton who thinks if you do this and this it'll all fall into place . . . I get very concerned about social deprivation . . . the decay of law and order, spread of violence, decay of parental authority, it affects working cla . . . er, less well-off people more than anyone else."

QUESTION: Aren't your policies, and the programs you're going to cut back on, going to intensify that situation?

HOWARD: I've talked to the Sydney Mission and the Salvation Army . . . there's a lot of criticism of the existing social welfare programs.

QUESTION: How will your policies improve that?

HOWARD: Improve family structure . . . improve the general economic situation.

QUESTION: Trickle-down effect?

HOWARD: Not every program is one I'd get rid of. There is an enormous amount of fat that can be eliminated that leaves intact certain programs . . . what we're proposing doesn't affect those who need unemployment benefits . . . OK, we have a work-for-benefit principle.

QUESTION: And welfare cutbacks?

HOWARD: I reckon if you gave the Salvation Army, St Vincent de Paul and so on the money to dispense, you'd have a far more effective distribution to really needy people and more hardnosed.

QUESTION: That sounds very much like nineteenth century charity.

HOWARD: Oh no, no, no . . . that's an example of my supreme cynicism . . . not cynicism, my feeling that governments have great limitations in delivering services . . . I'm suspicious of governments and government solutions.

QUESTION: Why?

HOWARD: Working for yourself is the ethic I grew up with. You didn't work for the government. It was part of the Protestant work ethic.

QUESTION: You're not beholden to that background, you didn't have to conform . . .

HOWARD: Well, I think it's right. I'm not a reactionary, I'm not a throwback to the 1950s. There were a lot of things about the 1950s that weren't any good. There are certain things you can't go back to. But society has become more conservative.

QUESTION: What's your motivation?

HOWARD: I do want to give something. A complex product of my background and values. I would like to feel I could leave the country, society better.

Headlines. Front pages, top to bottom: HOWARD BIG TAX GAMBLE. $7.3 billion in tax cuts, but axe for govt spending. THE DAY ANITA COBBY DIED. Nurse's killers expected to lodge appeals. How the killers were caught — Page 4. THE POLICY AT A GLANCE.

Qantas jet base. Bob Hawke's BAC-111 has had engine failure. Howard is left with the Mystere. The car drives on to the wasteland tarmac: Alphaville, The Future Desert. On, off, on, off. Howard's face is alternatively in darkness, in mirrored light.

What if he loses?

"I will win," he says determinedly. "I will be in politics for a long time. I'll be Prime Minister on July 11, and then I'll stay there for quite some time." Is there a life after politics? "Oh, of course, I'm not going to stay in it all my life. I wouldn't want to stay there forever, hell no." What would he do? "I wouldn't mind becoming a journalist, actually. I'd like radio. I write a lot of my own press statements." Law? "That's years into the future. I mean, I'm only 47."

But if he loses?

Howard refuses to answer. This is make-or-break time for him. In a few weeks's time he will be Prime Minister of Australia or the deposed leader of the Liberal Party; failed Opposition leaders don't get a second chance. But Howard is such a political animal he certainly won't resign form the Parliamentary party; depending on who the new leaders are, he could well be given a shadow portfolio.

As the election gets closer, the shadow lengthens. Three weeks. Counting down. Stand by. "Straight down the barrel." Under immense and self-imposed pressure, he's kept his control, and his sense of humour, and most of his integrity. He has also kept most of that deepest, ineradicable, Hard Right puritanism which he has never had the will, or the imagination, to shrug off and which maims him intellectually.

For John Howard the Western Suburbs, and Anita Cobby, and bikie gangs, and dole kids in black T-shirts, and gross and desperate social inequality, is another world. Unfortunately, its also the real world, more real than a (greasy) flagpole in Canberra. But, for all his personal charm, he can't see it.

The way things are going, John Howard may turn out to be the most pleasant but most purblind Prime Minister the Australian nation never had.

(This was published in the Sydney Morning Herald on 20 June 1987. John Howard lost the election. He is now the Opposition's shadow Minister for Industrial Relations.)

ELIZABETH EVATT

In a society like Australia where the people who are most admired seem to be corrupt, power-hungry, wealth-centred "heroes" it is good to find some people who aren't like that at all. Good people, in high places. They're usually women — "heroines".

Elizabeth Evatt is like that. She wouldn't agree, of course; the idea of heroes and heroines is pretty stupid anyway. Everyone has to be their own. But as a woman with a major public role — she is head of the Australian Law Reform Commission — she is perhaps the closest we have to a role model heroine.

She has been knocked about in her life so badly that it's possible to think of her as a tragic figure, whose humanity and stoicism have been forced upon her by fate. If the Evatt family, which is one of the great dynasties of Australian history, has had a curse laid upon it because of its brilliance and ambition, the weight of it has fallen unfairly on Elizabeth. But her friends and family say she has always been like she is: straight, dogged, unshakeably moral. No goody goody. A bit bloody stern and puritan at times. She has about her the presence and authority of a tribal matriarch. "She has a vision," says a close friend. "She's committed to it. She won't change."

That vision is something which you can only tease out of Elizabeth Evatt bit by bit, but it has something to do with the fundamental goodness of people ("most people are nice, they want to be friendly, unless something terrible has happened to them") and the need to change society to make it "fair and just and honest — I suppose I'm like that guy with the lamp, Diogenes, looking for an honest man!" she says, laughing in her gentle, self-deprecating way.

In pursuit of her vision, Evatt helped set up the Family Court and was Chief Judge for twelve years. Before that she was the head from 1974 to 1977 of the Commission on Human Relationships which Whitlam set up to delve into Australia's most urgent social problems, and which Fraser let die "a slow death". The Law Reform Commission may turn out to be her most important task yet.

And she held on to her vision despite an ordeal by fire which might have destroyed other people. While she was at the Family Court, pioneering a conciliatory no-fault concept of divorce which led the world, she experienced the gunning-down of one Family Court judge, the murder of the wife of another, bomb attacks, death threats, police guards and the introduction of a security system which turned the court into a fortress.

Then one of her two children, 21-year-old Richard, committed suicide in 1985; his body was found in Sydney Harbour after he was seen falling from the Bridge. Elizabeth was stricken; her marriage to Robert Southan, a British barrister, had broken up long before and she was living as a sole parent with Richard and her daughter Anne in a terrace house in Paddington, Sydney.

Today, however, Elizabeth Evatt seems as gentle and forgiving as ever. She is a big, heavy-boned, slow-talking, silver-grey-haired woman of 56 with half-glasses which she wears slung around her neck on a cord, and the black clerical garb of a judge, which can make her seem rather formidable; when she walks she hunches her shoulders like a burly front-row forward . . . at first glance an old-fashioned, Dickensian figure.

It belies the woman she is; close up she has a strong, symmetrical face, long nose, sensual mouth and a rather kindly ambience which signals: friend/mother/I am honest/lover? Her typical style, in fact, is rather old and grandmotherly; she affects the naivete and modesty of someone who doesn't know a lot about the workaday world; she speaks (like others in the Evatt family) in a rather broad semi-ocker drawl and her conversation is peppered with slang. She laughs a lot, too, in unexpected places; she has a straight, slightly sardonic gaze; and now she and her fellow commissioners are setting about the massive and thankless task of trying to reform one of the most conservative areas of Australian public life.

"There's a two-part legal system in Australia right now, a legal system for the rich and powerful and a legal system for the others. Parts of the system are out of touch with the community," she says. "It's a matter of maintaining a continuous process of reform, not just sitting back making sure law reform is pushed along. Even the idea that you should be doing that needs to be established. Society is changing, commercial life is changing, everything is changing, so the law needs to be constantly monitored and changed to keep up with what's needed of it. That means changing a very conservative world. It includes the structure of courts, legal aid, alternative remedies and so on, not just new Acts of Parliament . . . the whole way lawyers are educated and deal with people, that's all part of law reform. It's no use having the best laws in the world if your lawyers and court system aren't able to cope with what people actually need from it. I'm interested in the whole thing."

It seems so logical, so unobjectionable — yet Elizabeth Evatt and the Family Court have provoked extraordinary hostility in the legal profession. It takes a while to realise this is not directed at her personally, but at what she stands for: *a new court*, which upset the old court monopolies and their pecking order; *reform*, which included ripping lucrative divorce work away from lawyers; *politics* — I mean, she's a Labor appointee, she's an Evatt, isn't she? and she's *a woman*, in an area which is still male, hierarchical, privileged and old-(private)-school-tie.

Elizabeth Evatt was the first woman to be appointed a judge of the Arbitration Commission, the first woman to be appointed Chief Judge of a senior court, the first woman to preside over the Law Reform Commission . . . she wears it all lightly and says, sardonically, "I've been around so long I've ceased to be a wonder." But the suspicion and resentment in the profession remain. Says one critic: "She ran out of energy on the Family Court, had to be moved. She tried to keep it too much as Lionel Murphy had set it up." Says another: "A bit puritan. Disdain for excesses of any sort. Over-works. She doesn't bend with the wind, goes directly forward." Explains a senior judge, about the Bar: "They have nothing against women provided they behave like boys at a private boarding school. If you don't, you're in trouble."

People who like her believe she has been scarred by the Evatt controversies and the Family Court experience. "I'm not sure anyone ever knows Elizabeth terribly well," says one judge. "You're allowed to know what she thinks but not what she feels." Says another: "She's a first-class lawyer but she's withdrawn; she doesn't push her stuff to enthuse or motivate people." She is certainly reticent, even secretive; one of her peers describes her as "traumatised by recent events".

And Elizabeth herself?

She is drinking weak whisky and water at Giovanni's in Oxford Street, Sydney, under a garish illuminated sign. It's been a heavy day in Phillip Street, plus an equally heavy time the day before in Newcastle (she is the Chancellor of Newcastle University), but she seems as friendly and complaisant as ever; she is wearing a white embroidered hippie blouse, a rainbow ring where her wedding ring would normally be, and a family heirloom chain of gold links around her neck, and she is talking, with great reluctance and hesitancy, about pain — her own and others': "Am I happy?" Pause. "No. No, not really." Pause. "I'm not unhappy."

You haven't quite recovered?

"Those are your words. You have to find a way of incorporating pain without it poisoning your whole system; you have to acknowledge it first of all, be aware of it." A young couple at the next table are giggling together. "I'm a one-to-one person. I get on well with people. If you let the things other people do get into you and eat you up, you're damaging yourself. Then you give people more power over you, if you let them cause you that much pain."

She stops, shakes her drink bemusedly. "We see that in the Family Court, people are unable to accept the reality of what has happened in their relationship . . . they have to focus their mind and feelings on blaming someone else . . . they get so obsessed they blame the other party, and anyone involved with the other party, and then they blame the whole institution they are dealing with."

(The result: bomb attacks, displaced violence, a warning in the lift to solicitors not to identify any judge in public.)

"What you do to someone else, you do to yourself. Psychology? I'm interested in it, never studied it. No, I've never been to a psychiatrist. But self-analysis is quite important. I turn to people, friends, family. I have a lot of support around me, that's good."

Has what she has suffered personally helped her in her Family Court work?

"Aw, I think most people in the court have had a fairly broad life experience. Everybody has lots of knocks, being knocked around isn't an uncommon experience. There are always other people who have been through the same sorts of things, or worse, or different — everybody has if you can get under their skin a bit. You have to try to recover. Some parts of your life are good, fine, productive. I'm enjoying my work, it's stimulating. I don't have any major worries or problems in my life at the moment."

But?

"I'm trying to be positive. I don't want to talk about it. It's not going to affect my work." Later: does she feel isolated? She muses about that, swirling the whisky in her glass. "Yes, I'm very isolated," she says at last. "Yeah . . . well, I do get heartened sometimes. I feel optimistic. There are still plenty of people who want social and economic change." She laughs, finishes her whisky; cars are zooming homewards along Oxford Street in the early evening, their headlights spattering reflections in the cafe's wall mirrors. "But it's wrong to expect dramatic changes."

Elizabeth Evatt comes, of course, from an extraordinary family: the Evatts are probably the closest Australia has to the great privileged families of British history like the Churchills and the Sassoons, a brilliant and sometimes eccentric dynasty which has contributed massively to the political and legal history of the nation. Dr H.V. (Bert) Evatt, Elizabeth's uncle, was leader of the ALP, president of the United Nations General Assembly, a brilliant lawyer and socialist intellectual who split the Labor Party in the 1950s and ended his career in the bitterness and controversy of the Petrov case. Her father was Clive Evatt Snr, another outstanding lawyer and a senior Minister in postwar NSW Labor governments, whom I remember being driven around Sydney Showground in an open car to the cheers of hordes of schoolchildren when he was Minister for Education.

"They were all clever boys, their mother enjoined them to get well-educated, she was their inspiration," says Elizabeth of the six Evatt brothers, who all grew up as sons of a publican in East Maitland and came down to Sydney to set the world afire (two were killed in France in World War I, after surviving Gallipoli). "Dad was the baby; Uncle Bert was six years older. Dad? Of course I liked him, everybody liked him, he was an extremely charming person. Oh yes, he was irresistible!"

Certainly Elizabeth's mother, Marjorie Andreas, found him so; she came from a grand and wealthy Blue Mountains family and Elizabeth spent a lot of her childhood in the ancestral mansion, *Leuralla* at Leura. It is now a museum, open to the public for Devonshire teas, scones and guided tours.

By now the Evatt dynasty was well-established. The Clive/Marjorie branch produced three children who have all become well-known in their own right: Clive Jnr, barrister and owner of the Hogarth Gallery in Paddington, struck off as a barrister in 1967 and re-admitted seven years ago, a typical Evatt mixture of flamboyance, brilliance and eccentricity; Penelope, architect, arts patron and married to Harry Seidler, the architect; and Elizabeth.

Elizabeth is the serious one. Of all the Evatts, she's the one who has carried on Uncle Bert's legacy of high-minded commitment to reform and social justice. Says someone who knows the family: "She's everything her father wasn't: serious, dull, moral, heavy." A judge who went to the ancestral Evatt home for dinner as a young man remembers it as "the most excruciating experience of my life": at the table Clive Snr was reading a brief, Elizabeth was reading a Commonwealth Law report and Penelope was gazing at a blown-up photo of Neil Harvey, the cricket idol, while Elizabeth's mother vainly tried to borrow her own car back from her son, Clive Jnr! "Her mother was quite a beauty but swamped by the Evatt egos," the judge recalls. "It was like a parody of eccentric British upper-class life."

Penelope, who probably knows Elizabeth best of all, says: "She thinks I'm a bit frivolous because I have an interest in clothes, parties, ephemeral things like that! And I'm a bit of a flirt, which she's not. She was always a quiet sort of girl. Worked hard at university, kept coming top, won the medal when she was only 20 or 21. She's not groping around. She has goals, always has. Not for herself, but what she stands for. She's a true believer!" Pause. "I wish she could have spent more time on herself." Says Elizabeth of Penelope (they see each other nearly every week): "We're not only sisters; she's a great friend."

Is Uncle Bert, then, a model for her? "I've never thought of that," she says. He was a very kind-hearted man, very powerful intellect, enormous knowledge and understanding of things . . . set high store by intellectual capacity, that was the way those boys had been brought up . . . yeah, it was their mother, she was quite a remarkable woman. He liked to test out if you knew anything, liked to ask you about the principles of mathematics or legal concepts. [Laughing] Not in a difficult way; he was quite friendly about it. But y'see I never had an opportunity to talk to him about political or social issues or anything like that. I wish I had. When you think of the ideals and achievements he had, what he did when he was fighting the anti-communist referendum . . . Yes, I do admire him tremendously. He was a believer.

"Yes, I'm angry about what happened to him. But anger is not a very productive feeling to have. When the record's looked at, the vision and beliefs are there. They stand the test of time.

"I suppose I've picked up the crusading side of it all by furthering the ideals I have in the legal area, rather than in the wider political arena. No, I wouldn't have liked a political career. It's far too tough. Too many compromises. [Laughing] I don't think I've got the right personality for that. And yet you have to admire people who go through political life and seem to come through relatively untarnished. Yes, Bert Evatt was like that. And Gough. I think he's held on to his vision and ideas. God, it's not easy! You fight for what you believe in, in the ways you can. The role of Chief Judge or president of the Law Reform Commission gives a fair bit of scope. Yes, that's what I'm about. A striver for change."

She sighs, and then laughs at being so corny, so heart-onsleeve: "Hopeless idealism!" When she laughs her mouth widens into a self-deprecating grin, her face lightens and becomes animated. "Blow me down, I don't know why I'm talking about this . . ."

Is she very political? "As a judge I adopt a politically neutral stance," she answers; but she grew up in a socialist family which had "a broad liberal outlook on the world; it was open to new ideas, open to inquiring about things, not accepting things that didn't seem right", and she has never turned her back on that. "It's rather sad that the leadership of the Labor Party should be putting sound economic managment ahead of everything else . . . I mean, no-one can criticise that, but it's only part of what the goals should be," she says.

Her contact with politicians is at the formal level only. She has never met Paul Keating, and occasionally runs into the Wrans at social events. "What political support? I'm a judge! I'm sorry, you quite misunderstand me. I don't have any political connections." Doesn't that separate her, then, from potential support for what she is trying to achieve in law reform? She thinks about it. "Yes," she says at last. "But you should be independent of all that stuff. I guess you have to carry out the path that suits you, that you feel is right for you."

It worries her that other people have so little compunction in exercising power. "When you see how much money is spent in society purely for commercial exploitation, in advertising and so on . . . and you think, oh my God . . . when you see how forces can be mobilised, with enough money, to influence minds and attitudes . . . it's terribly frightening, the power that exists, when you don't know if that power is going to be exercised for good or evil. Who is there who is willing and able to make value judgments about that? I'm not setting myself up to judge any of that. What right do I have?"

It seems a strange stance for a judge to take. Indeed, one detects in her a final lack of self-certainty, of passionate belief, which seems to hold her back from fighting vehemently for her cause; she is no radical; if anything, she is rather apolitical and otherworldly, as though her attitudes are always vitiated by her scepticism.

The judge who refuses to judge.

Her career confirms this. All her life she has studiously avoided the classic judicial role, preferring areas outside the merely judgmental. It all chimes with her reticence, her unwillingness to condemn others, her emphasis in the Family Court upon conciliation; one of the court's successes, to her mind, is that only about 5 per cent of the disputes that have come to it have actually ended up in court for formal judgment. Says an outsider: "While the rest of Australia was rushing off to Vietnam, or arguing about it, she was getting on with something important to the whole human race — ridding divorce of blame." Says a legal commentator: "People need a fight; they need someone to be found guilty. If they don't get it, they feel cheated and they turn violent. That's what happened to the Family Court."

The Vietnam argument, re-run, in the rarified purlieu of Phillip Street, Sydney.

Elizabeth Evatt says she didn't leave the Family Court out of disillusionment, though others say she was bitter about the failure of the Federal Government and the media to support the court when it came under attack. The media, she feels, adopted a "blame the victim" approach. Various community groups and men's organisations, in Perth and Brisbane in particular, waged an active campaign against the court; individuals who felt aggrieved were able to get media attention; the judges operated in a climate of continual controversy and pressure.

Evatt says she realises that "there's an aggressive tendency in people, I know it, that makes people want to fight back, hit out". When a relationship breaks down, "people are willing to fight it out in court; they're reluctant to think you can resolve it other than through hostility". Nevertheless, she believes in the counselling and conciliation processes of the court. Other judges point out that Elizabeth Evatt had the task of "giving body" to a new area of the law, and did so; certainly she herself rejects any suggestion that it has been an "experiment".

"It's here to stay," she says firmly.

Then why did she abandon it to become head of the Law Reform Commission?

"I was offered the position — I've always been interested in law reform, it's not often you get an opportunity like that to work at something you're interested in, so after twelve years with the court I decided to move on," she replies. "I decided there has to be life after the Family Court." She smiles. "Yeah."

Evatt feels the Family Court will continue to evolve and likes some of the more recent changes, such as the strengthened maintenance provisions. "The maintenance changes mainly involve men; they won't be able to evade responsibility for paying for their children. This is a really good thing. The poverty trap that so many single parents fall into will be a litle bit alleviated," she says. But she is opposed to other changes, such as the wearing of robes by the judges. "I have never supported that. I don't think wearing robes is conducive to the right atmosphere. People don't come to the Family Court because of wrongdoing by anyone. They are there because they need help. No one is on trial, nobody is accused."

She feels guilty about coming from such a privileged background and there is much about her that is ineffably upper class: she goes to the opera and theatre and gallery openings, collects Blue Mountains paintings, plays clarinet, sings in the Messiah chorus each year, cooks mussels, likes lunch in the sun with a good wine, pate and pepper cheese, owns a Bang & Olufsen stereo and two houses (including Uncle Bert's old family home in Leura), learned Italian a few years ago, takes holidays in Florence and gets the *Guardian Weekly* from London . . . but guilt, like anger, is "rather negative and unproductive" and she tries in her work to make up for it all.

Also, there's a much more homespun and old-fashioned side to her. She likes gardening and slopping around in old sandals, she's very handy and virtually built an attic on her Paddington terrace herself, she taught herself computing, bashes out books for the Pearl Watson Foundation (which she set up in memory of the murdered wife of a Family Court judge), helped organise the Blue Mountains Festival, shoots videos of the family, has taken over Tim Seidler as a half-adopted son, and fills her house with mementos and photographs of the Evatts. She has close friends like Anne Deveson, former head of the Australian Film and TV School, who sat on the Commission on Human Relationships with her, flies to New York or Vienna once a year for a meeting of the United Nations committee for the Elimination of Discrimination Against Women, and is a member of various other foundations, though not of any political party.

Despite all this, her friends say she feels an outsider. Still. It goes back, no doubt, to her upbringing in blue-ribbon, Liberal, upper-class Wahroonga, where her family were virtually the only socialists. She spent a lot of time by herself, reading, listening to the radio, doing little woodcarvings or printing her own photos in a homemade darkroom, without ever feeling lonely. She went to Presbyterian Ladies College, Pymble, one of Sydney's leading private girls' schools, but has since written that "there is little of school I want to remember . . . I had a few good friends, but on the whole I was glad to leave . . . that sense of being an outsider stayed with me for a very long time."

She wanted to do arts at Sydney University, but her father insisted she do law. Dutifully, she complied. "I did quite well, I won the medal, I suppose . . . it has all become a bit irrelevant," she says now in her offhand way. Then came a year of post-graduate study at Harvard Law School, arranged by Professor Julius Stone; it was towards the end of the McCarthy anti-communist witch-hunt era and the beginning of the civil rights movement, and she found the experience "mind expanding". Then she went to London and lived there for the next seventeen years. She married Robert Southan, a barrister, had two children, practised at the Bar, and was invited to work for the first permanent Law Reform Commission. "So this is a bit of a re-run," she says. "It was a great experience. They were very intelligent, creative, reform-oriented people. I was really lucky to get in there while they were in their heyday, as it were."

London? "I loved it. I haven't been back very much." Did she become Anglicised? "Probably a bit. But I feel very Australian. Absolutely. Always have. You're born here, you feel it's your place, your country."

When, in 1973, Gough Whitlam asked her to come home as a deputy president of the Arbitration Commission, she accepted. Her marriage was breaking up; her husband came to Australia, but then returned to England. He flies out here every now and then to see Elizabeth and their daughter. A year after she arrived, Whitlam asked her to head the Commission on Human Relationships with Anne Deveson and Felix Arnott.

"That was an interesting and exciting time," she says. "We covered all the difficult social issues in Australia, then and now. It was a two and a half years' in-depth learning experience about the Australian people." The report showed the areas in which there was a desperate need for services, help and information and what had to be done "so that Australia might not remain a nation divided between haves and have-nots". The Fraser government ignored it in a way which she describes as "nothing short of scandalous". "No government wants to take a stand on issues like abortion and sex education. Australia is very conservative on some social issues; I'm not sure why. There's this desire for some sort of uniformity. I'm not sure to what extent multiculturalism is accepted deeply in the community yet. But there have been very significant changes. Even in Australia, opinions change as time goes by."

Then came the Family Court, and the Law Reform Commission, and personal trauma, and the most painful period of her life . . .

Leura. A cool, autumnal, almost English day, with brown leaves blowing off the deciduous trees and hedges straggling down towards the Lookout and children in scarves being tugged towards the tourist buses. Harry Seidler believes it feels like a European spa. He isn't there today but Penelope and young Tim Seidler and Elizabeth's daughter Anne are weekending in the ramshackle bungalow with its enormous backyard and overgrown garden which was Bert Evatt's home.

Elizabeth Evatt is relaxing. She is wearing, incongruously, masculine tracksuit pants, a buttoned-up old brown cardigan, severely straight Bloomsbury/Sapphic hair and an air of down-home casualness. Thick body, stout legs, sensible old lady's shoes. A matching old car is parked in the leaf-strewn driveway. The ambience is one of shabby gentility.

We walk down to the Lookout to see brother Clive's latest project, a stone amphitheatre with a stunning view over the Jamieson

Valley which he has carved out of the Evatt family land. Clive is taking tea on the patio of *Leuralla*, the grandiose mansion which was the Andreas (and sometime Evatt) family seat, with its stone balustrades and servants' quarters and stables and giant spruces and beeches and, inside, gilt-framed family portraits. Clive has rooms on the top floor, but has converted the rest into a remarkable museum which embalms the gracious way of life of almost a century ago: sitting room, dining room, retiring room, grand hall, even a children's playroom crammed with every imaginable Edwardian toy.

"That's my Peter Rabbit tea seat," says Elizabeth, a little sadly, pausing in the roped-off doorway to the playroom. "And that. And that, too, I think." She moves on. "I spent a lot of my childhood here; we used to come here for holidays. I'm very fond of it."

Above the staircase, Clive has turned one complete room into a Herbert Vere Evatt memorial; it is overburdened with sepia photographs of Uncle Bert with famous people, together with tattered newspaper clippings, books, framed certificates, mementos and a black barrister's gown. Evatt with Macarthur, Evatt with Ben Chifley, Evatt with Curtin, Evatt at the United Nations, Evatt with Molotov. Elizabeth peers at one small framed photograph on the wall, a family gathering. "That's me and Billy Hughes, and Bert and Frank Hurley, and Dad and Penelope with the teddy bear," she says. There is a lawyer's wig in a glass case on a stand. "Bert's?" I ask. "My Dad's," she replies, smiling.

We walk beneath a long pergola, between 30-metre exotic trees and old-fashioned shrubs and landscaped flower beds, back to Bert's more humble abode. As she trudges along, Elizabeth explains that she has never had any religious belief, never "travelled the road to Damascus" or had any blinding revelation in her life. However, listening to a daily reading from the New Testament at PLC Pymble gave her a respect for religion. "It's good stuff. If there weren't religious beliefs people would have to invent them. People feel the need for something beyond this chaos in the world. We're a pretty messy lot."

She has her own strong core of secular, humanist values instead. Truth, honesty, respect and consideration for other people

— the North American white liberal formula, with a fair bit of the guilt as well. She is also, in the words of a fellow judge, "absolutely dedicated" to the women's movement, where she is "much loved and respected"; although she is absolutely a shy woman, she is much more relaxed among her women peers than amidst the male camaraderie of the judiciary. She points to the way in which the Family Court "developed a way of recognising the equal worth of mother and father, husband and wife" and pursues the interests of women in international forums such as the United Nations Women's Committee. "It has the failings of other UN committees, the East/West, North/South business, but because it's all women on it, all twenty-three, it has something to hold it together."

Feminist? "I suppose I have been a feminist," she replies thoughtfully "though it wasn't a conscious thing to start with. My parents didn't treat me, or my sister, differently to my brother. The idea that I was discriminated against didn't occur to me; I never had to combat discrimination personally. Then suddenly, in the mid-1960s, I became conscious that there were lots of other women who did not have the sort of opportunities I had. I still thought it wasn't me, and then I realised it *was* me, trying to hold down a working life and a home life at the same time!

"I'm not a separatist or anti-male, though I understand women who are in separatist movements. We have to learn to live with one another. Eventually what that means is men have to make some changes. The level of violence between women and men is just extraordinary. It's not on. Domestic violence is a men's issue. I just feel quite strongly that men have to get in there and set other images for men. It's just as hard, right now, for men to find a role model as it is for women. This rather loud, tinny-waving model we often see on TV, a lot of men aren't like that at all; they don't conform to that ocker image. But somtimes they feel a bit bewildered. Changing stereotype roles leave a lot of people confused."

Will her own career help other women? "You hope it will make it easier for other women," she says. "Yeah. Helping to change things for women in a few ways."

The Law Reform Commission is one way of changing things. She is keen to take the initiative in areas the commission thinks should be referred to it by the government. "The Commission should be looking ahead. It's been worthwhile, it's working, even though sometimes its reports lie around for years. I feel optimistic about it."

Elizabeth and Penelope begin discussing how to get young Tim back to Killara, where the Seidlers live. Darkness has fallen on to the mountains; it is a sombre time. Elizabeth switches on a study lamp and checks the train timetables. The Seidlers and Anne depart. Later, talking quietly about her own life, Elizabeth Evatt explains: "You deal with people, you make all sorts of assumptions about who they are, what they are, but you don't *really* know what worries they've got, what burdens they have. So you should never assume that someone else hasn't got something awful that they're living with, that's affected them. You just don't know."

When she talks like that her voice rises, becomes almost plaintive. I assume she is thinking of Richard, her son.

Do you want to talk about that?

"No".

At all?

"No."

Later still, half-glasses perched on the end of her nose, she is discussing Gough Whitlam's philosophy of "go for broke" and she says, suddenly: "I've done all that!"

Including being betrayed?

"Well, the ideas we went for in the Family Court haven't been accepted. The idea that we should have an independent, specialised court of high quality, yet operating in a different way to the other courts, simply hasn't been accepted. By the legal profession. For their own interests, they want it to be like the other courts. I don't think that's what the people want." She breaks into that low, bemused laugh which she seems to reserve for the human condition, and its foolishness, including her own. "I've done a lot of that stuff, Craig. It remains to be seen whether I'm gonna do more of it."

When I leave for the city from the railway station, Elizabeth Evatt, Bert Evatt's niece, stays behind in the bare, shabby, darkened bungalow on top of the ridge at Leura. She is alone. Much as she was years ago at school, and later on, and now. It is cold. Mist is rising through the valleys and waterfalls and recommended walks of the Blue Mountains. She seems older than she is. She has buttoned her cardigan up a bit.

"I appreciate her singleness," says a close friend. "Good people get hit hard. She has no overwhelming passion to her — except her work. She's hopeful, intelligent, an idealist." There is a silence. "You know, I've only just realised what a great woman she is."

BOB HAWKE

1977

He drinks like a fish, swears like a trooper, works like a demon, performs like a playboy, talks like a truckie — and acts like a politician. Almost your cliché Aussie. Except in this case it's Bob Hawke, and the only typical thing about him is the way he's larger than average in almost everything. Bob Hawke is your typical Australian, oversize.

Hawke is in many ways the alternative Prime Minister of Australia. As the nation's top trade unionist he has been the man who has confronted Malcolm Fraser on all the major issues, attacked the government's policies, made the running on economic initiatives, and gained more media coverage than the rest of the Labor Party put together. It's an extraordinary performance for someone who, theoretically, isn't even a politician — yet. But, in fact, Hawke is running for the Prime Ministership as well as a seat in Parliament as the member for Wills; if Bill Hayden loses the 1980 election, as everyone expects, he will face a challenge from Hawke for the leadership of the Labor Party. Sooner or later, the Prime Minister, Malcolm Fraser, will face a similar challenge. Which is why we all need to know — *what's he really like?*

A few things first. Despite his TV image as a belligerent, confrontative, up-you-Jack union leader, Hawke is really a modedrate, a compromiser, a pragmatic wheeler-and-dealer who is distrusted by a lot of the union movement because he is too close to the bosses and too ready to make deals with them. HAWKE

STEPS IN is one of the commonest newspaper billboards around. When he does, the strike is usually soon over, the workers have gained a bit, and Joe Blow is happily back in his Holdy. Nothing is changed. Hawke's no radical. Those who think he is mistake the style for the substance.

Also, that glowering TV face is only half the man. Hawke is an extraordinarily warm, easygoing, open-hearted man whom most people respond to instantly. He attracts women, especially, like a sexual magnet. There's hardly any distance between his public and private selves; unlike most politicians, he reveals what he is and says what he thinks — and if you don't like it, to use one of his favourite expressions, "You can get fucked!"

He is aggressive, ambitious and highly competitive. He turns nasty when he's drunk. He relies heavily on his wife and kids for support, uses them, feels guilty, breaks down and cries in public. He can be emotional, compassionate and formidable all at the same time. He loves a brawl and likes to win; he can turn in a few hours from a suave persuader to a bitchy ogre. He's a bloody beaut.

What makes Bob Hawke run so hard? He's the son (born in 1929) of a Congregational minister, which means a poor but lower-middle-class background; his uncle was Albert Hawke, the former Labor premier of Western Australia, so he grew up in a Labor household. He went to Perth Modern School with Billy Snedden, did his own reading and thinking, became a socialist, and in his first year studying law at Perth University formed the first ALP Club there.

He gained his much publicised agnosticism when he went to India as a delegate to the World Conference of Christian Youth, and was appalled by the contrast between the wealth exhibited at the conference and the poverty which surrounded it. When he was 17 years old, a traumatic incident occurred: he was involved in a motorbike crash, ruptured his spleen and very nearly died. Lying in hospital on the critically ill list, Hawke decided to stop wasting his life. "It made me think a lot; it was like having a second time round. I knew I had a fair bit of talent and I thought, you're just bloody crazy if you don't use it to the full. And really from that time I've never stopped. I threw myself into everything, and I've done that ever since."

Hawke became a Rhodes scholar, went to Oxford, drank his way into the Guinness Book of Records by downing two pints of beer in twelve seconds, came back to the Australian National Unviersity to do a thesis on the basic wage, and was invited by the then ACTU president, Albert Monk, to become its research officer and industrial advocate. Hawke took off: he was a formidable advocate, won case after case before the Arbitration Commission and demolished John Kerr ("the Liberace of the law", Hawke called him) when he appeared for the employers. In 1969 he was the Centre Left candidate for the ACTU presidency, and won it.

And he's still running . . .

Thursday

10.30 a.m. Bob Hawke is sitting in his sparse, modern ACTU president's office above Bourke's, the cut-price store the unions bought in Melbourne. He's a surprisingly small, dapper bloke: gold watch, signet ring, stylish spectacles, rather a natty dresser, and that beautifully wavy, iron-grey hair. Appearances deceive. As everyone from Fraser down has learnt, Hawke can be as tough and bloody-minded as that heavily lined, scowling face would suggest. ("A little bloke?" says Hawke, when I ask him if he was bullied at school. "I'm fit-foot-ten-and-a-half, twelve-and-a-half stone; that's not so bloody small, is it?")

Hawke is listening to Parliament on a trannie. Phil Lynch is talking. "Wind him up, wind him up!" Hawke says, sneering. Bill Hayden asks a question, fatlers over the words. "Got a great voice, Bill," says Hawke. It's an ironic comment. Hawke once described Hayden as an "interim leader". He reckons he could handle the PM's job too. "It's a challenge I would enormously enjoy and hope I'd do well," he says. H'mmmnn.

Most of the time Hawke is honest to the point of rudeness; he has an abrasive, questioning style which has mellowed with the years, a quick brain, an extraordinary capacity for work and for summing up the intricacies of a situation — and a great sense of humour. Sometimes that leads people to dismiss him as a lightweight. But as his stand on the South African football tour showed, he has the courage to take an unpopular stand . . . and the tenacity to win it. He's a republican, and thinks Australia will have got rid of all the trappings of monarchy before the end of the century. He's interested in economics, trade and foreign affairs. When he takes a stand, he's usually thought about it beforehand and is likely to hold it to the point of dogmatism.

Yet some of his concerns, or lack of them, are disappointing. He doesn't talk much about Constitutional change, except to flog his ideas about non-elected Cabinet members. He tells everyone to forget about the dismissal of the Labor government, as though there's nothing to be learnt from it. A trade-union leader who knows him well says he's sidestepped reform of the ACTU: "Bob is a compromise." He's more of a performer (at which he is brilliant) than a policymaker; now, with the wage-price freeze and the settlement of an oil strike just behind him, no wonder he's looking tired.

There's a knock on the door and Bob Jolly, the ACTU's young industrial advocate, arrives with the Cost-Price Index figures for the latest quarter. "Two point three per cent," says Hawke, studying the figures carefully. He makes a point of never commenting on anything until he's read the full text. "Lower than everyone expected — including me. Food, clothing . . . rate of increase down. Recreation's up to buggery. Dunno what that means." The phone rings. Canberra. He chats about the CPI figures, then: "I must say, listening to Bill asking that question today, he comes across as a very bumbling sort of bloke . . ."

Already there are newspaper reports waiting in the office of his press secretary. The morning papers have been full of allegations of CIA influence in Australia. Hawke decides to meet all the media at 12.30 p.m. When he walks into the ACTU conference room, the place is jammed with TV cameras, lights, microphones, tape-recorders. "Where's the hot seat, over here?" quips Hawke, walking into the blinding glare of lights. There is a tense expectancy in the room, and if ever there was any doubt that Hawke is the alternative Prime Minister, the press conference quickly dispels it.

"I just want to mention one thing, off the record like, before we start: the states with the lowest increase in the CPI are the Labor states," Hawke says, grinning broadly. There's a chorus of comments from the interviewers; it's obvious they like him. "It's a stupid point, of course, so I certainly don't want to suggest anything to you . . ."

The first question is on the CIA. "I'll get my moustache," says Hawke. He argues that the Fraser government should get all the evidence it can and raise it with the US. What are the unions going to do?" "What would you like us to do? Declare war on the United States?" On the CPI figures, Hawke points out that the low rise has been associated with the full indexation of wages which Fraser has attacked. Is it true, asks the GTV 9 interviewer, that the Labor states had the lowest rise? "Thank you for that totally unexpected question," says Hawke, straightfaced, "Yes, it is true . . ."

Each of the TV news channels insists on its own interview. "This is where it gets boring. You keeping getting the same questions, and if you have any integrity you have to give the same answers," he explains between sessions. But he keeps at it, scoring points off Fraser and the government, ridiculing the claim that Labor Minister Street and not he had settled the recent oil dispute, cracking jokes about the Governor-General ("he didn't need the CIA; he had sufficient deficiencies of his own"), reiterating his call for a national conference on the freeze and tax cuts, scorning the Prime Minister's lack of response: "It's hard to believe the PM is capable of thinking rationally these days . . ."

Having to repeat everything he says, it would be tempting to turn it all into a charade; but Hawke remains serious, hunched over the table, frowning into the cameras, rubbing an eye ("I'm still a bit tired"), the beetling eyebrows and downturned mouth changing only when he makes a joke ("maybe Tony Street is breaking the guidelines!"), or when an interviewer stumbles into a spoonerism and asks him about "the CIA figures". Quick as a flash, Hawke launches into an equally bumble-footed parody:

"Yes, the CIA figures show a clear 2.3 per cent increase in activity," he pontificates. "We had expected a much greater infiltration, especially in the Labor states." The pressmen are in hysterics, Hawke is grinning, the cameramen get it down for a laugh, and when it's all over there's almost a cheer. Hawke jumps to his feet, the lights flicker out. "Let's have lunch," he says.

An hour later, in the Legend restaurant in Lonsdale Street, Bob Hawke is into his second Irish coffee, his second Havana cigar, and his first confession that he's changed. He used to be a radical, yes; but now he's a consensus politician. "I don't think in Australia we are going to be able to dramatically change things," he says. "We are a very conservative country. And you have to move within the constraints of what the nation's economic performance will allow. Whatever a future Labor government may achieve, it will live or die according to its economic performance. I've got no doubt about that. We need an economic plan: we're going to have to see some industries built up, others decline, and we have to plan for jobs to be moved from one industry to another. It's the haphazard way we go about things that worries me."

Hawke thinks he could preside over that process very well. He's proved he can consult with industry, and the employers, and obtain agreement. (Everyone agrees Hawke is in his element as a negotiator; he doesn't mind giving something away to gain something else; as you'd expect of a moderate, he's a great moderator.) "I communicate with the public; even though they may disagree with me, they believe me," he says. "Politics is doing things, and making people understand what you are doing, and why." Does that mean he believes the conventional wisdom that Whitlam moved "too far, too fast"? "No, that's all bullshit!" says Hawke. "It reinforces the conservative mythology. But they were too obsessed with all the bastardry of twenty-three years to communicate what they were doing; they just went hell for leather. I wouldn't make that mistake."

In promoting himself as an economic manager, Hawke points to his membership of the Reserve Bank board and his role on the Jackson committee on manufacturing industry. He thinks a society which can't provide jobs for its young people, condones poverty and won't redistribute its wealth to the poorer nations is under threat from "the dispensers of magic on the extreme left and the extreme right". Says Hawke: "If you have a troubled society, and ours is a troubled society, and you can't provide employment for the young, you are going to get an audience for quick, easy prescriptions." Whereas he believes in Parliamentary democracy, and a system in which "I can call an elected, conservative Prime Minister a bastard and stay free."

It's all conventional stuff — and a funny, trivial definition of freedom. He could be a small "l" Liberal speaking. A few years ago he would have argued for more public ownership of industry, now he's retreated from that. There are more "enlightened capitalists" around now. He has no ideas about the media, or how to free it up; you have to remind him about access radio and public TV and video and other standard countervailing techniques.

In fact, though Hawke prides himself on being an intellectual, he hasn't many real ideas or policies. He hasn't read much contemporary political theory. He admits he's not an innovator — he tends to react to issues as they arise, rather than create them ("I'm not an issue-digger"). Compared to Whitlam, who was an initiator, he is a counter-puncher, Laurel to Gough's Hardy, almost the advocate (he's the best the trade-union movement has ever had, or likely to have), not the thinker. On many issues he's surprisingly shallow; in Parliament he would need the help of a good Cabinet.

3.30 p.m. The business crowd in the Legend has begun to thin out. Hawke is trying to remember how much he earns; $24,000 from the ACTU, plus $5000 or $6000 from the Reserve Bank. His mother gave him some shares, but he sold those; he doesn't own any land, or a weekender, and doesn't speculate. But he gambles heavily on the horses, and boasts he lives off his winnings: "I bank my salary every week." He lives in a big old house at seaside Sandringham with its own sauna, swimming pool and tennis court — he's a keen tennis player, and a good one. And he sent his three teenage children (Susan, Steve and Rosslyn) to wealthy private schools.

There's some hypocrisy there. But Hawke explains that he moved to Sandringham years ago, just to be beside the sea, and that he deliberately refused to subject his kids to the "decrepit, bloody awful" Victorian state school system. Hawke wears his affluence lightly, shrugs off criticism of it, and just doesn't have time for any superficial display.

More worrying is what his success has done to his political stance. "Sure, there's been a change," he says. "I don't deny that. Twenty years ago I'd have said we know we're right, Labor knows the answers, we're going to impose them. Now . . ." Hawke calls for another cigar. "Now I think you have to get some understanding, some agreement in the community. Things have changed. It all sounds a bit banal . . ." selecting a large, gold-banded cigar from the tuxedo-suited waiter. "No one goes to sleep at night thinking that anyone is poverty-stricken. Look at how it used to be. Thanks very much, waiter. Terrible bloody . . ." lighting the cigar . . . "misery and . . ." puff-puff . . . "poverty . . ." puff-puff. "It's crazy. Our society is one where we needn't have one single human being . . ." speaking with the cigar clenched between his teeth . . . "who is hungry or cold. And if that meant me paying another one or two per cent in tax on my income, then we should do it."

But his current policy is to reduce taxes. Well . . . you have to take notice of the current economic climate. Also, he would have other objectives as a leader: like turning the Public Service into a real community service, instead of it being a private service to a Minister; planning the future of the economy; and he'd like to get "a great community debate going about education, so it became education for life instead of training for a clerk's desk or the factory floor".

Silence.

"I don't know what else I'm supposed to do."

Back at his office. Hawke plunges into paperwork. He doesn't like it, and a common criticism of him is that he isn't much good at administration; he tends to skimp his homework, or appoint offsiders whom he leaves to carry the burden. At least that leaves Hawke free to pursue his one-man-band style of operation.

The air controllers have decided on a twelve-hour strike. "Where's that note, Jean?" Hawke shouts at his administrative assistant, Jean Sinclair. Transport Minister Peter Nixon has been threatening the controllers, and Hawke's afraid it will provoke them to extend the strike — "which is just what those fucking bastards in Canberra want!" The phone rings. Sydney. "G'day. What's the score?"

6.15 p.m. Hawke dances down the stairs of Bourke's to his waiting Ford LTD and driver; he's due to appear on Channel 9's *A*

Current Affair in half an hour, and at a dinner of the Central Industrial Secretariat of National Employers afterwards. Gerald Stone has been attacking Hawke for refusing to co-operate in Fraser's wage-price freeze, and interviewing factory workers to prove the ACTU boss is out of step. Hawke bounces into Channel 9, lies back in the makeup chair, makes it on to the sound stage with a minute to spare. He's feeling good. He cracks a few jokes with Kate Baillieu, the program's anchorwoman, issues a challenge to Channel 9, and soon has Gerald Stone rocking back on his heels: "Just a minute, Gerald, I'm not in the habit of making deceptions." In a mini-repetition of what he did nationally, a week before, Hawke manages to turn the argument right around. A film clip of workers in a factory where the implications of the freeze have been explained produces an overwhelming pro-Hawke result: sixty-seven against the freeze, one doubtful.

Stone doesn't give up easily. He's organised a national phone-in on the freeze. Hawke agrees to help poll the answers, and for the next five hours answers phones in Channel 9's newsroom. Five hours! "*Hu-llo!* Yes, this is Bob Hawke. You're against the freeze? Good on yer! *Hu-llo?* You're for it? That's fair enough. *Hu-llo*. You're for a prices freeze? But that isn't the question, madam! It's a freeze on wages and prices . . ."

The telephone calls begin to go against Hawke. Most of them say they want a *prices* freeze. "Bloody eye-opener, this!" says Hawke, exasperatedly. The phones are ringing, one call every ten seconds. Someone hands Hawke a printed message:

THIS JEW HAWKE IS THE MOST TROUBLE-MAKER IN AUSTRALIA. HE SHOULD BE GOING BACK TO ISRAEL. FROM WHO SET THIS JEW HAWKE HIS COMMUNIST INSTRUCTIONS. WE THINK FROM RUSSIA!! BE CAREFUL MR JEW HAWKE NOT TO MUCH!

OBSERVER

Hawke shrugs it off, keeps his good humour. He gets a lot of hate mail. He's had his life threatened, and once he broke down in tears in an ACTU conference because of a death threat to his family. His family background is Cornish, not Jewish, he says, and though he has some good friends in the Jewish business community, it wasn't until he visited Israel after the Yom Kippur war that he became so passionately pro-Israeli.

The phones keep ringing. Hawke keeps answering, munching chips, joking and laughing, quipping about Gerald Stone's American accent, agreeing down the mouthpiece that "Bob Hawke should *not* run the country". The employers' dinner has been forgotten. After three hours I leave him to it. He's got Kate Baillieu in one hand, a beer in the other. Goodnight, Bob.

Friday

If ever there was a revealing day in the life of Bob Hawke, alternative Prime Minister, this is it. He starts off bright, optimistic and sober, and ends . . .

Hawke's in a natty light-grey check suit, spectacles and smiles. He's recuperated from the night before, is back into union discussions, paperwork, routine. Physically he's a resilient bloke, though he sometimes pushes himself so hard he breaks down; he loves fishing, tennis, getting out into the bush, and spends occasional weekends on a Gippsland farm owned by a doctor friend. He can even do one-arm pushups. But he's got a bad back, which he has treated by a Chinese acupuncturist. There seems to be a cycle to his behaviour: long boring spells which suddenly erupt into crises (like the wage-price freeze and the oil-tanker drivers' strike, which followed one after the other) when Hawke works day and night at a frenetic pace, overstrains himself — collapses back on to his wife and family to recuperate.

At lunch he's due to address the Farm Writers' and Broadcasters' Society. An assistant has written a speech, but Hawke decides to talk off the cuff. In the Sheraton Motor Inn banquet hall he takes his seat at the head table, and is somewhat surprised to find himself confronted with an opened bottle of beer in an ice bucket: "Your reputation has preceded you," they explain, kindly. Hawke drinks the wine.

He's introduced as "the Supremo of the ACTU" which gives him a chance to explain he was born in Bordertown on the South Australian and Victorian border, and how some left-wing trade unionists say "the bastard has been sitting on the fence ever since!" The audience, which is fairly conservative and could have been hostile, roars with laughter. Within five minutes Hawke has them eating out of his hand. "The trouble with Australia," he says, "is it's being run by five farmers and a sheep. Mr Fraser's a farmer, Mr Anthony's a farmer, Mr Nixon's a farmer, Mr Sinclair's a farmer, my little friend Tony Street is a farmer, and of course you know who the sheep is — Mr Lynch!"

He uses the lunch to call for a round-table conference between the ACTU, rural workers and all rural organisations, to see if they can't get rid of their traditional distrust of each other. (Next day it gets a good press: Hawke Calls for Burial of Hatchet.) He admits there are far too many unions, criticises demarcation disputes, but attacks the government's anti-union legislation as a "bash, bash, bash" approach designed to divert attention from the economy and make the unions the villains.

Afterwards he answers questions. He is reasonable, persuasive and very, very impressive. Political strikes? "I can understand your position, and why you take it, but trade unions are not here just to fight for better wages and conditions." High tariff walls? "To be honest with you, Jim, a policy of Australia First, Last and Forever is a recipe for disaster." How can he wear two hats at once, as president of the ACTU and (at the time) chairman of the Labor Party? Hawke quotes an American senator, and brings the house down: *"Look, if you can't ride two horses, you shouldn't be in the bloody circus!"*

In the formal vote of thanks the speaker thanks Hawke "for giving us the petrol to get here," but adds "I hate your bloody guts for the air controllers' strike . . ."

"NOT AFFILIATED!" shouts Hawke. And when the speaker wonders if the rural unions will attend the conference, Hawke interrupts again:

"I'M NOT A DICTATOR, BUT THEY'LL ATTEND!"

Afterwards people crowd around him. He is friendly, patient and absolutely unaffected, answering each question in turn. Hawke is one of the most gregarious men I have ever met. He has a naturally outgoing personality, calls everyone by their first name, hasn't got it all down to some phony style; in a politician, it's refreshing. Most people he meets like him. Especially women — and Hawke has a reputation as a great womaniser.

"Mr Hawke! Can I touch you? Are you human?" She is a pert, confident public-relations girl in a bosomy sweater, and she is running her hands over Hawke's chest, feeling him. "Who do you write for?" asks Hawke, smiling. "I'm just an ordinary citizen," she says, "and I can't believe you're *real* . . .!" Hawke chats her up, retreats to the LTD, then suddenly decides to call in at the Windsor Hotel to check on an ACTU function which will be held there in a couple of days. As he steps on to the footpath from the car, a pleasant-looking middle-aged woman swivels on her heels, rushes up, and gives him a big hug. "Bob!" she says. "I just wanted to tell you, I thought you were *marvellous* last night. You keep it up, Bob, keep giving it to them." Hawke, smiling, disentangles himself. "Who was that?" I ask. "Never saw her before in my life," says Hawke.

He strides through the main hallway of the Windsor, and as he does people call out to him, rush up and shake his hand, congratulate him on settling the petrol strike. The Carbine Club, a Melbourne sporting club, is just getting up from lunch and Hawke seems to know a fair number of them — including Ron Barassi, the Great Barassi of Aussie Rules, now coach for North Melbourne. Barassi comes up, hits Hawke on the shoulder, and they stand laughing and shouting at each other. "G'day fuckface," says Hawke.

But before Barassi can say anything in reply, an elegantly dressed woman in huge, fashionable sunglasses whom I had noticed walking into the lift walks out of the lift again, throws her arms around Hawke, and gives him a warm, sensuous kiss. "I adore you," she says. "I just couldn't believe it was *you*." The Great Barassi backs off enviously. "By Christ," says Hawke, "there's some bloody hope for Australia when women prefer politicians to footballers!" Barassi himself is a strong, handsome man with a rake's moustache. It's an instructive comparison of the power of sex appeal, and the sex appeal of power.

Suddenly a tall sportsman comes up behind Hawke, pinions him, and lifts him clean off the carpet. "Who the bloody hell is trying to fuck me?" says Hawke. It's another footballer. Hawke is a South Melbourne supporter, first name in the club. They all go to the Cricketers' Bar for a beer. The barmaid spots Barassi, demands an autograph. Hawke gives him his invitation card to the Central Industrial Secretariat dinner. "Ah, bloody Commo mob!" shouts Barassi, who's a Liberal supporter. "You dumb bastard, can't you read?" says Hawke. "It's the bloody bosses — your mob!" Score, Hawke 1, Barrasi 0. Barassi turns the card over, notices a name scribbled on the back, guffaws and demands a proper autograph book. Score, one all. Then the barmaid recognises Hawke, and wants his autograph too. Hawke signs above Barassi's signature, adding, ALWAYS ABOVE BARASSI. Score, Hawke 2, Barassi 1. But when Barassi notices, he grabs the book back and scribbles, WHAT ELSE WOULD YOU EXPECT OF A POOF? Score, 2 all. They stand opposite each other like a pair of gamecocks, Hawke with his feet apart, legs bent, shoulders slightly hunched like a bantamweight prizefighter, Barassi bigger and more athletic, smacking one hand into the other. They're a good match, slinging jibes at each other. But when Barassi disappears to say hullo to a birthday-party admirer, Hawke grabs the autograph book, scribbles a final comment, slams it shut. "I can beat the big bugger in anything but football," he says.

Half a dozen drinks later Hawke starts to leave. Throughout it all it's become obvious just how popular, how widely admired, Hawke is; he is the focus of a great deal of affection right across the spectrum: men, women, workers, sportsmen, businessmen. It buoys him up, even exhilarates him, but he remains easygoing, serious, arguing or defending himself when necessary.

Just as he reaches the door, however, Hawke runs into George Polites, director of the Employers' Secretariat, an old adversary and a good friend. George grabs Hawke's arm and drags him protesting back to the bar. George wants to have a sing-song; Hawke suggests "Keep the Red Flag Flying"; they compromise with an old parody of the "International":

> *The working class*
> *Can kiss my arse,*
> *I've got the foreman's*
> *Job at last . . .*

When finally Hawke gets out of the bar, the five-minute visit has taken a couple of hours. When I remark on the whole extraordinary sequence, Hawke replies, "You only get that if you've done all the hard work beforehand. That's just the icing on the cake. I couldn't stand it if it was all the time."

Back in his office Cliff Dolan, secretary of the Electrical Trades Union, is on the phone. Troubles. "It's a hard year, my son," says Hawke. More calls. The air controllers have voted to limit their strike to twelve hours. "By Christ, it was close, though," says Hawke. "Bloody Nixon, stirring it up."

There's a telegram for him, too. From Sir John Dunlop, former head of CSR. It describes Hawke's question on the freeze posed to viewers of *A Current Affair* as "emotive and unworthy", and accuses Hawke himself of being a demagogue. "Get him on the phone," Hawke says into the intercom. Laurie Oakes, political correspondent for the Melbourne *Sun*, is on the other line; did Hawke ever stay at the home of a US labour attaché who has now been revealed as a CIA agent? Hawke starts to deny it, thinks better of it, and says he may have stayed with him overnight in Washington once. "If he's in the CIA, it's news to me," Hawke growls down the mouthpiece. "I never knew him as anything other than a labour attaché."

Hawke is getting tired. He's still taking drugs for a virus infection. And the grog is taking effect. He looks pale, washed out. Fifteen minutes later, when I come back to ask yet another question, the president of the Australian Council of Trade Unions, Robert James Lee Hawke, is asleep. At his desk. Head in hand. Elbow on chair. Mouth open. His face is creased like a crumpled ball of paper, unravelled.

6 p.m. Hawke is on his feet again, lively, ready for his evening engagements. He's driven to Prahran to a Chinese restaurant and has a hasty bowl of fried rice with his wife, Hazel, some friends and Ken Davidson, economics writer for the *Age*, whom he is to join at 8.00 p.m. in a symposium on unemployment at the Prahran College of Advanced Education. But first he has to put in a return appearance on *A Current Affair*.

The phone-in has resulted in a three-to-one rebuff to Hawke's stand on the freeze. Hawke stares into the TV camera and tries to defend himself by arguing that people didn't understand the question (which they didn't) and that, strangely, some people had begun ringing up *before* the program came on. Gerald Stone needles Hawke, demanding to know if he is accusing Channel 9 of rigging the program. Hawke, for once, comes close to losing his temper, and threatens Stone that he is close to defamation. The sweat stands out through his makeup. The TV monitor closes in on Hawke's glowering, pugnacious face. In the studio people are holding their breath. Kate Baillieu is worried, jittery. Gerald Stone is six hundred miles away, safe in Sydney; Hawke is arguing with a monitor screen. The moment passes, and the program ends with a friendly Keystone Cops film clip of Hawke answering phones. But there are bad vibes all around, and even a quick drink with the Channel 9 hierarchy and program staff doesn't dispel them. On the way to Prahran, Hawke is silent, depressed.

The symposium is worse. Because of the Windsor Hotel diversion, Hawke hasn't had time to prepare his speech: he talks slowly, badly, without any of his usual verve. When there is a question about the need to share unemployment right through the community, because technology makes high unemployment a permanent feature of modern capitalism, Hawke doesn't understand it. And though he maintains he is still making up his mind about uranium, he admits his "personal view" is that Australia should export its uranium. When the predominantly young audience hisses, Hawke sneers at them. He is full of hostility. You realise suddenly he is an ageing man, a compromiser and proud of it. The trouble with "going through the mill" — Hawke's phrase — is you emerge damaged on the other side.

The questions and Hawke run down together. He and a few others repair to the principal's office for drinks. Hawke slumps into a chair, puts his legs up on a woman's lap, gulps at a whisky. There are a few young people there, including his daughter; they start arguing with him about uranium. As the night wears on, Hawke gets more and more belligerent and drunker and drunker. He starts shouting, swearing, hurling abuse at anyone who disagrees with him. He is a bellicose, maudlin, spiteful drunk, beyond reach of reason. It's a shock to see him in such a state. If the morning showed Hawke at his most lucid, and the afternoon showed him in full grandiloquent flight, this was Hawke at his worst. Two hours after midnight, he is dead to the world.

"We're worried about him," says a friend. Says another, "We've been telling him for twenty years to conserve himself." Someone who works with Hawke thinks he drinks out of sheer frustration, at being unable to do everything he has set himself. There is no doubt that Hawke, a minister's son, sets himself high ambitions and judges himself harshly. He's pessimistic about man's ultimate fate, about atomic weaponry, about terrorism. Perhaps the most perceptive summation came from someone who admires him: "Bob's sacrificed himself, and his family, to his causes. There's a fair pressure of guilt there. That's why he can be so maudlin."

It's not as though Hawke hasn't got himself together; in fact, he comes across as a remarkably confident, well-integrated personality. But he spends less than a third of the year at home, he's missed out on a lot of his kids' growing-up, he plays up, and I get the feeling he sometimes doesn't like himself for what he does. "It's been a necessary price to pay," says Hawke, briefly.

Saturday

Hawke gets up late, feeds the Siamese cats, trots around his Sandringham home in a batik kimono. He's recovered — almost. He's decided to spend the day pottering about at home, placing bets: "Big win at the races today — I can see it coming up!" The telephone has already started ringing: GMH, for Christ's sake, has decided to stand down its workers for a week. In between Hawke manages to call a few mates, discusses the Moonee Valley form. With one of them he goes into his Jewish act. To another: "If I went out to the track today, I'd just get earbashed the whole time."

Despite the night before, he is as funny and friendly as ever.

OK, so why does he come on so strong? "It's a world in which strength is required," says Hawke. "This stuff about the meek inheriting the earth is a lot of bullshit. The weak need the strong to look after 'em."

What are his main qualities? "Scepticism, probably. I'm not prepared to accept anything on its face value. And I've got a concern about whether people get a fair go or not. No, I'm not driven by any passionate sense of injustice to myself. But I'm concerned about others."

Anything else? "I suppose I'm a funny sort of mixture of toughness and softness. You've got to be hard in the job I'm in. But I'm a soft touch for anyone, really. I tend to say yes rather than no. And for some reason I cry easily." Hawke scratches his bare balls reflectively. "I suppose I must be emotional."

Why did he cool the trade-union movement down after the Kerr coup? "My judgment was that it couldn't be done; mobs in the street, protests — it wouldn't work. I'm not even sure that I would have done it even if it would have worked." Why not? "The processes of democracy were underway; we were having an election. I don't indulge in the luxury of what if, if, if . . ."

What's his assessment of Fraser? "He's a man of moderate intellectual equipment — that's a kind way of putting it — who has an inflated idea of his own capacity for sound judgment. And that leads him intuo dogmatism and intransigence. Up until this last meeting I'd found it almost interesting talking to him; but he seems to have made a decision for confrontation. It's eyeball-to-eyeball stuff now."

Will he last? "He's started to go bad; that's why he needs the unions as a diversion. He's a desperate man."

Will Robert Hawke stick to his promise to give up booze if he becomes Prime Minister? "Hell, Craig, I might give it up before then!" He goes to the refrigerator. "Hazel, where's the orange juice?"

So that's Bob Hawke. For all his faults, and contradictions, and massive blind spots, there's a warmth and integrity about him which appeals to people. If charisma means anything, I suppose it means that. He is now, according to the Morgan Gallup polls, the most popular political leader in Australia. "He's got more conservative as he's got older — like everyone else," says a plumber I know. "My mates have a bit of a go at him. But he's the best bloke we've got."

The best bloke we've got? Driving along the cold grey rim of Port Phillip Bay, I suddenly thought, of all people, of Nikita Kruschchev: swearing, farting, telling jokes, getting drunk, the peasant-politician come to scandalise the Praesidium, a United Nations shoe in one hand and a threat in the other, and everyone standing around with a bemused, begrudging look of admiration on their faces, shaking their heads: *what a man, what can you DO with him . . .?* It's a funny comparison, half-right.

No country in the world but Australia could produce a leader like Bob Hawke. In a way he sums up the best, and the worst, of us. For that reason alone, if no other, he could make a great Prime Minister. Looks like we may soon know.

1983

It is one of those smokey, heat-hazy days you get in Canberra in summer: the hills around this improbable city are smudged blue-grey with smoke, the Molonglo shimmers, the bitumen shines. Bushfires have been burning down near Burrinjuck; it is ten days before the worst bushfires in Australian history are to burn across Victoria and South Australia, but there is a smell and taste of smoke in the air. It could be a city after a bombing raid, except it is too peaceful for that. The taxi wheels hum along the border of the lake. Ahead, the white, old-fashioned citadel of Parliament House remains intact. Unlike Chile, there has been no revolution.

On the twin glass doors outside the room of Her Majesty's Parliamentary Opposition is a lopsided sign which reads: CAUCUS MEETING. TODAY 10.30 A.M. It is 8 February 1983. There is to be a national election in exactly twenty-five days' time. Behind the closed doors, the Parliamentary Labor Party (caucus) is meeting to choose someone to lead it into the election. Nobody doubts who it will be.

One floor up, in the press gallery, and on the stairs leading up to it, teams of photographers and camera crews are waiting for the result, but the caucus meeting is expected to take some time and the green-carpeted corridor outside the caucus meeting room is strangely deserted. I sit down on a settee as green as the carpet, just outside the chamber of the House of Representatives. Parliament House, when the politicians aren't sitting, is like some gigantic democratic funeral parlour: there is a palpable hush and everyone seems to talk in whispers.

Bursts of applause come from behind the closed doors. Something is happening. But before we can find out what it is, Hazel Hawke, Bob Hawke's wife, strolls in carrying a briefcase which is obviously not hers and a freshly laundered suit labelled BOB

HAWKE. Last night she had allowed herself to be interviewed on the ABC's *Nationwide*; although she has avoided publicity in the past, it was a good interview, one which elicited her warmth and integrity. Now she is looking for her husband, who is still in the caucus meeting. She wants to get rid of his briefcase and suit, symbols of power to be, and thinks of leaving it in Bill Hayden's room, but I suggest not. At that very moment the official leader of the Opposition's room is a scene of frantic and desolate activity. His staff are ripping files open, throwing documents into wastepaper baskets, packing other papers into cardboard removalists' cartons which are piled up outside the door. 'All this stuff is for Ipswich,' says one of his staff. Hayden has been through it before, on 11 November 1975, when Sir John Kerr dismissed the Labor government; there is the same sense of frantic, despairing abandonment now. There are random piles of paper on the floor, desks and open filing cabinets everywhere; it looks as though it's been ransacked.

"They chopped his legs off," a former Whitlam Minister had told me earlier, talking of Hayden. "A lot of us are very angry. I only hope it doesn't blow up in caucus."

Hazel Hawke changes her mind and trudges on down the gloomy corridor to Hawke's room, tucked away one floor up at the end of the new wing of Parliament House. "I can never find Bob's room," she says, peering at the room numbers. I remind her that it won't be his room for much longer; maybe half an hour. She stops. "Of course," she says quietly. "I keep forgetting."

Back in the corridor outside the caucus room everything is quiet. Suddenly the door opens and Bill Hayden comes out. He walks quickly down to the leader of the Opposition's room, turns inside. Everyone stops packing. All his staff — there seem to be almost a dozen — rise silently to their feet and stare at Bill: Nick Nagle, Alan Ramsey, Louise Holgate. They look tense and deeply troubled, as though afraid of what he might do; the atmosphere is charged with pathos. Hayden, as brave and courteous as ever, nods to them all, walks into his private room, and closes the door. Above it is a brave red sticker: GIVE BILL THE TOP JOB. Whose task in Hawke's entourage, I wonder, will it be to tear that down?

"A Hayden government would have been dangerous to established interests," a Labor politician had told me earlier. "It would have changed things. They had to get rid of him." Labor paranoia?

The caucus meeting drags on. Then Les Johnson, the balding, silver-haired Hermes of the ALP, who delivers all the news, good and bad, comes out and announces to the waiting media that Bob Hawke has been elected, unopposed, to the leadership of the Australian Labor Party.

It's an anti-climax. Nobody rushes to the phones. Since the Thursday before, when Hayden announced he was stepping down from the leadership, nobody had expected any other result. For the last four days Hawke has been acting as leader of the party, giving press conferences, announcing his plans, defining his policy directions. Johnson tells the reporters that Hayden has been elected to the executive and will be shadow Foreign Minister. Lionel Bowen, who held the post before, will become shadow Minister for Trade and will remain deputy leader of the party. Stewart West has Finance. Mick Young has added Employment and Youth Affairs to Immigration.

Finally, just before midday, the caucus meeting ends. Members of the Labor Party drift out like Brown's cows. Hawke stays behind to have his photograph taken with a few of them. There is a glimpse of the familiar, natty figure, the head of immaculate hair. At last, when the room is almost empty, Hawke appears in the doorway, for the first time, as the duly elected leader of the Labor Party. He is wearing a plain dark blue suit, patterned red tie, white shirt and a winning smile.

I hesitate, step forward, shake his hand. 'Congratulations.' Hawke grins, friendly as ever. Next to shake his hand is Blanche d'Alpuget, his official biographer. Then Alan Reid, the grand old man of the press gallery. Maximilian Walsh. The TV cameras spin and glitter from the press gallery stairs. Hawke turns and walks, alone, along the corridor to the room where Hazel is waiting. He has now achieved the leadership of the Australian Labor Party. Next, the Prime Ministership of Australia?

Half an hour later, Robert James Lee Hawke did what he does better than any other man in Australian history: he gave a press conference. Like all such occasions, it was a spectacular affair; a press conference by Hawke isn't just a *conference*, it's a media extravaganza, a glamourfest, a promotional wonder like those MGM spectaculars of old, in which Hawke plays King to his adoring court, fences and jibes with his carping Lords, puts down the media Fool, works himself up into a lather of anger at The Enemy Outside, and finally sends his audience home, as after an Aristotelian tragedy, exhausted, admiring, and experiencing the exquisite pleasure of catharsis. They were all there: the banks of TV cameras, with their numerological symbols displayed like the mystic signs of some occult society, the radio interviewers with their bulky Japanese recorders and proboscis microphones, the reporters with their mini-machines (hardly anyone relies on the old hand-held biro and notebook any longer, this is not linear time, this is techno-audio-visuality time we are dealing with), Blanche d'Apulget in her beach sunglasses and on her way to Jerusalem where she is setting her next book, fiction, love, though she *is* rewriting the last chapter of her *Robert J. Hawke: a biography* if he wins the election ("the more pressure he's under, the better he is," she says with the certitude of one who really knows, "just watch his hands!"); Richard Carleton, tieless, tousled, safari-shirted, whom Hawke tore to shreds on *Nationwide* on the night Hayden resigned and who now looks unaccustomedly ruffled; Alan Reid, slumped at one of the tables arranged in a huge U around the empty chair which, resplendent under the arc lights and TV spots, sits at the end of the room like a vacant throne ("G'day, comrade," says Alan when I sit down next to him; he's old now, but I remember him from when he used to slouch around the press gallery in riding boots and bushman's hat, a roll-your-own smoke dropping from the corner of his mouth, a battered Land Rover parked outside Parliament House steps — if he'd been the Green Dragon, he'd have been booked for overacting); Maximilian Walsh, former editor of the *Australian Financial Review*, now TV personality and Grey-Haired Gallery Guru; all the heads of the gallery services, correspondents, reporters, lobbyists, cadets, commentators, at least a hundred in all, talking, bustling, chattering like lorrikeets, awaiting the arrival of the New King. This is exactly what Versailles must have been like.

You can tell when Hawke is coming because the TV cameras

near the door switch on their lights. Everyone turns, falls silent. Hawke strides through the door, thrusts his way up to the vacant chair, sits down. The lights blaze. He is going to read a statement and then invite questions. The familiar raspy voice begins:

"I am deeply honoured to have been elected today as leader of the federal Parliamentary Labor Party.

"The sole task now before the party is the defeat of the Fraser government.

"In taking on the task of leading the Australian Labor Party in this critical election, I must pay tribute to Bill Hayden. He has acted with great courage and dignity in putting the interests of the party ahead of any personal considerations.

"The Australian Labor Party is united and determined to form a government which will heal the division and confrontation of the last seven years under this Prime Minister and, with a sense of common national purpose, begin the path to economic recovery.

"Any questions?"

For a moment the press gallery, stunned by the confidence and utter panache with which Hawke has delivered his statement, is silent. "No questions?" says Hawke. He allows himself, for the first time since striding into the room, a faint grin and makes as if to get up and go.

It's a joke, a lovely feint; everyone laughs. The questions start to pour in: "Mr Hawke! Mr Hawke! Mr Hawke, sir!" The first question is about punitive clauses in the arbitration system and Malcolm Fraser's controversial Industrial Relations Bureau; what will he do about them? Hawke's reply is unequivocal: "Clearly, the IRB will go. You'll remember that in one of his more whimsical moments Billy Snedden, when he was leader of the Opposition, appointed Malcolm Fraser as shadow Minister for Industrial Relations *(laughter);* one of the first things that will happen under my government . . ."

And on it goes: more questions, Hawke promising a referendum for a fixed four-year term of Parliament, withdrawal of Australian troops from the Middle East peacekeeping force, a resources rental tax on mining companies, the references to "my government" and "I will" becoming more constant and rolling more and more easily off the lips; rebuking a questioner who asks about his stance if he is in opposition with, 'Let's talk about what's going to happen!'; swivelling around in his chair to face questioners, pulling the skin beneath his left ear, talking fast and furiously most of the time, then slowing down to exchange quips and jokes with his audience. What's going to happen to John Stone, head of Treasury and ironclad monetary conservative? "Ah, my old schoolmate!" replies Hawke, grinning. Maximilian Walsh, perched high on a dais above the milling throng, asks about the double dissolution correspondence with the Governor-General. "Ah, the pulpit! the pulpit!" shouts Hawke, in mock genuflection, and goes on to reaffirm that even though he regards the electiorn Fraser has called as contrived and opportunistic, the Labor Party's stance is that the Governor-General *must* obey the advice of his Prime Minister (no more Kerr-style dismissals, especially of Bob Hawke). What will he do with top public servants who may be opposed to Labor politics? "I will say to them, you will be aware there has been a change of goernment *(laughter)*, and a change of policies . . . I don't want sycophants . . . but if you cannot in all honesty put these policies into practice, then you go."

By the end of it all the audience is won over; Hawke has captivated them yet again, whether through humour, or directness, or sheer force of personality, and has demonstrated for all to see the qualities which have made him so popular. A few questioners persist; Hawke demurs, explains he has to "save a few bullets" for the policy speech, and walks towards the door. He exudes confidence, and is so immaculate in dress and demeanour he seems to positively glisten. A flash of blue suit and hair-halo and he is gone.

"They ought to give him the Prime Ministership right now," says a press gallery man next to me. "They might as well," says another. I'm reminded of what Mungo MacCallum, the Canberra columnist had said to me when I arrived in Kings Hall early that morning:

"What are you doing here? Come to see King Hawke ride up the steps of Parliament House on an elephant?"

Just about.

Later that day, outside the House, I ran into Bill Hayden. We walked down the steps together, Hayden quick, nervous, greyer at the temples than when I had seen him last, dressed in an unfashionable fawn Queensland suit. "I can't find my car," he said, smiling in his wry, self-deprecating way. I couldn't think of what to say: sympathise? joke? tell him that he brought the Labor Party to the brink of victory, and that's enough? Hayden solved it for me. "You'd think you'd have something left . . ." he said.

He walked on down the steps, coat flapping open, turning his head left and right. The last I saw of him, he was a dwindling figure at the end of the carpark, alone in a blaze of Canberra asphalt, walking away from the Elephant House.

1990

The rest, as they say, is history. Bob Hawke won the 1983 election, and the 1984 election, and the 1987 election, and in 1990 became the first Labor Prime Minister to win four elections in a row and the longest serving Labor Prime Minister ever.

You could speculate that, for all his faults, Hawke has achieved two remarkable things for Australian politics: he got rid of Malcolm Fraser when Fraser seemed set to become another Menzies in our nation's history; and he enabled Australia to resist the tide of Right-wing economic and political conservatism which swamped so many other Western democracies in the 1980s. During the age of Reagan and Thatcher, Australia had a Labor government. It still has.

Hawke resisted the tide, of course, partly by giving in to it. He presided over a government which moved the ALP decisively to the Right, deregulated the financial system, moved close to big business and almost gave up on the party's traditional reformist agenda. Hawke pursued the middle class vote so avidly and took such a conservative stance on issues from uranium mining to privatisation to the ANZUS alliance that it was sometimes impossible to distinguish the ALP from the Opposition. Yet he proved to be such a consummate leader of the party that he was able to hold the warring factions together and, using his habitual give-and-take methods, obtain a consensus which enabled the ALP to hold on to power under the most unlikely circumstances. The 1987 election was probably the crucial one; it is sometimes hard to remember that it was a time when Howard was riding high, the Joh-for Canberra push was a serious political move, racism was on the agenda, Reaganism ruled and it was the New Right which seemed to have the answers. Without Hawke's personal popularity Labor would have gone the way of so many other Western social democratic parties and Australia would have faced a prolonged period of ultra-Right government. Instead the ALP was able to proceed, as it had since 1983, with a limited series of progressive programs: Medicare, the Accord, support for women's issues, more school and child-care places, a fairer tax system and a slow but important expansion of social welfare.

As for Hawke himself: as he has worked his way through his Prime Ministership he has become thinner, frailer, more controlled, honed down to the pursuit of the one thing that always meant more to him than anything else — success. For its sake he has given up drinking, and cigars, and even, perhaps, women (though he tearfully confessed to adultery on national TV). The gruelling personal and political ordeals he has gone through have changed the legendary lair/punter/drinker/player/good mate/extrovert of yesteryear; he's got sterner, greyer, more lined about the face. He doesn't smile as much as he used to.

To some, Bob Hawke is the Great Betrayer. He is certainly the most conservative federal leader the ALP has ever had. He doesn't see any need for profound changes in Australian society; he has virtually no reformist agenda except the economic one. In Hawke, the old socialist ideal of a radical transformation of society has withered away to talk about stimulating the private sector and keeping the key pressure groups on side. He has no desire to challenge the class system, private wealth or corporate power. These days he plays percentage politics. No risks, no worries — and not much hope for those on the bottom of the pile either.

The middle classing of the Labor Party has disenfranchised the very people who originally created it. Hawke is not out to change Australia; he simply wants it to work more efficiently. Co-operate, don't transform. Tune it up, compromise, find some common ground. Nothing extreme. And stay in power. For all his personal vivacity, which people still respond to, he has no passionate grail to lead him on; his program for the future is simply ''more of the same". He has been revealed, to the disappointment of those who hold to the idealism of the Labor Party, as just a responder, a synthesiser of other people's ideas, the ultimate communicator. All technique, no vision.

And yet in a funny sort of way Bob Hawke has never pretended to be anything else. He's always said he is about reconciliation, compromise, consensus — they're his theme words. When he was elected Prime Minister in 1983 he was something of a folk hero; people expected him to be a saviour, a leader of inspiration. What they got was a skilful middle-of-the-road politician whose Messiah role (remember that?) shrunk year after year to the point where, in 1990, one Canberra commentator could say "that's the last election victory Labor will be able to squeeze out of him".

But he is unique in other ways: a Common Man, an absorber, a listener, and in some mysterious way a bit of a mirror of the qualities and demands and inputs which Australians project upon him. If the Australian people are content to be pragmatic individualists, Hawke will be precisely that. If they want idealism he may be able to accommodate that too; there is a genuinely humane, even sentimental side to Hawke which his readiness to cry in public betrays. In many ways he reflects us more exactly than we realise. He is ourselves writ large — or small. If the Australian people demand more than that of a leader, they'd better look hard in the mirror.